The Two Conversations Classroom

A Complete, Student-Centered Approach to Teaching a Second Language

Copyright © 2022 by Mike Peto

All rights reserved. No part of this book may be reproduced or used in any manner without written permission of the copyright owner except for the use of quotations in a book review.

First paperback edition August 2022

ISBN: 978-1-957729-05-3

Published by My Generation of Polyglots

 My Generation of Polyglots

http://MyGenerationOfPolyglots.com

With gratitude to

many students

who have passed through my life

while I learn

What you'll find in these pages

This book presents a **highly student-centered approach** to teaching a language.

Language courses are often designed around thematic content. It is traditionally assumed that it is the teachers job to make sure that students are interested in a thematic unit, such as a unit on parts of the house. The teacher develops activities to force students to use language that may not interest them. In the end, the teacher develops assessments to force students to pay close attention. The students' interests are the last to be considered when planning the school year.

However, if we focus on **who** we are teaching, rather than **what** we are teaching, the class content emerges naturally from our class conversations. Not only is it easier for the language teacher to develop a compelling and enjoyable language experience by centering the lives of actual students as the content of each class, but it is also **more likely to generate language that students find relevant**. Class time is no longer wasted on a list of words that students resist learning; instead we focus on communicating messages that are pertinent and interesting to the students in the classroom.

This book presents many classroom techniques to structure conversations in the target language with the goal of discovering **who we are teaching**. As these class conversations grow, our students' proficiency in the target language also grows.

After years of focusing class on my students' lives, I realized that I also wanted to carve out more time discussing the target language cultures that are foreign to many of my students. We developed a balance between two class conversations: a student-centered conversation that I call "**Student Voices Activities**" and another conversation where we explore what I call "**Voices of Others**".

Finally we added a **beginning of class routine** and an **end of class routine**. The beginning of class routine develops the **skills of independent readers** and eventually leads to a full pleasure reading session in the first ten minutes of class. The end of class routine provides a written summary of the class through a community writing technique called **Write & Discuss**. There is also an extremely easy **daily exit quiz** about our class conversations that ensures that all students are following along with the content generated in class.

And thus was born "**The Two Conversation Classroom**". This approach supported an extremely successful language program in a high-poverty public school system. While we still dealt with high-absenteeism and a culture of not doing homework, our program developed a 100% pass rate on AP and IB exams. More importantly, we became **happier students and happier teachers** as our classrooms became refuges rather than sources of conflict.

- Index -

How to use this book 9

Starting the Year

    The Flow of a Daily Lesson 10

    Planning a day, a week, a month, a year 15

    Identify the High-Frequency Verbs in your Target Language 21

    Using the Verb & Question Word Posters in Class 23

    What if I leave English translations visible on my posters? 27

    Are the Sweet 16 verbs just a longer Super 7 list? 28

    Setting up a classroom 30

    Classroom Management 39

    Get Buy-in from Parents 43

    First Days of School 47

    Class Jobs 49

Basic Skills to Maintain a Class Conversation 53

    Ten Essential Techniques for Easy Communication 54

        Write on the Board 54

        Ask Artful Questions 56

        Require Choral Response 57

        Point & Pause 58

        Increase Processing Speed 59

        "What did I just say?" 59

        Default to the Sweet 16 60

      Choral Translation 61

      Write & Discuss 61

      Exit quizzes 66

Bailout moves & extending the input 70

Fluency Writes 74

Student Paired Retells 79

Encouraging Student Voices 82

What does a Beginners Class look like? 85

What does an Advanced Class look like? 89

Language Spoken at the speed of a native-speaker 97

The Reading Program

Leading students to love reading 100

Book Talks 102

Whole Class Reading 103

Build a Class Library 111

The Flow of an Independent Reading Session 114

The best bookmarks 116

What does intermediate reading look like? 118

Books I like to read with advanced heritage learners 121

Browsing Strategies 125

Powerful Display of a Class Library 134

Reading Activities & Assessments 137

Boys Reading 141

Troubleshooting a reading program 143

Encouragement & Good Reading Quotes 144

Student Voices Activities 147

Picture Talk from Student Pictures 148
Card Talk 151
Card Talk Database 154
Student Interviews 156
Student Interview Database 158
Calendar Talk 161
One Word Images 163
One Word Images for Advanced Classes 170
Matava Scripts 175
Whole Class Community Creative Writing 179

Voices of Others Activities 185

Picture Talk – illustrations from books & photos from target cultures .. 186
Movie Talk 190
Cultural Presentations 198
Oral Storytelling 202
Using Target Language TV & Movies 208

Essays about Teaching

Letter to parents about advantages of a deskless classroom 214
Aligning with a textbook 216
"Common sense" activities that simply waste time 221
Keeping it fresh all year long 227
Fear & Creativity 230
The Art of the bailout move 234
Extra long & extra short classes 236

The Cool Generation 237

'Calm & Clear' is Better than 'Loud & Lively' 238

The Problem with a Grammar Syllabus 241

Do Word Walls Help the Flow of Conversation? 244

Cognate Recognition Routine: Béisbol Baseball 248

Comprehensible but Rich Language 249

You are not on stage 252

5 Scaffolds to Improve Class Outcomes 254

The Balance of the Two Conversations 257

Crosswords: Boring or Fabulous? 259

A Small Bucket of Language 263

Is 'Non-Targeted' Language an Efficient Use of Class Time? 265

Harness the power of choice to develop a smooth-running class 268

What are grades good for? 272

Acknowledgements 276

- How to Use This Book -

This book is a complete description of my language teaching.

When I give workshops, I usually spend most of our time together demonstrating activities from the "Student Voices" and "Voices of Others" sections. **If you are new to this approach I recommend that you first find an activity from one of those two modules that you can imagine doing in class.** Find your strengths first, before building on your weaknesses. Movie Talk (on page 190) is an activity that many students and teachers enjoy right away. Try it out, and then read the Basic Skills chapter (page 53) to refine your technique so that it leads to the most language acquisition.

If you are already familiar with this style of language teaching then I recommend that you start from the beginning of the book with Starting the Year. There you will find how I organize my classroom and plan loosely to create an environment that elicits true conversation. Experienced and new educators alike will benefit from broadening their language acquisition toolbox in the following Basic Skills chapter.

Even if you do not yet have a classroom library of language learning novels, comics, picture books and non-fiction books, I still recommend that you plan a short session at the beginning of class dedicated to the reading program. This is more than a time to read. Starting with just one novel, you can still develop readers' skills through a short book talk.

However, **if you received this book at one of my workshops**, then you also have a year's access to the online Master Class Library on my website. The Master Class Library is a collection of language learning texts for French, German and Spanish teachers. Project part of a book against a white screen and read one scene together. Use the short stories, explore the comics and the non-fiction texts.

The last section of this book contains 19 essays that I have written over the course of my career. These essays address deeper elements of my teaching. As you get further along, I think you'll enjoy these reflections that tease out complex and subtle dynamics that make The Two Conversation Classroom such a powerful approach.

- Starting the Year -

> This section describes the classroom organization and curricular preparation that sets the stage *before* the first day of classes.

The flow of a daily lesson

Many teachers who are new to these techniques report feeling anxious about standing in front of class without a textbook to guide the lesson. I want to show you how easy it is to plan and feel prepared for your lessons using these activities. There is no need to feel anxious about whether students will contribute or what to do if a conversation flops, in the same way that you should not feel anxious about talking to the cashier at a supermarket. Yes, some cashiers may not respond when you greet them just as some students do not provide lots of chatter when being interviewed, but that is actually a blessing in a lower level class. You just need a little bit of information that you can then use as fodder for classroom chat.

In my school I teach 55 minute classes, so I will start with that as an example. Here are my lesson plans for an entire week. I know that the beginning of my class will be dedicated to the reading program, so let me block off the first 10 minutes to reading.

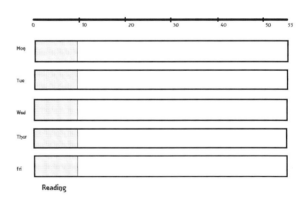

To be clear, a reading program is a lot more than simply giving kids a text and telling them to read for 10 minutes. In this time we also do various browsing activities which you will read about in the chapter on the reading program. Once students can choose their own independent reading, this is a heavenly way to begin class. Regardless of whatever craziness may be happening outside of the classroom, starting the class with 10 minutes of quiet reading calms and focuses everyone so that the remaining 45 minutes are much more productive.

At the beginning of the school year in a level 1 class you clearly cannot expect students to read what they do not understand. Some level 2 or higher students who did not have a reading program in their previous class may also need to learn to build their reading stamina. However I still do some book talks to introduce my students to my library, in the first days in English and then gradually transitioning to the target language over the course of a couple of weeks. I want my level 1 students to be familiar with all of the easiest reads in the library before we start the independent reading in second semester. Therefore in reality the lesson might look more like this:

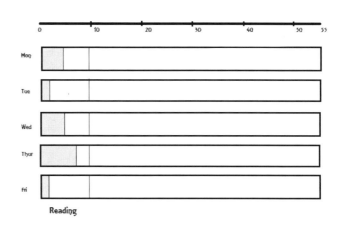

As Stephen Krashen says, if students can only handle 7 minutes of independent reading, give them 5. If they get antsy after 3 minutes, stick to a 1 minute book talk. Slowly build the reading time as they can handle more and they will eventually beg for more time when the 10 minutes end.

The other thing that we can count on in our lesson plan is the last 15 minutes dedicated to an activity called "Write & Discuss" and the exit quiz. Both of these activities are vital to the long-term success of the language class, so don't skip them.

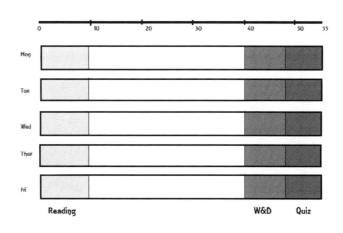

It is easy to get sucked into a good activity and feel like we run out of time, so I developed a routine to make sure we never miss W&D and the quiz. Have a student act as a time-keeper who will warn you everyday, 40 minutes into class, that it is now time to start the W&D. I told my timekeepers that if they warn me exactly 40 minutes into the class, regardless of how much fun we are having, then I would fly through the W&D in 6 minutes and the quiz in 6 minutes as well, leaving students 3 "free" minutes to fetch their backpacks and check their phones. Once students realize that they will not be given time to pack up if the timekeeper does not interrupt me, I am reminded promptly every day.

A teacher who has trouble fitting a daily exit quiz into her 44 minute class period recently wrote to me to ask if she would get the same benefit if she gives Friday quizzes or sporadic, unannounced quizzes instead of a daily exit quiz. Answer: *I don't recommend it.*

We want to give students a solid incentive to be present and engaged every day. Sporadic quizzes encourage students to 'gamble' on whether there will be an assessment. Friday quizzes encourage students to tune off with the mistaken belief that they can get the notes and study Thursday night. **It is not the quiz that leads to acquisition, it is the consistent engagement with the language.** Choose the tool that leads to consistent student engagement, even if sporadic quizzes lead to a grading curve that looks more like 'school'.

Now we only have thirty minutes to plan. I have two types of activities that I do nearly every day. **The first is called a "Student Voice" activity.** This might be simply describing a photograph of one of your students when he was a child, with the student helping you along in English to establish the correct details and you, the teacher, slowly turn the description into the target language. It might be a student interview aided by a power point slide with the questions in both the target language and English, but all of your spoken language and the comprehension questions you pose to the rest of the class will be in the target language. The student voice is also the creative One Word Images

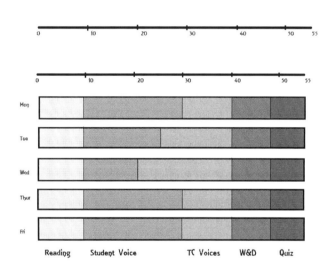

and the little stories that your students create about these lovable characters. **The key idea to understand about the daily student voice activity is that the students themselves are the curriculum.** Students acquire best when they are highly interested in the messages being spoken; that is why we purposely talk about the students, their lives and their ideas every day.

The second type of activity that I do is called "the voices of others" or sometimes I refer to it as "Target Culture Voices". I personally believe that we should be engaging our students with "the other", that which feels foreign to them, on a daily basis.

It troubles me that adults in the USA lack empathy for so much of the world's population. What I really would like to do with this portion of the class period is present the lives and voices of admirable people from around the world in language that is as simple and as comprehensible as in our student interviews. My cultural presentations known as Las Maravillas, for instance, are great examples of the kind of activity suitable for the "Target Culture Voices" component.

However, these activities do not have to be overly didactic. A simple but powerful picture talk can also be a bridge between our students' world and the world of the target culture. We can use simple language to open up the worlds of our students. Yes, this is also the place for movie talks... some of them silly and delightful. We love people with whom we can laugh. But most of all this is where we use language to connect our students with the rest of humanity.

One last thing that we bring into every class period: a well-planned **bailout move** (or transition activity) for when the activity loses energy. This is the net beneath the teacher and the reason none of us have to experience the slightest bit of anxiety, knowing that there is a student-directed activity ready to go. I actually do a bailout move almost every single class period because my bailout moves are in themselves good language acquisition activities that I want my students to experience. I do not have to be the entertainer on stage at all moments, and so the way my lessons often actually play out looks more like the graphic to the right.

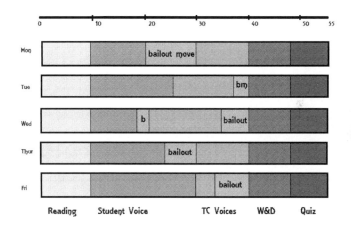

In the following chapters I will describe each of these activities in detail. I will also supply quite a few ready to go materials, many which can be adapted to any language. My recommendation is that you should not try to do everything at once. Get good at one technique at a time.

Better yet, you'll notice above that **I planned one lesson for the entire day regardless of the levels that I'll be teaching.** *That is really how I teach!* With the exception of the TV series that I choose for each level, I tend to use the same pictures for picture talk, often the same interview questions, and if we are creating a OWI in period 1, we'll do that all day long. The difference comes down to how I speak to my students. Sometimes I get a level 3 student who seems to understand like a level 1 student; there is nothing to be done but look the student in the eyes and speak comprehensibly.

As students can understand more, you will naturally expand the conversation paying close attention to signs of wavering or lack of comprehension. Every class relies on the highest frequency word posters, but the content of each class is as unique as any conversation. The W&D activity verifies comprehension, the daily exit quiz quickly verifies that every student is engaging, and you will see that your more advanced classes will naturally engage in more complex language.

At a regional conference I once witnessed a celebrated teacher burn half of her presentation time fiddling with manipulatives during her live teaching demonstration. We all have bad days, and my heart honestly went out to her. But I began to have a sneaking suspicion that this wasn't simply a bad day. The idea of the lesson wasn't so bad until you watched not only the class time squandered to organize the manipulatives, but also realized the amount of time dedicated to printing out and cutting out the tiny pieces of paper before class.

You might be asking yourself: "is he seriously going after manipulatives?!" Well, if there is an easier, lower-prep way to run a class then the answer is yes.

It is much more **effective** and **efficient** to focus on simple activities with a maximum amount of *conversation created in the moment with your students*.

The key to being a teacher that **comes to class each day refreshed** and **who enjoys being with students** is to:

- (1) learn how to remain **comprehensible** in the moment,
- (2) develop a repertoire of activities that are **low to no-prep conversations**.
- (3) follow each activity with a quick **Write & Discuss**, and
- (4) end every class with a **brief exit quiz** to verify that students engaged and understood the class conversations of the day.

If you do that, you can go home at the last bell and leave everything behind.

It is a beautiful and stress-free process.

Are you nervous about planning the entire year?

Take a look at the next section mapping out the entire year.

Planning a day, a week, a month, a year

If you have not yet read the previous essay, I recommend that you start with that simple approach. It describes a way to barely plan a highly successful year by combining two main activities every day (a 'student voice' and a 'voices of others' activity) and finishing the session with a Write & Discuss and exit quiz. If you have a classroom library, start the class with a short pleasure reading session. Regardless of the level of your students, this simple approach will guarantee that your students receive bountiful, perfectly appropriate input every day.

The phrase 'barely planning' is used in a positive sense; over-planning is the surest way to create a course that is a mismatch for your students both in terms of interest as well as language proficiency. **Instead of spending all of your available prep time developing a beautiful content lesson that students are frustratingly uninterested in, perfect your skills drawing out student responses in interviews, calendar talk, and picture talk.**

Instead of developing a complex lesson that artfully provides the opportunity to use advanced grammar, focus on developing the skills to foster student creativity through one word images (which will lead to rich language use). These activities work best when the teacher is truly *with* her students, highly aware and ready to seize the moment without a secret agenda to sneak in contrasts between the preterit and imperfect verb tenses.

Nonetheless you do not want to use all of your best activities in September before students are ready to take full advantage of their possibilities. You could theoretically do movie talks all year long and, as long as your students engage, they will acquire the language just fine. But you might want some change throughout the year so that your class feels fresh and students feel like they are making progress. On the next page is a graphic roughly showing when I introduce certain activities in my beginner classes.

As you can see, August in my level 1 classes is mostly Book talks, different kinds of Picture talks, Card Talks and Student Interviews. In August we are moving very slowly as I develop their speed processing the highest frequency words in the target language. I do not have to dazzle them with videos or exciting games... a simple picture talk is novel enough in these early days of the school year.

Picture Talk is the basis of movie talk; teach students to listen closely to your input without blurting in August so that they are ready for movie talk in October. In September I also introduce One Word Images, but that does not mean I stop with the other activities. Truthfully I conduct student interviews throughout the entire year, as long as they are interesting. The student interview database gives you questions to last 9 weeks, or roughly the first quarter. The card talk database gives you enough prompts to do one each week for the first half year of instruction.

Year plan for a level 1 or 2 class

August **S**eptember **O**ctober **N**ovember **D**ecember **J**anuary **F**ebruary **M**arch **A**pril **M**ay **J**une

Book talks and other browsing activities all year long
Introduce the easiest to read books in class library but no independent reading for level 1 until January

Start independent reading & do a monthly gallery walk

Start the year with lots of Picture talks, student interviews and card talks

Keep doing occasional Picture Talks, student interviews & card talks throughout the school year

Short Movie Talks (that last one period)

Start a TV show and watch two scenes every day until Spring Break

After Spring Break do two or three cultural presentations per week

One Word Images and their stories twice a week

Continue to occasionally make One Word Images throughout the school year

Matava Scripts (which may lead to creative writing)

"Good Stories" once every two weeks & **Telling Tales** (i.e. Aesop's fables, etc.)
"Good Stories" is the reader available in French, German & Spanish that accompanies the Master Class

One of the strengths of the Two Conversation Classroom is that the teacher and students have a lot of flexibility in choosing the activities that work best in their classroom. I absolutely adore the creative activities like One Word Images that, with the guidance of a strong teacher, can lead to the creation of empowering short stories that teach life lessons.

Once we get into the One Word Images, however, I make sure that we are making a new OWI twice a week, on Mondays and Thursdays. On Tuesdays and Fridays we follow up creating with a short story about the OWI. I do this because **the OWI creation process is the most remarkable language acquisition activity that I have in my toolbox. The language that comes out of the process is very rich but highly comprehensible and leads to the kind of comprehensible input that I think is optimal.** I would spend all year making OWIs, but students begin to get punchy by late November, although I keep pushing them as long as possible! When they groan I jokingly tell my students that I have to mail two OWIs to Mexico every week or I will not get paid. Push them to be creative even when no one takes the bait. It will do incredible things to build their language.

A TYPICAL WEEK WHEN WE ARE CREATING ONE WORD IMAGES

	MON	TUE	WED	THUR	FRI
10m	reading program	-- reading program	--- reading program	reading program	rogram --
15m	chatting about the weekend	picture talk	student interview	telling tales	chatting about the weekend
20m	OWI	story from OWI	movie talk	OWI	story from OWI
5m	W+D	W+D	W+D	W+D	W+D
5m	exit quiz	exit quiz	exit quiz	exit quiz	exit quiz

But if you find it difficult to spin these stories in class, or worse if the stories spin out of control and the class is left with objectionable texts, try another technique while you develop your skills. I will say that, even in a student-centered classroom, the teacher should always be in control of the narratives. So if you feel like you are losing control, chose a bail-out move and shift to a technique like a Picture Talk that has clear boundaries in terms of content creation.

You may also notice that around mid-October I start leading **movie-talks** and "**telling a tale**" activities. In part this is because students are gratified to find a few more "passive" activities such as movie-talk in this part of the year. Students listening abilities have developed considerably but they are self-conscious of their speaking, so this is the perfect time to give them rich language in "telling a tale" activities.

With the movie talks I am also training them to participate appropriately before we begin a TV show in January. In October students will whine because they want to chat with friends during the movie-talk and not have the teacher pause and discuss. **Teach students to expect the teacher to interrupt the video while talking about what is on the screen, and to maintain a silent room** so that the activity will work in January. It is not the worst thing if you burn a movie talk or two in October because your students are not listening to your input… there is no ongoing plot line. However, in January if students are not paying proper attention to the movie talk each day, they will become hopelessly lost in the complexity of a plot that lasts until Spring break.

Throughout the entire first semester I start my class with **reading program activities**— brief book talks, a few read-alouds and such. I want students to be so familiar with the class library that, by January when they actually start independent reading, they will already know what all of the easy readers are about. Ideally I want them thinking about which book they will grab first, when I finally let them start reading on their own. In January they finally get to choose their pleasure reading books. Let them build their reading stamina gradually. At first they may only be able to handle 5 minutes before they begin to fidget, so only give them two minutes and let them long for more reading time. By fourth quarter my students might be spending up to 20 minutes quietly reading every day, as long as they can handle it. I like to end the school year slipping deep into reading. While the rest of the school is slipping into chaos and other teachers are dedicating more and more time to playing movies in class, our TV watching has come to an end and we are becoming more and more quiet as we silently read. I hope that students remember how pleasant our quiet reading sessions have been and keep it up –in any language– during the summer.

In January I also start movie-talking 1-2 scenes **of a TV show** every day. This lasts until Spring break, when students either binge watch the series or decide not to. Either way, it is a logical break to stop watching the series because student interest has either played itself out by completing the series at home or waned to the extent that we need a new conversation topic. After Spring break I replace the time we spent on the TV show with some non-fiction cultural presentations. If you have access to the Master Class online you'll find my *Maravillas* presentations in Spanish and the *Merveilles* presentations in French. We might occasionally conduct a student interview or a picture talk, but the end of the year is often satisfyingly dominated by pleasure reading, book browsing activities, a few chats about the weekend or after school activities and the cultural presentations.

Year plan for an intermediate level class (high school levels 2, 3 or 4)

August **S**eptember **O**ctober **N**ovember **D**ecember **J**anuary **F**ebruary **M**arch **A**pril **M**ay **J**une
Book talks and other browsing activities all year long Start independent reading & do a monthly gallery walk
-Cultural presentations like the Spanish Maravillas are appropriate all year long-

Start the year with lots of Picture talks, student interviews and card talks to develop class culture	Keep doing occasional Picture Talks, student interviews & card talks throughout the school year	
	Short Movie Talks (that last one period)	Start a TV show and watch two scenes every day	During second semester either choose a new show or watch a variety of films, still only 1-2 scenes per day.
One Word Images and their stories: try to develop stories that "go deep"	Creative writing with **Matava scripts** as a starting point. If you are not creative writing with students then continue to occasionally make One Word Images throughout the school year to give a creative outlet.

"Good Stories" and / or **Telling Tales** (i.e. Aesop's fables, etc.) every two weeks
"Good Stories" is the reader available in French, German & Spanish that accompanies the Master Class

Intermediate classes, on the other hand, follow a slightly different sequence because they already have the skills to delve into pleasure reading on day 1. Inevitably there are students new to the school, so I start with Picture Talk and Student Interviews in order to norm the classes and get to know everyone.

Also note that I place level 2 in both the beginner and intermediate graphs. You know your school; if your level 2 students truly come to class with the skills of beginners, you have to teach the students in front of you. Starting off slow is better than going too fast and losing them.

You will notice that in the intermediate courses I start **an authentic TV series** in Autumn semester, but not before six weeks of picture and movie talk to be sure that every student is ready. I have about 50 movie talk videos in my movie talk archive, so I am not worried about saving certain movie talks for level 1 and others for level 2. Instead, I do the same movie talk all day long and just change it up next year… or not. Being exposed again to a movie talk is like rereading a book; great for acquisition!

During the Spring semester I can follow the level 1 calendar if I want, but I like to do two things differently. First, we delve into authentic film which is movie-talked scene by scene. Certainly read the part of this website about **using film in class** before doing this. The other thing I do, sometimes, *if classes can handle the long-term attention needed*, is work to create a longer narrative that could be transformed into a full CI novel. If they bail after a week, okay, we can do more pleasure reading, but an outstanding class will dedicate twenty minutes every other day to writing a new scene from our class novel. Generally I create a plot outline based on one class conversation in February and when we imagine a paragraph together, I tell them what we need to accomplish. "Today", I might say in Spanish, "our character meets the villain. Where do they meet?". Then the brainstorming happens in Spanish, ending with a Write and Discuss text that I add to our ongoing novel. If kids lose interest by March, we abandon the activity.

If writing a full-fledged novel with your students is too much, consider writing a few short stories based on **Matava scripts**. Even with my level 1 students I am surprised at the texts we create. Ann Matava's skeleton scripts are easy to personalize to your students' lives.

Identify the High-Frequency Verbs in your Target Language

The linguistic backbone supporting daily conversations in class are the **high-frequency verbs posters and the interrogative words posters** that you'll refer to often to make yourself comprehensible. In Spanish I originally chose 16 verbs that I called the "Sweet 16 Verbs". French teachers talk about 14 key verbs. I have considered adding one or two to my original list. The number of verbs is not as important as finding the verbs that occur most often in your target language so that you can quickly develop a conversation-based classroom.

Here are the English translations of the verbs that I post in the 3rd person singular form:

Can	Leaves	Says	Goes
Puts	Is	There is / are	Sees
Wants	Has	Does	Hears
Knows	Gives	Makes	Comes

Once you can refer to these most often used verbs, you'll see that conversational possibilities are extremely varied. Before I developed this concept, most teachers who followed approaches like mine used long lists of target structures to guide their curriculum. The problem with that approach is that is easily distracted with less frequent vocabulary and ultimately reproduces the massive vocabulary lists from textbooks that were far too heavy for most students to actually acquire a basic conversational fluency in the language.

If you limit the vocabulary used in a beginners class and focus on developing a native-like speed processing that limited language, your students will acquire faster. At first they will understand faster. Eventually they will start writing and speaking faster, and with comfort. The purpose of limiting our vocabulary in the first year is to develop a micro-fluency. We choose the highest frequency verbs because that will give students the widest communicative range for their limited vocabulary.

This is not to say that I don't use other words in class! We choose words as they come up in discussion, as they are needed. Most words are taught in context. If they come up repeatedly and are important to students, they will be acquired. If not, then they may have been important to express an idea one day but will fade away from memory. The highest frequency verbs, however, will constantly be used in conversation.

There are a few verbs that I teach right away because they are important for the stories that hold students' attention in the first days of classes. There are stories about students **looking for** something, **finding** something, and often **hiding** something. We discuss fears and a character that **is afraid of** something is sure to be compelling.

Don't feel trapped, like you must remain a prisoner of the high frequency verbs. Instead, ask if you can express yourself with those limited verbs and, if not, take the time to slowly introduce new vocabulary embedded within language that students already understand.

Embedding new vocabulary within comprehensible messages is how language is acquired.

Using the Verb & Question Word Posters in Class

In the front of the room I hang the question words posters. These are huge and used frequently both to maintain student engagement and to verify comprehension. I most often require a choral response to my questions, so I need to be able to point and pause repeatedly wherever I happen to be standing in class.

I have since removed the subjunctive and past tenses of the Sweet 16 verbs to reduce clutter on the walls. Now I just have the present tense verbs and, when I use another tense, I write it on the board. Simply pointing to the correct verb with a laser pointer while telling a story, or asking a question, is amazingly effective.

I have found that you don't have to remove the English— students will internalize these crucial verbs & interrogative words and stop glancing up when they've got them. On the other hand, I glance at them throughout the year as I am talking spontaneously in class and trying to remain comprehensible. I use them as a crutch to remember to stay in bounds. If I can avoid introducing new words and just work on getting students to process the basic words faster and faster they will eventually use the words naturally.

It is essential that the letters are so BIG that lazy adolescent eyes cannot help but read them even when exhausted from watching Netflix all night. Having a big list of small letters encourages students to not read anything, while a limited list in large letters makes a strong impact. I like letters that are at least 10 inches high. I write on the board when I use a yo form, and that is a good way to slow the conversation down so that students have time to process the language.

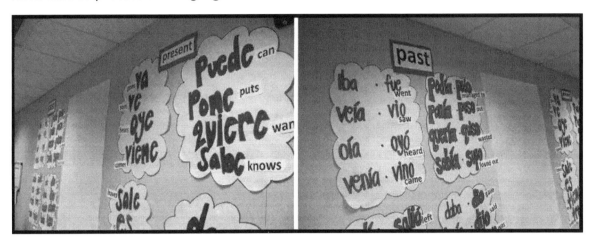

Use the verb posters to introduce new vocabulary

After I posted the question words in a spot that I frequently look at during instruction I noticed that I was asking many more questions in class. In fact, I asked a greater variety of questions. Suddenly interrogatives like *¿cuál?* Were popping up everywhere. My students acquired these words rapidly because I frequently used the poster as a crutch to help me generate questions on the spot.

In the same way, the sweet sixteen verb posters are as much a crutch for the teacher as the student. After a few weeks students will occasionally glance over at the posters (which is valuable for me to recognize what has not been fully acquired), but for the most part posters become invisible if they are not an active part of the class. To prevent these verbs from becoming buried, I recycle them whenever I introduce new vocabulary. The posters really help me come up with questions during the heat of the moment, unscripted but perfectly comprehensible.

Here is an example: one day in November a level 1 class was imagining a situation in which a man, allergic to Pepsi, wants a Coke. However there is no Coke in the restaurant, so the employees keep coming up with excuses to give him a Pepsi. At the time I used to teach with target phrases (that day we were targeting "pide" and "le ofrecen"), but even today I might spontaneously go through this process when some crucial new vocabulary expression is introduced into class conversation.

¿**Puede** beber un Pepsi el hombre? No, él no **puede** beber Pepsi, por eso pide una Coca-Cola. ¿Los empleados **salen** para comprar Coca-Cola? No, le ofrecen un Pepsi porque ellos no **quieren salir**. ¿Por qué no **quieren salir**? Porque **quieren ver** su programa favorito en la tele. Entonces, ¿qué **ve** el hombre en las manos de los empleados? El **ve** latas de Pepsi, pero no **ve** una lata de Coca-Cola. ¿Le ofrecen una lata de Coca-Cola? ¡Qué va! ¡Le ofrecen una lata de Pepsi! ¿El hombre **pone** el Pepsi en la boca? ¡Claro que no! Él **puede** morir si bebe Pepsi. El hombre pide una Coca-Cola. ¿Los empleados **saben** que el hombre **quiere** Coca-Cola? Sí, ellos **saben**. **Saben** muy bien, pero **son** flojos y **quieren ver** la tele…

Even if you are not creating stories in your classroom, you can embed new vocabulary into sweet sixteen verb phrases so that students develop an ability to handle the highest frequency verbs with ease. Suppose, for example, your district requires that students learn thirty words related to camping. Rather than spend an equal amount of class time on words that are extremely low-frequency I might create a conversation centered around one of the low frequency words.

(Holding up a can of beans) Aquí **tengo** una lata de frijoles y necesito (holding up a can opener) un abrelatas para abrir la lata. Pero… (placing a can opener discreetly on a student´s desk) ¿dónde **está** el abrelatas? ¿Quién **sabe** dónde **está** el abrelatas? Ay Dios mío, no **puedo** comer (pointing and pausing at the verb puede) sin el abrelatas. (A student answers correctly that Susan has it). ¿Susan?
No **es** posible que Susan **tenga** (point and pause at "tiene"—they´ll get it) el abrelatas. Ella **es** una chica buena. (Turning to class) Clase, what did I just say in English? Class says in English: she is a good girl. (Turning to the Brian) Brian, what would I say if I wanted to say she is a bad girl? Brian: es una chica mala. (Turning back towards class) Susan **es** una chica buena, ¡ella no **tiene** mi abrelatas! Clase, ¿cuál **es** el problema? (They might not know how to articulate an answer to my question, or someone might rudely say "¡usted!", so I rephrase my question as an either/or question): Clase: ¿**quiero saber** dónde **está** la lata de frijoles, o **quiero saber** dónde **está** el abrelatas? (Hopefully they respond abrelatas, but if the response is not strong I simply ask the question again slowly, pointing and pausing). Clase, ¿quién **quiere** abrir la lata? (They answer "el profe"). Sí, correcto, yo **quiero** abrir la lata con el abrelatas. (Turning towards Sally) Sally, what does the —o on the end of quiero mean? (Sally says "I"). Y clase, ¿qué necesitamos para abrir la lata? (If they can´t say the answer then I write the word on the board and ask them an either/or question).

As you can see in the above description, the questioning is a bit plodding as I am trying to find something interesting to say about a can opener. More importantly however, the students are now processing the present tense fairly quickly if I were now able to speak like that without too much pointing and pausing. Yet they understand the message at all times as they can answer my questions, and hopefully we will soon move on from can openers to a more interesting conversation topic.

Once the high frequency verbs have been acquired there is no reason to not continually sow them into your classes. It really should be part of your daily routine throughout the year. Students will gain more experience with a variety of conjugations. If your focus is limited enough, by the end of the year they will be using these verbs fluently in multiple conjugations because they have heard them many times in meaningful contexts.

Key point: New vocabulary should be 'embedded' within language that students are already processing fluently. Rather than present "dormirse (ue): to fall asleep", ask students questions and make statements using posters to scaffold a relatively spontaneous conversation.

What if I leave the English Translations Visible on the Posters?

My initial belief was that, if I left the English available, students would never memorize the words but simply glance up whenever they need the word. However, over the course of the semester I noticed students glancing up at the posters less and less. They still would look during a quick write, for example, but I was never sure if they were seeking a translation ("what is the word for *to leave*?") or if they were seeking inspiration ("what else could I write... ah, *salir*, I could mention that he left!).

So I designed a little experiment. During midterm exams I let two of my level 1 classes take the exam in my classroom with posters visible. The other two sections of level 1 were brought to a French classroom where there was no textual support in Spanish. They were not informed previously that they would be brought to the French room, nor were the other sections that stayed in my classroom specifically instructed to not look at the posters. On the midterm exam I feature the sweet 16 verbs heavily because I think this is the bedrock foundation of level 1. I want to know if these verbs have been acquired so that, if necessary, I will dedicate the rest of the year to really nailing down these verbs. To my surprise, there was absolutely no difference between any of the sections.

So, what is happening here? I think the key to understanding my students' retention is to look at the difference between (1) teaching students to memorize vocabulary and (2) guiding them to process the vocabulary quicker.

I try not to ask questions that my students cannot answer; instead I am giving them so many meaningful repetitions that their minds eventually move faster than their eyes. The first time they hear the word **tiene**, their eyes will dart up to the posters. If I keep using the word tiene repetitively, they will stop even thinking "**tiene means has**". Tiene will just mean tiene. The next day I will have to repeat the process and some students will process it very quickly while others will need more time. Eventually, they will all be processing at the speed of native speakers.

I recommend that you do your own action research. If you are a travelling teacher who uses more than one classroom, try covering the English part with post-it notes in one of the classrooms after introducing the verb. See if there is a difference between your classes. Or try covering the English after two weeks, or two months.

In any case, actively use the posters in your teaching every day so that students are seeing, and hearing, many meaningful repetitions of these high-frequency words.

Are the "Sweet 16 verbs" just a bigger "Super 7" list?

I often see people misunderstand how these two concepts are different. Someone recently let me see a presentation she was giving and she said that the "Sweet 16" are just more verbs. As I responded, I realized that the concept of the Sweet 16 verbs is deeply rooted in a non-targeted approach.

The idea of Terry Waltz's "Super 7" verbs was to quickly get your class to a point in which you can tell simple stories, rather than spending months learning thematic vocabulary lists. That was a gigantic leap forward. However, the idea behind the "Sweet 16" verbs is not simply some more verbs tacked on to Terry´s list. When I first proposed the sweet 16, Terry was describing her Super 7 as an anchor for meaningful communication within the first few hours of class. My contribution was to take an expanded list of sixteen high-frequency words and describe them as a full four year curriculum.

Many people miss how this point is a dramatic step forward. In fact, teachers who want a highly-controlled curriculum (i.e., "every teacher does the same exact lesson") often totally misunderstand this contribution. As a department chair trying to design a common experience for students in different classes, with a half dozen different teachers on staff, I could have sought to limit the creativity of students and teachers by insisting that every teacher follow the same collection of story scripts, movie talks, and novels. That is, "all Spanish 1 students will read X novel and discuss Z movie talk. All Spanish 2 students will acquire this list of target structures so that they will be "ready" for Spanish 3".

On the other hand, the Sweet 16 verbs represent a different path towards creating a common experience between classes. Of course we do not simply repeat sixteen words for four years, but we do agree that structures with these verbs are the ones that are recycled and given priority at every step in the journey. The only other guideline we follow is to simply strive to provide compelling CI, for four years.

> **We recognized that in any classroom there will be many different interests, and that when students are following their own interests then they perceive the input as more compelling, which leads to faster acquisition.**

That is the funny thing about those studies which try to count how many times a student needs to hear a word to fully acquire it... teachers know that swears might be fully acquired the very first time they are understood whereas an abstract transition word that the student never uses in their own L1 could be uttered comprehensibly 500 times and not be fully acquired.

> **The Sweet 16 gives a department the flexibility to allow their teachers and students to pursue different interests in class, to use different language, but**

guarantees that there will be a common communicative foundation throughout the entire program.

For example, the Sweet 16 verbs allow one teacher to develop an **independent reading program** for her students in which students are all reading different books (and thus developing their own idiosyncratic vocabularies), while another teacher develops his CI skills by using an **authentic Spanish TV show as an anchor text** for his class.

There is another major advantage to running a department this way. When any of my teachers get students at the beginning of the year, we do not have a list of target structures in our minds that we assume our students have acquired. We do not get angry if our level 3 kids do not understand X phrase; instead we are trained to start the conversation assuming nothing and paying close attention to their eyes.

At all levels, as we think about how to phrase our language so that it will be comprehensible, we all return to the Sweet 16 verbs and posters. It is a common experience in all classes, even though I spend a week talking about whales and my colleague spends weeks talking about football.

This is necessary because **students move into our district at every level, and we cannot just leave them behind because they did not start with us**. We need to provide a comprehensible experience at all levels, even if students missed the first 3 years of our communicative classes because they were learning thematic vocab in another district.

Setting Up A Classroom

My preference is to have no desks. Chairs only, with tables on the outside for students to place their backpacks (and cell phones) underneath. Students come in and take out a notebook and pen and then put their notebooks under their chair. In classrooms that I have a class library they will also grab the book that they are reading and, once the reading session is over (after about ten minutes) they place the book under their chairs too. About 35 minutes into the class they will pass their books to the class librarian, who carefully returns the books to the correct place in the classroom library.

I have to fit forty students into a classroom designed for twenty-eight; it was necessity that first led me to remove desks just to free up space. But now that I've done it, I would never go back! On the days that my AP students complete a formal essay I reserve the library. But writing is not the backbone of any language acquisition class; **listening and reading in class develop speaking and writing skills**.

They can place their notebooks on their laps as they write during the last ten minutes of class. I have heard of teachers who buy clipboards for every student; the clipboards are inevitably covered with swears and unsavory drawings by January. My advice: don't bother. Writing in a notebook balanced on their leg is fine for the few minutes that they do it. If you are new to a deskless classroom consider **printing the letter** that I wrote to parents explaining the shift (see page 214). When I first removed desks I had to confront a parental rebellion until they understood why we removed the desks. It is best to explain before the rebellion forms.

My word wall focuses on the main sixteen irregular verbs that are used over and over again in conversation. Simply pointing to the correct verb with a laser pointer while telling a story, or asking a question, is amazingly effective.

I want to leave the bulk of my available wall space to display the best One Word Images created in class. Displaying great OWIs encourages every class to raise the bar on their creativity and they also provide a text rich classroom.

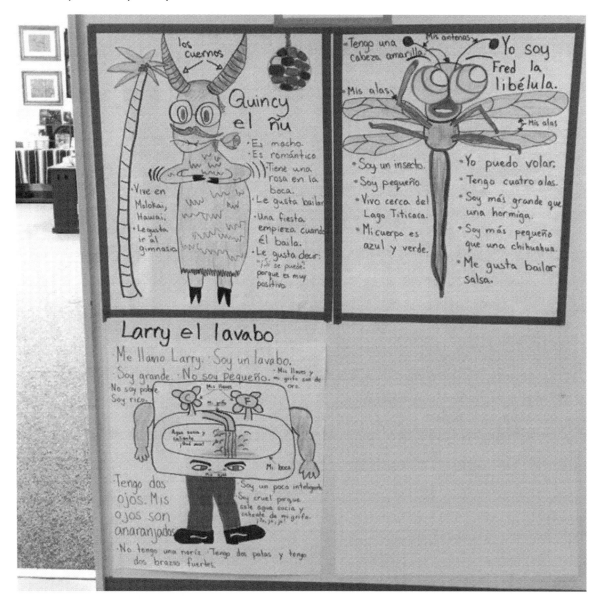

Photo of One Word Images hanging in classroom courtesy of Cameron Taylor

In the front of the room I hang the question words posters. These are huge and used frequently both to maintain student engagement and to verify comprehension. I most often require a choral response to my questions, so I need to be able to point and pause repeatedly wherever I happen to be standing in class.

Changing the lights from industrial office park lights to soft, friendly lamps has a surprising impact on the mood of the class. These are perfect for telling class stories.

One of the biggest changes over the past several years is the size of my classroom library. After years of purchases it is finally a functional size to maintain not only an FVR program for beginners but also a full heritage speakers program. I have tried to create a room that is more "a library with a classroom space" rather than a class with an isolated library nook. The module on developing a reading program provides many more ideas on how to surround students with texts that intrigue and encourage them to read.

My classroom library is large enough that at a certain point I had to confront a major problem: it was too big for students to navigate! My heritage learners read anywhere between a first grade reading level all the way up to college level, and despite my book talks I felt like I needed to do more to get them to explore the library further. This inspired me to create a wall of books of the week so that students looking for a new FVR book have a more manageable selection to choose from.

Currently the "active library" only consists of easy readers to encourage a good first reading experience, but as the year goes on I will encourage students to visit different parts of the classroom library where I have books displayed cover up on tables that surround the room. In the photo below you can see my room before the beginning of the school year. During the school year every one of the tables surrounding the room will be covered with books, and students will place their backpacks and bags in the space below the tables. I moved my main book shelves back to my desk so that these shelves become a "passive library".

In the photo below you can also see the **sets of colored index cards** for each class, hanging on the wall behind my chair. Students start the year providing a few details about themselves on the cards, but for the most part these cards are empty right now. As we find out more information about them through student interviews I will pencil in details so that I can remember and seed the information into future classes. Not only do I include biographical information, I also take notes whenever they were a particularly memorable character in a class story or if they contributed particularly memorable details to a One Word Image.

The best part of all is that I can later flip through these cards in class and immediately identify which students have been passing "unnoticed". **A blank card is an invitation to find a way to make that student a star.**

Expectations in a deskless classroom can never be too clear if you do not want chairs migrating all over the room. It is a good idea to consult with your custodian before placing duct tape on carpets or you will risk creating a very bad relationship with someone who can make your life miserable. I spoke to my custodian before doing this and, with his blessing, we both have agreed that he will never clean the dark marks left behind when the tape is removed. He actually likes the order that this has created and often comments that my classroom is one of the cleanest in the building. There is something about an orderly room that discourages mess. In addition, he loves it when my last class stacks up the chairs against the wall, making it easier to vacuum.

I have experimented with several kinds of tape. Super strong duct tape from Home Depot worked well, until I decided to remove it and it has left disgusting black gooey marks. Blue painters tape worked well for a semester, at which point the chair order was an ingrained routine. Now I change my chairs almost daily depending upon activity, so I haven´t replaced the painters tape. In either case, after putting the tape down I had to spend about an hour pressing it down with my feet, scuffing it into the carpet, going over each section three or four times or it would not stick correctly.

It is absolutely necessary to develop strong classroom management skills so that all students are actively listening to all of the language said in class. In my room I have one very strict rule: one person speaks & everyone else listens. A conversational class will not be effective until students have internalized this essential rule. During the first two weeks I am often stopping class to enforce this rule, and I repeat the rule at the beginning of every period all year long.

Nonetheless this rigid, "everything in its place" organization will give way to seeming anarchy by second semester when students are literally sprawled out on pillows laying on the floor, draped in comfy chairs or sitting with their friends. That is fine for second semester when they are well-trained to maintain their exclusive attention on class, but for me August is all about establishing respect for this all-important class rule.

At the beginning of the year, here is how I fit 36-40 kids into a classroom designed for 25. There are nine chairs per pod. I often sit on the stool in front, but can stand next to any student.

With the independent study kids, a kid sitting at my computer and another couple hanging out back, it is not uncommon to have 40 people crammed in focused on one lesson. Organization is crucial to quickly eliminate distractions while students learn to focus on the class conversation... especially on those days when I am not being a brilliant conversationalist. It is crucial to be able to move around the room easily and be able to stand next to any particular student who needs me there in order to stay focused on class.

Craig Klein Dexemple from **Spanish Cuentos** gave me permission to trace parts of his "**Storytelling Characters Poster**" against my wall. This is so wonderful. I use it throughout the year to spice up a story or unblock a students writing block when they sit down to do fluency writes. Either order from Craig's website or do a Google image search for "black silhouette character" and you will find plenty of characters that you can either print out, trace or use as inspiration to create your own character wall.

I am proud to be able to offer an independent pleasure reading course to heritage speakers. They sit in this little reading nook in the back. I never let kids in my normal classes sit back there (because it is designed to tune out the rest of the class) unless they are heritage learners who are held accountable for their reading in class. They read 20-30 pages per day and are allowed to pick a new book if they grow disillusioned with their current selection. That is, after all, what I do as an adult reader... I don´t finish boring books. Outside of view I have a clipboard where they keep track of what they liked, what they finished, and the suggestions that were rejected. I use these lists to help me make good suggestions and to guide future purchases.

I do have a group of comfy chairs that I bring out to the very front of the room in late October when class routines are firmly set. The comfy chairs are not a place to hide from class!

I have five posters that I made especially for class use. The first is in English and I use it to encourage students to stop me if they do not understand. Of course, the responsibility for remaining comprehensible is all my own. If I were to grade a exit quiz and find many of my students did not understand class then I would not put those grades in my grade book. Nonetheless this poster is a good way to emphasize that they **have the power to slow the class down** if they choose.

The second poster is one that I occasionally use when I have a student who blurts out in class. The last thing I want to do is respond to his blurting by speaking. Instead **I calmly walk over to the "no blurting" poster, point and pause.** Students must learn that choral responses are not a race; everyone needs time to process the language and some students need more time than others.

The third poster keeps me from speaking English when enforcing the "One person speaks, everyone else listens" rule. I simply point to a poster with the rule written in English. Or perhaps a long thin banner that is right above the front board that reads, "**One person speaks, everyone else listens**". You do not want to have to repeat that aloud or some students will enjoy provoking you. Instead, simply stop the conversation whenever there is an interruption, point silently at the banner and smile to show that you have not lost your calm… *but you will not allow this one rule to be broken.*

The fourth poster is so effective that I actually had it printed on a free-standing banner like you might see at a convention (you will see it at my live workshops). This system comes from French teacher Cécile Lainé and acknowledges that there are different types of responses that we may expect from students. This poster clues them in on what kind of response I want right now.

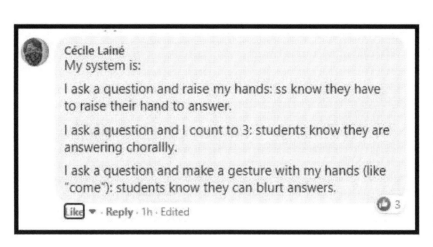

I like how having the teacher raising two hands in order to prompt students to raise one hand is so purposeful. I also like counting down, if only I can train myself to do this consistently. I *love* that Cécile has included an option for allowing students to blurt, because honestly that has its place in my class culture too.

A poster helps teach this class routine and, more importantly, maintain it as part of the class culture. **The poster reminds me to perform this routine.** I recommend that the poster be written in English (unless you only teach heritage learners) so that you can silently point and pause when the rule is broken. All posters should be large enough to be seen from the back of the room. I would draw this on a huge sheet of butcher paper.

Why English?! I think it is a novice teacher's mistake to fill their classroom with a scolding voice; experienced educators draw and maintain clear behavioral boundaries but rely on silent routines so as not to poison their relationships with students. I want my teacher voice to be consistently warm and inviting; I don't want to confuse students. Consistency is important. As much as possible I react to breaking of class rules silently. My silence is loud. I silently point and pause with a neutral gaze (neither smile nor frown, but rather relaxed facial muscles like I am bored), hand raised

indicating the appropriate poster whenever the rule is broken. Slowly... I maintain my posture a few beats longer than socially comfortable. When I resume speaking, it is still a warm and inviting voice.

One advantage of adopting Cécile's system is that it builds in a tiny amount of wait time into the response, slowing down your instruction and giving students time to process the language. I recommend making an effort to adopt this system if you are like me and tend to forget routines when immersed in class conversation... it's worth it.

Classroom Management

In a conversational classroom it is essential that students listen and mentally process the meaning of everything said by the teacher. If you do not provide the environment in which this is possible, your students will acquire much less and your classes will quickly become stratified between the haves and have-nots; those who pay attention will *have* acquired while those that *have not* will become a problem and prevent everyone from acquiring. **Don't let students choose their path; allow only the path of acquisition.**

Classroom management requires strength of will.

It is the rare teacher who can manage a high-energy class while also effectively policing students so that they do not go off-task. From a teaching perspective, it is inexcusable to execute high-energy activities while permitting side conversations and distracted behavior, which undermines the overall objective. Worse yet, it is nearly impossible to reel back a class once students claim their "right" to have side conversations, check their social media, or otherwise not engage 100% in class.

For this reason **I recommend that teachers start the school year with a very controlled, decidedly low-energy classroom**. Don't aim to be their most fun teacher; aim to be a respected adult who firmly enforces boundaries. It is a lot easier (and effective) to be perceived as a strict teacher who eventually reveals a warm, caring side than being perceived as a goofy teacher who, in October, desperately screams at class in an attempt to control the spiraling chaos.

1: Tell students what you want them to do

This sounds simple, but it is THE MOST IMPORTANT step which many teachers fail to do. Alina Filipescu, a teacher with incredible classroom management skills, says that she starts every class, every day, reminding students of the most basic classroom rules. **Never let it slide!** In my CI classroom I start every class reminding students of how I want them to behave during class conversations with the three rules below.

2: One person speaks, everyone else listens

My ironclad first rule of classroom management is: "**One person speaks, everyone else listens**". In a room with 40 people this feels so unnatural, and it is!, but for students to acquire it is essential that no one is distracted. Therefore the first thing I recommend is that you print out a banner with this phrase to hang in a central location at the front of the room. This will save you from having to speak English in class; just point at it when necessary... which will be frequently at the beginning of the year.

Side conversations in any language cannot ever be permitted. If there is a warm class community, your students' natural urge will be to chat with each other. You must nip this in the bud at the beginning of the year and remain vigilant throughout the year to make sure that there are never side conversations. Every day start class telling them your expectations, and stop class whenever there is a side conversation regardless of how much you might be enjoying class. Side conversations surge forth when the class conversation is getting good, so you must always be vigilant and never get entirely swept into the drama of the class conversation. **You are your own worst enemy if you get swept up in class and fail to stop side conversations.**

3 & 4: Look at the Speaker & Raise Hand to Speak

Virginia teacher Brett Chonko adds two more important class rules:

> "I think "**Look at the Speaker**" and "**Raise Hand to Speak**" are particularly important when it comes to managing the CI classroom. "**Look at the Speaker**" is how I call on students whose hands are raised. Instead of just calling Justin's name. I say (in the target language), "*Class, look at Justin.*" It is a small tweak, but has a huge effect. If done well, which means constant reinforcement, making students look at the new speaker is like 50 attention checks every class. It constantly directs them to the content of class, and it's a wonderful soft skill to teach them the importance of eye contact as a form of respect in interpersonal communication. "**Raise Hand to Speak**" is an obvious extension of "one person speaks, everyone listens", but kids definitely have to be trained and constantly reminded."

Post a rules poster on your classroom wall with rules 2, 3 & 4 written in large font. It should be in English so that you can walk over, point & pause at the rule when broken in class, make eye contact with the entire class while pointing, maintain a neutral gaze as if you are bored, and then proceed with instruction without ever speaking English.

CLASS RULES

ONE PERSON SPEAKS, EVERYONE LISTENS

RAISE HAND TO SPEAK

LOOK AT THE SPEAKER

5: Talk to the 'troublemakers' when they are not in trouble

I don't even like to think of these students as 'troublemakers'; instead, think of them as kids who need more attention. And they'll demand it!! But seriously, ignoring students who enter the classroom looking to disrupt is a mistake I occasionally see among new teachers. The teacher knows that the class will be interrupted at some point, so the teacher starts off focusing on the quiet obedient students in order to model the way they want class to run. **It is an unconscious instinct that you have to avoid.** A student who is aching for attention will perceive this as an empty stage beckoning for his performance.

Instead, greet everyone and make sure to greet the talkative, rules-averse students by name in a friendly but authoritative manner. Engage them in small talk at the beginning of class. Touch base with them frequently. When conducting a student interview take three seconds to survey the entire class and make eye contact with your rule-breakers. Give a thumbs up, smile, keep a positive stream of social signals flowing outward. Make sure that when you have to quickly reseat them, it is not the first time they were noticed.

6: Pre-plan smooth transitions to limit student chatter

Smooth transitions: Limit opportunities to chat by planning smooth transitions and **bailout moves** so that students do not fill "free moments" speaking in English. Have a student sitting at your computer if you have the projector on and talk about what is happening on the screen rather than disappearing in the back of the room to fiddle with the computer yourself. Sit strategically with your class when they are doing the bailout move, even better right next to a likely source of disruption. I like to have a **music activity ready** on one of the tabs in my computer so that the moment we need to transition I call a student up. When you disappear from view and students are not engaged in doing something, side conversations start.

7: A wordless way to limit English usage in class

Assign that can be flipped in class to indicate on one side when (a) the use of English is forbidden, and on the other side when (b) "2 words in English" is allowed. There are times in which I feel comfortable with students using a few words in English, such as when we make "One Word Images" or I conduct a student interview. I often say *"una palabra o dos palabras en inglés" ("one word or two words in English")* which prevents entire discussions in English, but if they need to communicate that they have a hamster I will let them say that one word in English and then I will translate it on the board (the word "hamster" in Spanish happens to be "*hámster*").

However there are other times when I do not want to allow English and I communicate that by having a sign that on one side reads "*Prohibido el inglés*" ("*English Prohibited*") and on the other side is blank. I flip the sign when I want to eliminate code-switching. I stop mid-sentence whenever there is a side conversation in English, point at the "*Prohibido el inglés*" sign, and then chant the rhyme *"uno, dos, tres… ahora sin el inglés"* ("*one, two, three… without English*", which rhymes in Spanish). Keep in mind, however, that I more often allow code-switching, especially in a lower level class, so my sign is most often displaying the blank side. I only flip it consistently during upper level classes or if I feel that students are abusing the ability to offer a word or two in English.

8: Class chants to redirect student attention

Class chants redirect student attention without having to annoyingly whine at the class. Working with elementary and middle school teachers has impressed me with the power of song, especially when coupled with hand gestures. I once observed a third grade class that was melting down after a "turn and talk" activity went too long. The teacher stood up straight, raised her arms above her head and formed a circle by touching her two index fingers together and her thumbs. Gently she made up a rhythm on the spot, "Vamos a hacer un círculo, ¿un círculo?, ¡un círculo!". Students began noticing and instinctively started to form a circle. She kept singing… it was marvelous. Add a double clap between verses and you have a powerful attention-getting routine.

The following chants also work well when kids are trained to repeat the second half after hearing the first part: "**Clase, ¡Escucha! ¡Estamos en la lucha!**" *(often accompanied with pumping fists in the air)*, "**¿Hola hola?** *(raise hand to ear)* ¡Coca cola!**", " ¿Qué te pasa, calabaza?** *(shrugging)* **, nada nada limonada**", "**Uno, dos, tres… ahora sin el inglés**", "**Otra cosa,** *(put outstretched hands together at thumbs to form a butterfly)* **¡mariposa!**". It is best to start the chant before you have lost control. Just as you begin to feel control slipping away, launch straight into a chant.

9: Harnessing a Running Horse technique to regain control

Harnessing a Running Horse: If you are talking about interesting things in class you will occasionally find yourself in a situation in which everyone suddenly gets so excited that side conversations erupt spontaneously. Clearly you should try to prevent this from happening, but when it does you have about 20 seconds to regain control of your class. I have a technique called **"harnessing a running horse"** that allows you to maintain a pleasurable atmosphere in class without yelling or unpleasant reminders about rules. Keep in mind, however, that *this is a tactic of last resort*. It stops working if you are doing it every 5 minutes! Watch a video of the technique in action: **tinyurl.com/2p8wxdrv**

Harnessing a running horse: technique to quickly regain control

Get Buy-In from Parents

If you are in a new district, or substantially changing methods and shaking up the status quo, you may need to preemptively defend your program so that you don't face parental misunderstandings before you get started. Let's take a look at some ways to get parents on board before misunderstandings brew.

Sometimes the best approach is to fly under the radar.

Is your classroom your castle, or do you have a department chair keeping a close eye on you? Are you a tenured, established leader in your school, or a new hire that has yet to map out how power is expressed in your district? If your principal receives parental complaints, does she ask parents to first speak directly to you (thus empowering all involved) or does she pass on anonymous complaints to you (thus enhancing uncertainty since you cannot even communicate with the stakeholders involved). Consider your teaching situation carefully.

Unfortunately, your power to influence other educators and the school community is not rooted in the strength of your opinions or even the depth of your knowledge; **your power to defend change emanates mostly from your reputation as an excellent and beloved teacher.** Build that reputation first.

Make sure that the first impression of your class is a good one.

Your school probably has an online grade book, and if not then your students are certainly wondering where they stand in terms of grades. Release that tension as quickly as possible. I make sure that my first two weeks of daily exit quizzes are recorded immediately so that when parents and students log-in for the first time there is inevitably an A there. Those first two weeks are all about developing class routines anyways… consider seriously what you are losing by letting that first impression be a D! If a student were to actually fail my first really easy comprehension quiz, I just would not record it and then pay very close to her the next day during class to make sure she gets an A.

After two weeks I tell students that I am now confident that everyone knows how to play the game and I am going to start giving slightly more difficult comprehension quizzes, "so pay close attention to what we say in class". Everyone has an A at that point, and most students keep the A throughout the rest of the year. Nothing motivates like success.

Demonstrate a technique that is your strength during Back to School Night.

The parents who attend are the community voices that will either defend you or band together to run you out of town. Don't waste your chance to impress them with a research-filled power point or a lecture about homework; they will trust you if they feel in their hearts that you are competent. I spend my 10 minutes on a quick demo of card talk because I can easily personalize and remain 100% comprehensible. I want to show them that our class might not be like the language course they once took in high school, and that might be a good thing.

On the way out the door I have a student volunteer handing out an information sheet with my absentee policy and other details. Some parents read it, especially those who approach school like a perpetual courtroom where they are the lawyers defending their children, but most leave my classroom with Spanish buzzing in their heads and a nebulous sense that they can trust me.

Don't let your policies blind you.

In my class, grades reflect whether students engage and, well, if they actually attend class. I know that they will acquire the language if they are simply present and understanding… it is my job to make sure I pace the conversation so that everyone in class understands. However, we cannot be successful if they don't come to class. I now have the track record to prove to administrators that this approach leads to success on outside assessments (in my case, the AP and IB exams). However, in my zeal to make sure that students attend my class I have, at times, imposed draconian punishments for absences.

Let me explain something peculiar about my district: I am frustrated that so many extracurricular coaches can excuse students from my classes. All the time. I even caught the ASB secretary changing my online attendance records. It was outrageous. I reacted strongly with policies to try to keep kids in my class. Strongly! It took me a few years to perfect my grading system so that students would not skip class to make prom posters (yes that really happened, absences excused by the ASB director), **but I was still burning relationships with students, parents and other educators who believed that they have the right to routinely pull kids from my class.** Even worse, at times I was blind to the ways that my attendance policies failed to adequately distinguish between students shirking class and students missing class because they were living in debilitating poverty. If you are a new teacher in your district, understand that your policies may upset the culture of your workplace. **Be flexible and avoid confrontation until tenured.** If tenured, keep in mind that any confrontations you take on, even unwittingly, may impact your entire career. You might decide that the fight is worthy, like I did, but remember that 'burning bridges' is long-lasting.

Get in the habit of looking at your grade book and identifying students who need an intervention.

Leave behind your sense of indignation, even if students chose this path. Dig them out of their hole. If like me you have one of these crazy policies that attempts to deal with an even crazier school culture, recognize when to throw in the towel. If the kid is already failing, the policy clearly does not have the intended impact. Dig the kid out and find a new way to motivate the student. Parents will be grateful.

Allow parents the ability to find evidence of rigor in your classes.

For some parents it is all about the grade, but not for all. Some parents may be upset if their children say your class is extremely easy. Many people still associate the concept of rigor with difficult mental exertion, which is not the case when acquiring a language.

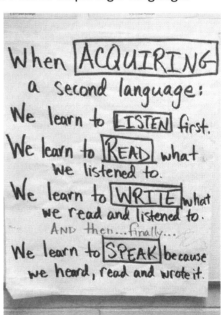

Luckily we have the evidence that will impress many parents. Have your students copy the Write & Discuss text that the class creates each day into a notebook. For homework once a week, have students translate one of the W&D's to their parents and ask that a parent or guardian sign the page. Some parents are still looking for conjugation charts, but many will be surprised by the richness of the language that their children already understand.

Now, some parents will leap to ask their children to start speaking. In that case it might help to coach your students on the order in which skills emerge, beautifully expressed in this poster written by Grant Boulanger.

Grant's posters are available at http://www.grantboulanger.com/products/

Cultivate signs of success in your classroom.

I like to build a text-rich classroom with the annotated One Word Image posters covering the majority of my wall space. Not only does the text inspire my students, but the colorful student-created images speaks to a class in which students are truly engaged in their learning (um, or "acquiring"). Be sure to display your classroom library during Spring parent-teacher conferences so that parents can see that there is substantial rigor in your classes; in the month before you meet with parents track student reading so that you can show them the exact books that their child has chosen to read. I like to take this moment to also talk to every parent about literacy during the summer months, encouraging them to bring their children to the public library once a week.

Don't try to be the fun teacher.

Parents like teachers that their kids like, so it is tempting to try to build a 'birthday surprise party' of a class where everyday is a constant string of new surprises and delights. Most teachers burn out after a month of being a constant entertainer, and students quickly grow bored. **It is better to learn to become a good conversation partner rather than a theatrical entertainer**.

If your students just stare at you and never participate, I get it. Schooling has trained them to turn off. Tell them to answer with just a few words in English. Use the "verify comprehension" techniques in the basic skills module. Then put their ideas in the target language, slowly and deliberately. Are they still silent? Turn and write it on the board. Point at it, read aloud and pause. Then ask another question. Don't give up. Don't respond to the need to fill the space. You are not on stage.

Seek to fill the role of a **respected adult**, not a summer camp buddy. Learn all of their names and more through student interviews. Become comfortable with awkward silence. You are not there to entertain them; you are building social skills that many young people have not developed. When students become engaged, curious and actively consider your questions, they enter into a state of flow where language is acquired effortlessly through good, comprehensible conversation.

The First Days of School

The first hours of language class can be difficult to imagine for many teachers, even those accustomed to leading a free-flowing conversational class. Where to begin *when they know nothing!?!*

It may be tempting to start with thematic vocabulary ('head, shoulders, knees & toes' anyone?) or memorizing a few basic greetings just to find a starting place, but I want to convince you otherwise. You'll never have the opportunity to make another first impression, and you want to *firmly cement the idea that conversation and their contributions will form the backbone of this class.*

Save thematic vocabulary such as body parts for a later **bailout move**. First things first: you want to get everyone familiar with the highest frequency verbs (and the interrogative words) as quickly as possible so that your class can be immersed in communicative activities.

There are three goals that I have for the first days in any class:

- Set in place the **most important class management rule**: 'One person speaks, everyone else listens'.

- **Get to know students**. It is not only the teacher who needs to get to know students; students need to get to know each other as well.

- Build a communicative foundation by making sure everyone acquires the Super 7 verbs, **the Sweet 16 verbs** or whichever high-frequency list of verbs along with the interrogative words that you will need to verify comprehension.

You will never have goodwill like on the first day of school. If your administrators permit it, don't blow the first day on administrative blah blah blah. Kids are getting syllabi in every other class. Worse yet, kids are being switched in and out of classes and you'll need to go over it again. Save it for the third or fourth day. Instead choose some of the following activities and, **when you eventually give out your syllabus, go over it in 5 minute brain breaks**.

Card talk, described fully on page 151: This is the ideal first day activity because it is easy to talk comprehensibly using student drawn illustrations while personalizing the conversation, talking about their interests. I think it is not a bad idea to spend 15-20 minutes on card talk, then introduce students to **Write & Discuss** (see page 61). Co-create a text about the content of the card talk session, and then give them a four question oral quiz based on the Write & Discuss. Within the first 30 minutes you will have demonstrated not only **how they will acquire a second language** (by listening and understanding the class conversation), but you will also show them **how to easily get a good grade** in your class. After you have verified that everyone passed the first 'quiz', you can either attend to administrative mumbo jumbo such as student handbooks, or you could continue for another ten minutes of card talk and then give a real **exit quiz** (see page 66 for details) that goes into the grade book.

Student interviews: I usually have a power point with five questions in both the target language and the translations in English. On the first day there is typically a ton of code switching (switching from target language to English and back). In the first few days of class I am all about the message, about the conversation, and over the course of a week I slowly transition to a 90% target language classroom. You might feel like it is important to remain nearly 100% in the TL from the very beginning, but I like to emphasize that I am first very interested in my students, and then putting that information into the target language.

Have a photo ready to project against the white screen for a **picture talk** (see page 148) in case you get nervous and blow through the planned activities too quickly. An interview chat, a card talk, a picture talk and a quick Write & Discuss activity plus the exit quiz is more than enough for an hour-long class. In fact if you are going slowly, pointing and pausing and writing on the board, you'll probably be lucky to finish two activities. The conversations will produced a full paragraph of comprehensible language in the target language. However it is important to make sure that class is legitimately about the students, not just a pre-written 'mad lib' type activity in which you plop student names into a prepared script. **You want to have a *real* conversation. If you already know the answers to the questions you ask, it's not a conversation.**

The main thing that I want to communicate is that, *in my opinion*, you should not freak out about remaining in the target language in these first few days of class.

Focus on the three goals that I list above:

1. **Class management** ('one person speaks, everyone else listens')
2. **Getting to know each other**, and
3. **High frequency verbs**.

    Complete at least **one Write & Discuss** per period (at the beginning of the year I might even do two, one halfway through the class period and the other at the end of the class period) and **end every class with an exit quiz** so that your students can see how much language they are processing each class.

    As you feel comfortable, write on the board more so that you speak English less, but **keep student ideas and conversation in the center of the class**.

Class Jobs

Much has been written about assigning students a job so that they feel essential to the class community and so that the class runs smoothly. In my own practice I only assign a handful of class jobs because, unless I truly need the job for my own sanity, I find unnecessary complexity to be a drag on my energy.

If you love creating complex systems, "hire" one of your students to be the human resources dept that keeps track of who is doing what job so that you do not have to (a simple notebook will do). You might even arrange your grade book so that a certain amount of "community service" is necessary to earn an A (otherwise the highest grade achievable would be an A- or a B+). If you do that, be sure to publicize that fact loudly and consistently during class and reach out to parents so that they understand in August that their children need to volunteer for class jobs. **But ugh!** I hate the idea of bribing students to pretend to be good members of the class community. It's better to simply encourage students to truly be good class members without a hidden agenda (i.e. grades).

The first six student jobs listed here are the ones that I could not teach without. Keep in mind that **the value of a student job rests in the way that it makes your class run more efficiently**. If a student distracts others when sitting on their special stool, if a student stops paying attention to class herself when she is sitting at the computer, if an artist makes a commotion or makes an inappropriate illustration, just end their employment and return them to their normal seat in class.

- **Computer kid:** Consider abandoning your teacher desk so that **you can always be sitting among students** throughout the class. When I was tethered to my teacher desk, I found that classroom management issues broke out whenever I had to retreat back to my desk to fiddle with the computer, whenever I disappeared into the back of the room, whenever I was not visibly *with the class*. Now I sit on a stool at the front of the class and see issues well before anyone else in class is aware of them. Or I sit with the students, right next to the kid who needs me there during pleasure reading. I tend to have my projector on most of the time with a movie talk file ready to go, so I can just tap on the projector screen to indicate to the computer kid what she should press. During movie talks the computer kid is watching me closely to make sure she presses pause the second that I twitch. **I am not sure how teachers do a movie talk without a computer kid!** Obviously, this is a job the requires trust between student and teacher. It is a highly-prized job among students; generally I settle on a computer kid by September to do the job for the rest of the year.

- **Dictionary kid:** Nobody knows every word, not even the teacher, and if you did not have a childhood in the target language then it is likely that activities like One Word Images are going to test your vocabulary. I think it sends the right message that you do not have to be a dictionary to be fluent. All of my students keep their phones in their bags, which are kept under the tables on the outskirts of the room, except for two students who retain their phones. The dictionary kid is called on whenever we need a word. I encourage them to use wordreference.com because Google turns up some silly translations.

- **Artist #1:** Responsible for the black outlines of characters when we create One Word Images. Uses a thick black sharpie and makes a large figure, while leaving space on all sides for me to include text afterwards. Often we have more than one Artist #1 in class. We switch back and forth and generally settle on two or three students who perform this job when called on. Don't have them compete on the same day to create the best drawing; the competition will burn fragile egos.

- **Artist #2:** After Artist #1 creates the black outlines, he or she will tell Artist #2 what color to use to fill it in. Artist #2 uses crayons. Usually Artist #1 picks their artist #2, and the pair always works together.

- **Student librarians:** When reading period is over students pass all of their books towards the wall rather than getting up and returning their books. If students all get up they will inevitably push and shove when trying to return their books, some books will get tossed in the anarchy. Prevent the damage by having one or two students act as student librarians who carefully return each book to their proper place. This will prolong the useful life of the books in your library.

- **Time Keeper**: Don't let activities drag on. When starting a Write & Discuss I will tell my time keeper to give me 7 minutes, and after 7 minutes the W&D is finished regardless of what has been written because we need to move on to the exit quiz. I do this throughout the class; I tell them to firmly interrupt me during movie talks, interviews, any activity except for the pleasure reading time. I think that other students like the feeling that there are transitions, that we are making progress and not just chatting aimlessly. I like that the time keeper prevents me from focusing on any one thing for too long. Occasionally I will ask for another five minutes to finish a story, but being aware of that time allows me to effectively keep to my lesson plan. The Time Keeper is one of two students who is allowed to have a phone during class time.

The following jobs are valuable additions to CI classes. I might assign them if needed, especially to keep a fidgety student busy. I would not assign every job listed on the first day of class. Instead, assign them as they are needed.

- **HR manager:** Keeps a notebook indicating who was hired for what job, and when. Essential if you give extra credit for doing jobs, or need to keep track of 5 or 6 different classes. The HR manager highlights the student name once the person has completed a job for two uninterrupted weeks or crosses out names of students who have been fired, and records the date that they were fired.

- **Class note taker**: I assign this job if a student insists that they need to take notes during class. Truthfully, just copying the Write & Discuss texts are enough notes for any learner, but some students have an affective need to record everything... particularly in the beginning of the year when the way the class & assessment works is not transparent. The notebook is kept in class at all times; I tell the student that this is for me to refer back to after class to remember what we did in class.

- **Calendar Kid:** Some teachers have the calendar kid announce weather and date at the beginning of class. I prefer to simply have the calendar kid place the appropriate butcher paper calendar for the class on the front white board at the beginning of the class period so that it is there once we finish our pleasure reading (first ten minutes of class). Immediately after the teacher checks in with the calendar ("*Calendar Talk*"), the student returns the calendar to where it is stored (along with calendars for other classes). This is an essential job if you are doing Calendar Talk every day; everything runs so much smoother if the students are in charge of moving things around.

- **Impartial Game Controller:** When we play games on the computer we replace the "computer kid" with the "impartial game controller" who controls the computer while the game is projected against the screen at the front of the room. That way the "computer kid", who is often a little removed from the class, joins us in a competitive activity.

- **Gesture leader:** When the teacher comes up with a gesture for a new vocabulary phrase, this is the student who keeps track of the gesture. If students do different gestures, the teacher calls on the gesture leader to demonstrate the official way to do it. Then everyone closely imitates the gesture leader. The gesture leader has final say over what is correct.

- **Actor**: A student who will *SIT ON A STOOL* at the front of the room and act out from waist up any Write & Discuss text. The teacher reads one phrase and the student acts that particular phrase, as best they can. I find that students who are not tethered to a stool will add movements that are not part of the text and end up distracting the class, so I require that they sit on a stool and only act from waist up.

- **Class cat:** Whenever someone not from our class community comes into the classroom, the class cat starts whispering the words *gato gato gato* (*cat cat cat*) in a steady voice to inform me that there is someone new in the classroom. I may be deeply absorbed in the story we are creating… or I may just want to finish whatever we are doing, but the class comes first! The rest of the class, however, is sitting on the edge of their seats waiting for their signal to act. They are waiting for me to utter the phrase "*había un gato*" ("*there was a cat*"), at which point every student says "**MEOW**" at exactly the same time in a loud, confident voice. No smiles, no giggling… the purpose is to make our visitor wonder what craziness is this. At that point I address our visitor as if nothing unusual had happened. My kids really enjoy this, but practice it to get the classes timing perfect without giggles.

- **Movie/TV show Summarizer:** If you teach an ongoing movie or tv show as an anchor text, I recommend that you teach one or two scenes every day rather than have a "fun Friday" movie day. Yet, seeing a bit every day, you will still come across kids who missed class or cannot remember what happened. The "Summarizer" stands up as the Computer Kid is cuing the video and, in one or two sentences, summarizes what happened last time. In lower levels the student chooses which language they want to use, while upper levels use the target language. This is very useful on Monday after a weekend has erased the memory of students.

- **Idea generator**: This kid has a ridiculous idea ready whenever the class is not generating ideas. Don't over-rely on this kid… I only call on her once per activity maximum, and only if the room is otherwise silent. The idea generator is allowed to participate as normal, so be sure to tell her that she does not have to curb her enthusiasm.

If you include class jobs in your grades, be sure to rotate jobs frequently so that everyone has a chance to volunteer. I would require two weeks of uninterrupted service (i.e. without getting fired or being absent). Better yet, consider erasing the lowest exit quiz or homework grade of everyone who completes two uninterrupted weeks of service. I would even let students build up their awards in a bank so that my athletes (who miss classes during their athletic season) and drama students (who also have specific seasons in which they tend to miss class) would be inspired to really work on becoming an active member of our class community.

- Basic Skills to Maintain a Class Conversation -

> In this module we address the basic techniques that form the foundation of a conversational classroom. Most of these are not activities, but rather make our activities comprehensible and engaging to our students.

You may be tempted to try to 'master' these skills before trying any of the activities presented in the third and fourth modules; I think this would be a mistake. Instead, read through this module and then return to it repeatedly throughout the year. **These are skills that most teachers spend *years* perfecting.**

Do not feel defeated if your first attempts feel like frustrating attempts at conversation. We expect student laughter and delight immediately when, if it happens, it is the product of learning to become a good conversational partner. Resist the urge to entertain and play to student laughter. Return back to this module and reflect on how you can go slower, how you can provide even more opportunities to revisit a text, and how you can drill down with a student interview and really concentrate on getting to know one person without the need to entertain everyone in class.

Ten Essential Techniques for Easy Communication

Remaining comprehensible is *the essential concern*. On the following page are listed the foundational techniques that I use to remain comprehensible to my students. I recommend that you photocopy the page and post it on the wall near where you position yourself while you teach so that you can refer to it in the moment. Even if you are a skilled conversational teacher **there is a good chance that you rely on a few favorite techniques** to verify that your students comprehend what you are saying. Today I want to encourage you to broaden your reach and solidify your skills, because ***remaining comprehensible is everything***.

Write on the board: I know, it seems silly, but I list this as our first legitimate technique in order to SLOW DOWN and RECOGNIZE new words that are being uttered. At the beginning of the year I write an entire sentence on the board along with a translation, and then I use the "artful questions" technique to repetitively use the words in new combinations until students are responding quickly and with confidence. You want to avoid switching oral languages because you want their brains to feast on a single stream of the target language. However, speaking the target language is a waste of time if students do not understand you.

You point & pause at the posters but inevitably you need more words. The poster says "pone: puts" and you just said "pones", so you calmly write "pones: YOU put" on the board and then point and pause, smiling. Then I would ask a few comprehension questions using a variety of interrogatives which lead students to process the new word several more times without having to write anything more on the board. It is okay to break into English and ask, "what did I just say" to make sure that their understanding of the question/statement is exactly correct.

When you write on the board it may be a new word or phrase, but **also use this technique to emphasize a point** that is not using difficult language. The idea is to slow down conversation and focus student attention on an unexpected development in the class conversation. It could be as simple as discovering that your level 5 student does not like chocolate! "*A Ellen no le gusta el chocolate*", I write as I digest this shocking piece of news. There is a good chance that, despite years of input, there is a student in class still acquiring the special way that the verb *gustar* is used in Spanish. I frequently meet *Spanish teachers* who forget the "a" in front of Ellen! Slowing down and writing it on the board will help them acquire.

Remain Comprehensible

Write on the board

Ask artful questions
Who? What? When? Where? How? yes/no this/that

Require choral response

Point & pause at language frames (online) & posters (on walls)

Increase processing speed; don't memorize

Ask students, "what did I just say?"

Default to Sweet 16 when talking in class

Choral translation

Write & Discuss

Exit quiz

Ask Artful Questions: This may sound like a strategy to verify comprehension, and it is, but once you have established the meaning of a new phrase, hearing it used several times in slightly different contexts will help your students acquire it. The key is not to be mechanical and predictable with your questioning. If I were conducting a student interview with Penelope and she revealed that she likes to draw, I would write the phrase on the board (le gusta dibujar) and then glance up at my question words posters to consider the logical questions that I could ask the class. In Spanish I would say, "Class, who likes to draw?" thus repeating the new phrase and requiring a choral response from the class indicating that they understood. They would respond "Penelope"... no need to require full sentences because they simply need to demonstrate comprehension.

Ask artful questions
Who? What? When? Where? How? yes/no this/that

Asking students to repeat or **practice speaking will not lead to quicker acquisition**, it will just slow the process down and likely expose students to hearing the incorrect responses of their classmates who say something like "Penelope gusta dibujar" rather than the correct phrase, "A Penelope le gusta dibujar". Instead, in the target language, continue to ask questions using the new language chunk: "Class, does Penelope like to draw or run?" Then, turning to Penelope, solicit further information using more of those question words (continuing to ask in the target language): "Penelope, where do you like to draw? When do you like to draw? What do you like to draw?"

Penelope can answer in Spanish or one or two words in English, but consistently translate her responses into Spanish and then follow up with choral response questions to the entire class. I like to pose many "either/or" type questions for the choral response, especially when Penelope's responses are free-flowing and out of bounds (meaning, the words have not been experienced before by students in the class). **Key observation: you are trying to ask easy questions that everyone can answer correctly, not difficult questions that trick students and lead them to being unsure of themselves.**

You want to develop their confidence. Hearing the language develops their ability to speak, so find as many opportunities as possible for you the teacher to speak and be heard. Your students' speech reflects what they have already acquired; there is no reason to force them to speak in the early stages of acquisition.

Require Choral Response: Responding to an artful question in chorus keeps students minds engaged with the language. If you require a choral response with a specific correct response, preface each of these questions with the word "Class" (in the target language) and count down from 3 (see the poster on page 37). **This helps build in thinking time for every student and alerts students that you are expecting everyone to respond.** We often ask questions that do not require choral response, for instance when we are soliciting new details while building a class story. If you do not have a process to distinguish between choral response and individual, creative response questions, you are training students to retreat into silence and doubt as they try to read your mind: *"Is this a choral response? Am I supposed to come up with my own answer? Ah, it's easier to remain silent!"*

The choral response questions are comprehension questions, but I think it is best to think of them as **a way to develop the processing speed of your students**. We are getting students to think faster and faster until they are processing the limited language we provide at the speed of a native speaker. For that reason, we are not asking difficult questions!

The teacher, who is observing the eyes and faces of the students, may notice a student who does not respond. This is not always due to non-engagement; that student might be confused. The student may be daydreaming, or she may have gotten lost three minutes ago.

When I see a student who does not join in the choral response, I often ask an individual question to one of her peers sitting near her. Instead of starting the question with the word "Class" (or *clase* in my Spanish class), I say the students name. Upon receiving the correct answer I turn to the student who originally caught my eye and ask, in a different tone of voice, the exact same question. For the first student I ask in a doubtful, quiet tone of voice while the second student hears the same question in an incredulous, roaring tone of voice, or a smiling, inquisitive tone of voice. Either way, I am drawing the non-responsive student back into class without accusations, threats or reprimands.

If you cannot get students to respond in chorus, try getting a non-verbal response. The key is to maintain student engagement. You could ask for students to "raise an open hand or a fist", or you could provide two different colored pieces of paper. "Raise the red paper if Penelope likes pizza or raise the yellow paper if Penelope likes lettuce". I once fabricated a YES/NO paddle for each student (actually it was a Sí – No paddle in Spanish) with an answer in a different color on each side attached to a thick popsicle stick. Students held it up to respond to my many yes/no questions. They quickly realized that repetitively raising an arm is more work than opening their mouths.

Point & Pause: Point & Pause is one of the bedrock techniques to remaining comprehensible. Research shows that an average adult speaks their first language at the rate of approximately 170 words per minute, while the average adolescent processes their native language at the rate of only 130 words per minute. Even if we were teaching in their native language, we need to slow down dramatically to make sure they can process all of the language that is flooding into their ears. Imagine how much they need us to slow down in their second language!

I hope that you display the Sweet Sixteen verbs and the Interrogative words (in both L1 and L2) towards the front of the room. This will give you a perfect reason to pause every time that you say the word, casually stroll over to the poster, lift your arm up and physically touch the word. Repeat it. Some students will roll their eyes. Some students will react with impatience as if this were the worst thing they have experienced today. Keep doing it. You are teaching for the slowest processor, the student who is just putting the language together and who will not speak up. Even the fast students are benefiting from your deliberate pace because they are learning to process the language at the pace of a native speaker.

When you place your hand on a verb and you notice that part of the class does not follow your hand with their eyes, **that is the time to simply ask the whole class, "What does —- mean?"**. Ask in English and if they respond without glancing up then you know they've really got it.

- If you see students glancing up at the poster with the translation written below the verb, get in the habit of asking more comprehension questions so that students have to look up and acquire the word.

- Start with choral response questions so as not to single out any particular student.

- As the class progresses choose a few specific questions aimed at students who are not tracking you with their eyes. By not observing, they are volunteering to be asked individually to show that they have acquired the word.

- Then return to the whole class questions in which you require a choral response.

Increase Processing Speed, don't memorize: When I say that we do not memorize, I mean that we are not drilling a list of isolated words to commit to memory. Increasing processing speed implies that students already understand the phrase when given enough wait time. If we continue to use the language that they already understand in new ways, students will process faster. That is the principle purpose of **asking artful questions**.

Memorizing and tricking students to memorize is so deeply embedded in traditional approaches to language teaching that we need to consciously pull ourselves back. When a student doesn't know what a word means, just write it on the board with the translation! And truly, vocabulary games that drill discrete words (such as the flyswatter game) are incredibly inefficient and, in the long run, ineffective uses of time. The flyswatter game is fun, but after doing action research with classes I found that **a year of unstructured conversation did more to build spontaneous vocabulary use** than a year of flyswatter. In fact, in my classes, the discrete vocabulary games only developed temporary ability to play the vocabulary games—the words rarely showed up in unrehearsed written or spoken samples in class whereas words acquired through spontaneous conversation (when repeated through artful questioning) did show up again in later unrehearsed language samples. *Please see the essay "Activities to leave behind" on page 221.*

Ask Students, "What Did I Just Say?": Use this short technique to verify comprehension with 100% certainty. I usually use this phrase when I believe students are following the change of a verb tense or an idiomatic phrase that we have encountered previously. If they surprise you and you find that students did not in fact understand, consider creating a gesture in the moment for the phrase. **You can develop a gesture** for anything-- absolutely anything! A gesture does not *have to be* for a recurring high-frequency phrase. If the wolf licks the door in your class-created story, create a gesture for wolves that lick doors and then have your students do that gesture as you retell the story.

Too many gestures may feel absurd, but a few humorous gestures prevents students from daydreaming. Eventually (hopefully within that same lesson) we want students to be able to process the language at the speed of a native speaker, but to get the repetitions necessary we may need to first slow down and use techniques that require students to engage in physical and even silly ways. The moment you recognize a misunderstanding: slow down, write on the board and ask artful questions until students are processing the difficult language chunk at a normal speed.

Default to the Sweet 16

: Using the high-frequency verb posters in class will help you speak in a comprehensible manner while also reacting to spontaneous student contributions. When a student reveals something in English during a student interview, my first reaction is often to slow the conversation down while I consider how to express that using the limited language with which we are working. Students will hear me mutter as I look at the verb posters, "which verb can we use" and students will often suggest a verb. For instance if during the first week of classes my student Marie says in English that her cat **stays** in a cardboard box under her bed, I am likely to look at the high-frequency verb posters and simplify her sentence using "está" (is). I'll say, "el gato **está** debajo de la cama" (the cat is under the bed). Then I will repetitively use that sentence, asking a variety of artful questions, so that students acquire the entire message and can process when I speak at the speed of a native speaker.

Later in the semester, after students have fully acquired the Sweet 16 verbs in the present tense, I am likely to continue defaulting to the Sweet 16 but explore other tenses. I'll ask Marie where her cat **was** this morning when she **left** for school. I'll ask if her cat **were** not under her bed, where **would she be**?

Eventually I'll introduce the verb "stays", which is actually a high-frequency verb in Spanish and comes up often enough in level 1 that it is worth introducing in class. But for the first weeks I'll certainly default to the Sweet 16 verbs to gradually build students' mental paradigm of the verb system.

There is a lot of unconscious acquisition going on that will not emerge in students' writing or speaking for a long time. However, if you expose them to rich grammar early on, and you make that rich grammar comprehensible, it will "sound right" in their minds and they will adjust to using the rich grammar when developmentally appropriate. **If, on the other hand, you avoid using the subjunctive until level 3, they will need a very long time indeed before they start using the new grammar in their own spontaneous language.** Don't expect beginning students to output (write or speak) using all of the verb tenses that you expose them to in class, but **default to the Sweet 16 so that you can use rich language while remaining comprehensible in class.** Early on this will help them with their independent reading as they are exposed to language that they may not have seen before in class.

For more on using the verb posters to default to the Sweet 16 please read the section on using verb posters on page 23.

Choral Translation: Like a choral response to a question posed in class, a choral translation is a technique that helps the student identify misunderstanding without having to become the focus of class attention. Leading an effective choral translation is a skill worthy to hone. I typically stand at the board and touch each word as students translate the text, **but don't let students jump ahead!** The teacher must demand that students say each word in unison, without skipping ahead to read the whole phrase.

If students create a loud, unintelligible rumble then you are undermining the purpose of the activity. This is important because the translation is not for the purpose of assessment, not even informal assessment. **The purpose of a choral translation is to make sure that timid students entirely understand the reading**. The students themselves must be able to hear every word.

We frequently use this skill after completing a Write & Discuss text. However, a choral translation does not have to be done with a long text. You can simply write a single phrase on the board as you are speaking and say to your students (in the target language), "Everyone, let's say this in English", and then point to the words as your students translate.

Every time students actively interact with the language, you are pulling minds back into the class conversation.

Write & Discuss: Write & Discuss is a short end of class routine that lasts from 5 to 10 minutes. **Do this every class period for deep acquisition and build a class library of easy texts that your students will have no problem reading.**

Whether you have spent the class interviewing a student, chatting about the weekend or even watching YouTube videos, W & D is an excellent way to get one last repetition of the input by summarizing the class period and getting that information into their notebooks. The W & D texts are also a great answer when parents ask what their children are supposed to study for midterm or final exams.

I stand at the board and simply ask in the target language, "what did we talk about today?". If we interviewed a student I might write that student's name as the beginning of the paragraph. Or I might simply write the word "there is" to start us off. Students suggest the next word or two, no more. They don't suggest full sentences. I ask for just one or two words. As I write a word or to students start calling out ways to complete the sentence. **Write & Discuss is a community text**: don't turn this into a teacher-driven summary. Have a time keeper allot 6 minutes to the process and write as much as you can, but limit yourself to the time. You don't have to summarize the whole class.

I have a group of transition word magnets on the board that I use in all levels. Authentic Spanish sentences tend to be longer and more complex than the average sentence in English, so I add a transition word when students think they are finishing the sentence. I'll add a transition word even if I have no idea how to complete that thought. My rule is once a word is added, it stays and we are stuck to figure out how to finish the paragraph. This leads to a text that summarizes our class conversations but is inevitably more complex than our actual conversation. Yet it is entirely comprehensible!

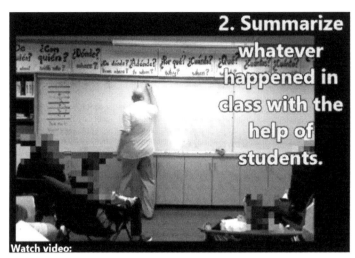

https://vimeo.com/729347325/4d091a2330

But what do you do with the text once the Write & Discuss is complete? Despite the video, I almost never have students take their notebooks out WHILE we are doing the W&D because I want students to be actively participating in the activity. However, once we are done creating the text together I do often (but not always) have them copy the text because I believe there is some value in having them quickly interact with a text that they have already mastered.

The manner in which they interact varies on my whim, but they know that something is up and therefore have an incentive to make sure one last time that they really can connect each word with meaning. **Every class there is always an exit quiz, but maybe once per week, upon copying the paragraph, they may only have 4 minutes left in class and I ask them to quickly translate the W&D,** writing the exact translation for each word in Spanish just above so I can quickly glance at it and match the two. I count that as the exit quiz. To correct it, I certainly don't read the translations word for word. I just glance at them and if it looks on first glance to be all there, they get 100%, almost all 85%, some gaps 75%, significant gaps 60%. I can grade the entire class in the 5 minutes between classes because most students get 100%, it is just a question of flipping through and quickly identifying the students who did not get 100% and placing their quizzes on top so that when I put grades in at the end of the day those quizzes are right on top. I never return the quizzes (same with other exit quizzes), just record the grade and in the trash they go.

Maybe twice a week after copying the text from the board I then tell them to go home and translate the paragraph aloud to a parent or guardian and have that adult sign underneath. I never, ever waste class time checking these signatures. Instead, this is my

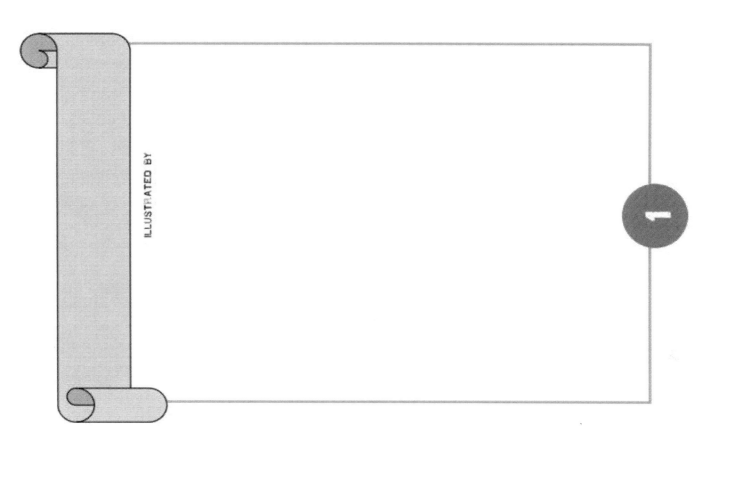

public relations campaign to impress parents with how much their children can understand. I tell students that if I ever speak to their parents, the very first thing I will ask about is the at home reading. Students with helicopter parents know that day will come!

When parents see the W&D notebooks, it preempts the expectations that speaking is the only way for their children to prove that they are learning in class. Parents are generally impressed with the ever-growing notebook packed full of rich L2 text that their children can easily understand. Parents no longer ask, "do you actually do anything in class?!" because the proof is in their hands. Students may often go home saying we do "nothing" in class; the notebook is the physical evidence that we do a lot.

Sometimes I will notice that a student has lost their notebook. That is when I threaten notebook checks. Sometimes parents ask me how their children can study for a midterm or final exam when so much of class content is just made up on the spot each day. I tell them that the best thing their child can do to study is go back and read through their class notebook. If the parent says that the student does not have a notebook, well I AM SHOCKED because the parent has supposedly been signing off twice a week that their child has orally translated the class text. **If you have anyone questioning the rigor of your classes, the notebook is the most eloquent response**.

The notebook can be used as a last resort for reading in class during pleasure reading period (the first 10 minutes of my classes) if the student reports that all of the books in the class library are too difficult. That happens occasionally, especially with students who switch schools midyear. After a while in class they build the reading skills they need to be able to independently read the easiest books in my library, but until then they can read from their own notebook.

The best use of Write & Discuss text is to use the text as the basis of a cartoon that students illustrate over the weekend. These cartoons then form the basis for your classroom library. Not all students will enjoy reading these during independent reading at the beginning of the period, but that is okay. Those students who reject everything that you have as too hard to read independently need an easy read, however, and what could be easier than a packet of readings that were created by the students themselves! It is a smart solution to a problem that could otherwise cripple your independent reading program; every kid needs to be able to read something.

Photocopy the template from the last two pages of this book on to a single piece of paper, double sided. Then fold it; you'll have a four page booklet. Split the text of a W&D text over the four pages and have students illustrate it at home over the weekend. Better yet, do this with several W&D texts from the week and give each student only one so that, on Monday, you'll get a dozen new illustrated pamphlets to add to your classroom library.

Exit Quizzes: This last basic skills technique focuses on daily assessment. There are many approaches to assessment. Some teachers rely on performance rubrics; I think these are too easily challenged by students and parents who claim that the teacher could not possible observe everything that happens in class.

> ***Parent***: *"have you ever been to a child's birthday party? Can you honestly claim that you heard everything said by every child? You only see my child when he is misbehaving, you never praise him for all of the good things he does"*.

Rubrics are great when we have the time to calmly evaluate a writing sample or a recorded conversation, but I do question using rubrics to evaluate the simultaneous participation of an entire class, evaluated in real time while the teacher is teaching and attending to the thousand details of managing a classroom. **Implicit bias** is a real concern.

Whether parental complaints are an attempt at "playing the game" or are based in a profound sense that their child is being wronged, there is no way to respond satisfactorily. You are the professional, you are reporting your professional observations… so why are you putting yourself in a position that begs parents to question your competence?

In situations like these it is better to have hard data that cannot be questioned on the grounds of subjective observations. I am not saying that I don't use rubrics; I prefer not to use them for the daily assessment that forms the core of each students grade.

There is a simple solution: **end each class with an exit quiz.** Collect hard data that are objectively correct, not subject to incomplete observations taken while juggling other tasks and recalled later with questionable accuracy. Base your exit quiz on comprehension of what was said and created in class so that the grade truly reflects what each student understood. Exit quizzes have several other advantages:

- Get a reliable data point from every student, every day.
- Identify slow processors whose eyes did not show signs of misunderstanding
- Identify who you need to focus on when introducing new language
- Lead students to engage every day, even if they are not super interested in the activity
- Communicate the true basis of success in this class– understanding messages in the target language

Simplicity is the key to exit quizzes. During every class period, after completing the Write & Discuss, we complete a **quick four or five question exit quiz**. The questions are based on class discussion, but more often than not many of the questions come straight from the Write & Discuss text. Sometimes I leave the W&D on the board, sometimes I erase it to provide a greater challenge.

On Monday my students rip a piece of paper into quarters to get the paper for four exit quizzes a week, but if you need something more orderly try using index cards. On the fifth day of the week the exit quiz is often a quick written translation of the W&D text. They write their name at the top of the paper before we start; when we finish the quiz everyone puts down their pencils at the same time. Most questions can be answered with one or two words. I tell them not to write full sentences because I want to be able to correct them quickly between classes. I give my quizzes in the target language (Spanish); responses in either Spanish or English are fine. I am interested in their comprehension, not their spelling.

During the first two weeks of school the exit quizzes are ridiculously easy as I norm the class. As the year proceeds the quizzes become harder and I get useful information from each of my students. I never make the quizzes too hard; **I want to stay true to the idea that simply coming to class and listening with the intention to understand is enough to acquire the language.**

I grade them quickly between classes; since most students earn 100% I can quickly flip through them and place the few that do not earn 100% on the top of the stack, fastening them together with a paperclip before the beginning of the next class. These daily quizzes are weighted as 65% of their overall semester grade because they best reflect the hard, rigorous work of acquisition that we do in class every day. Since they form such an important part of the overall grade, I also do not want to make these quizzes tricky because I do not want to encourage a class culture of cheating.

I simply excuse the occasionally absent student from the quiz. A retake is too much of a burden on student & teacher. Frankly, if you have a quiz every day then you have enough data points to surmise general trends.

If you do find a culture of cheating developing among your students, respond with the following multi-pronged strategy:

- Explicitly name the problem without identifying any particular wrongdoer: "*I have the impression that some people are whispering the answers under their breath. That is cheating*".
- Name the solution: "*I am making these quizzes easy so that you do not have to cheat. If any question is too difficult, tell me so that I can replace it with an easier*

question". Now give the quiz and after each question ask people to quietly raise their hands if they want a different question. When a hand is raised, tell them the answer and then either give the same question or a much easier question. You are learning a lot about who needs help in your class, and you are teaching your students valuable life skills concerning honor and honesty. By giving away these answers you are building a culture of trust between student and teacher. In a culture of cheating the teacher is an enemy to be fooled; **you need to build a bridge to a culture where the teacher is a coach that helps every student shine**. It's not a bad idea to explicitly say that last line so students understand why you are acting so strange, giving the answers away!

- While doing the above, sit directly behind the group that was cheating. Temporarily switch a student's seat if you must, but recognize that the students who are most involved in a culture of cheating may likely see the above speech as evidence that you are easy to fool. You need to sit directly behind them so that you can hear every whisper. Separate them if necessary. The speech above prevents the rest of the class from adopting the ethos of cheating as they observe that you are not a fool. **Make honesty the easier and more gratifying path in your class.**

- If the group that you have identified continues to cheat, quietly inform them that if they need to be closely watched during the quizzes then you will require that they take their exit quizzes during lunch every day. It will be a different exit quiz, of course.

- Over the next week continue to purposely ask the class whether an exit quiz question is valid whenever a question flirts with trivia. Encourage students to advocate for themselves so that they see you as the coach who helps them improve rather than an enemy to undermine.

A daily exit quiz provides actionable data for the teacher to use to modify instruction. After all, **the reason we spend any time on assessment is to improve instructional outcomes**, not to rank students or simply get some grades in the grade book. If you are not reacting to the grades, why are you assessing?!

In my own classes I glance through the daily exit quizzes and make sure that none of my students develop a trend below a B. If I see that Tammy earned a D yesterday, I will direct more of my attention to her when checking for comprehension. I will make sure that I am speaking at the correct pace for her. If she offers, I will be sure to incorporate her suggestion into the *One Word Image* that we are creating so that the class feels more compelling to her. Not every class period will be a home run for every student (some classes aren't home runs for anyone, student or teacher), but I will make an effort to personalize the class towards Tammy on that day so that she is drawn in and then finds it easier to pass the exit quiz. I might even check in with her during the quiz to make sure she feels strong about her answers. I will certainly check to make sure we broke the emerging trend and put her back on a path of success.

I know that I cannot be *everything* for *every student* on *every day*, but using the results of the previous day's exit quizzes helps me pace my classes to the slower processors rather than the vocal fast processors. Being able to react immediately and prevent any student from ever falling through the cracks will make administrators love you. And in a perfect world, parents and students would love you for this too.

Bailout moves & extending the input

Repeated exposure is a key factor in language acquisition.

In class I often manage to say something new and make it comprehensible to my class. I think I am at my best, however, when I am able to find **many clever ways of repeating the comprehended message** while still remaining compelling to my students.

Linguist Paul Nation emphasizes that re-reading and second encounters with a text is very beneficial for language acquisition. I think this has to do with the lesser cognitive load demanded of students on the second pass through. Think of the brain as a computer; the second pass through, less energy has to be dedicated to understanding the message allowing the unconscious brain more energy to piece together the way the language is put together. In my own classes I notice that my heritage learners improve spelling when they read easy *easy* texts, whereas when I used to dedicate the majority of our reading time to difficult but rewarding classic literature there was very little impact on their spelling. **It is the light cognitive load that allows them to soak in so much.**

A good repetition could be as simple as restating a message with a different emotional tone. For example, imagine in a student interview that we just established that Tom has three older sisters. After making this comprehensible through writing on the board (or pointing and pausing if you are using a power point to conduct the interview) then simply turn to one side of the class and whisper the phrase in a questioning tone, "he has three older sisters". Take a moment to look stunned. Turn to the other side of class and announce astonished, "Tom has THREE older sisters!". Look straight at Tom and say with fear, "You have three older sisters?! Is it hard to live with three older sisters!?"

You can do this with any new fact established in class; "the cat is blue?" I ask quietly, then astonished, then with fear as I ponder the reality. Or I could respond happily, as if that were the best twist I had heard all day. This repetition remains compelling to my students because each repetition actually communicates slightly different information about my emotional reaction. However I am leading my students to process nearly the same phrase, over and over again.

Emotional reactions can go very far to help you repeat phrases in the moment, but much of the repetition in my class goes beyond the moment and leads students to revisit language that was previously spoken or read in class.

Film a freeze-frame version of your class conversation in which EVERY student acts out your narration. You read one line and students arrange themselves in a frozen representation of what is happening. The teacher walks among students with camera in hand, commenting on their poses. The "freeze frame" conceit is useful because it prevents horseplay and focuses students on expressing the action in the phrase read. A good video can be saved to play again later in the year, ready as a five-minute bailout move.

Jenny Robbins shares a strategy called **Hallway True or False**. Students line up in one long line in the middle of a hallway. The teacher reads a sentence from a longer text that everyone has read (whole class novels are ideal for this, but non-fiction articles, *maravillas* or other texts with lots of details could be used as well). Students simply touch the right wall if the statement is true, or the left if it is false. Watch the video to see how great this looks in practice.

If you have a lively pair of students who are in the school's drama program, don't miss the opportunity to harness their energy with an **"actor in a box" activity**. Choose two students to act out the text as you read it. To keep the

watch the video:
https://vimeo.com/729409909/167bd05f04

attention on the text, I have two stools that I place on the right side and left side of the front of the room. Student actors remain planted firmly on the stools and use their upper bodies to be as expressive as possible. This prevents them from moving about the classroom, getting too physical and embellishing the text with actions that are not actually in the reading. Film it to watch again later in the year.

A game of mysterious person is a great way to recycle information from weeks of student interviews. In the video German teacher Ben Fisher from Washington state paces his speaking carefully for his audience and does a great job demonstrating the almost imperceptible things we do while speaking that reinforces comprehensibility.

watch: https://vimeo.com/729412170/afbc875731

I recommend that you get a subscription to the **Textivate website**. Every once in a while you will make a W&D text with your class that you really want to save in all of its wonderful complexity. I put these texts into Textivate and then save them as a bailout move for some later day. Perhaps a month later we will have trouble being creative, so I cut the story activity short and pull

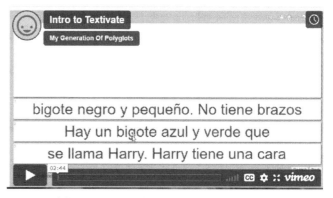

https://vimeo.com/715795159/5d8c5f1849

up the Textivate activity that reminds us of when we made a really great story. There is so much that Textivate does to help students revisit the text that I have made a short video. It really is worth the expense of the subscription and, personally, this is my all-time favorite bailout move as well as one of my favorite ways to extend the input.

A simple game of "Yes or No" feels novel when Ben Fisher has students stand in a circle, scream the answer and use hand gestures. Never underestimate the power of a teacher's optimistic enthusiasm to make an activity feel interesting.

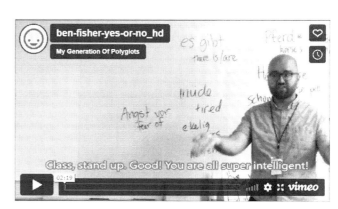

https://vimeo.com/729425755/5f65d66b29

Trashquetball: In the video Texas Spanish teacher Andrea Schweitzer demonstrates the game after having watched a video with her class. The questions are improvised in the moment and you see a lot of other skills in this video, including use of class chants and movement to maintain students' attention. One crucial thing that I love about this video is the way Andrea takes advantage of the moment to create a lot of comprehensible class conversation within the game. The spontaneous game narration becomes a wonderful source of comprehensible language.

https://vimeo.com/359819087/f258dead65

A Running dictation is a reading activity designed to burn calories. Created by California teacher Jason Fritz, a paragraph length text is posted outside of the class in the hallway. Students work in pairs: one runs out into the hallway and memorizes as much as possible, then returns and recites it to the other student who copies it on a piece of paper. The student who memorized the text must make sure that there are no spelling errors, but cannot touch the paper or pen. Then the two students switch roles and the student who wrote now runs out into the hallway to memorize the next part of the paragraph.

Depending on the length of the paragraph, this activity usually takes 5 to 10 minutes. There is a variation in which the text is split onto several pieces of papers and, after copying them, students have to arrange them in the correct order.

I made a version with crossword puzzles designed for classes reading my novel *Superburguesas* as a whole class novel. The crossword puzzle clues are posted outside while the answer grid stays in the classroom. The activity requires reading, but less writing, so it is a quick burst of physical activity that can be finished in less than 5 minutes.

The eBook versions of Superburguesas are free for members of the online Master Class. If you are reading Superburguesas with your classes, you can find my crossword puzzles and other free activities for teaching the novel here:

https://mygenerationofpolyglots.com/crosswords-lame-or-fabulous/

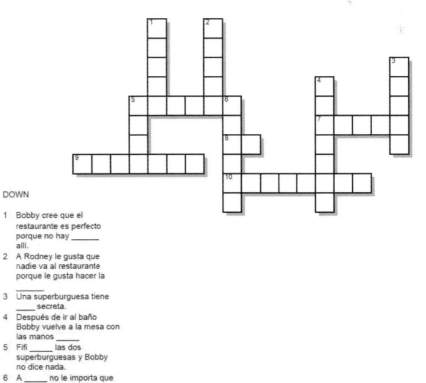

ACROSS

5. El señor Superburguesas tiene que _____ el restaurante porque nadie quiere comer las hamburguesas.
7. Rodney es un empleado que nunca se lava las _____
8. Bobby le _____ la comida a Fifi porque no quiere comer.
9. Rodney grita el número trescientos _____ y ocho.
10. En el baño Bobby ve a Rodney, el _____ malo.

DOWN

1. Bobby cree que el restaurante es perfecto porque no hay _____ allí.
2. A Rodney le gusta que nadie va al restaurante porque le gusta hacer la _____
3. Una superburguesa tiene _____ secreta.
4. Después de ir al baño Bobby vuelve a la mesa con las manos _____
5. Fifi _____ las dos superburguesas y Bobby no dice nada.
6. A _____ no le importa que haya perdido el trabajo en el restaurante.

Superburguesas - capítulo 1

Fluency Writes

Build student confidence with this simple output activity

Speaking and writing are not the center of my class for a good reason; linguists who specialize in second language acquisition emphasize that **language is acquired through a steady stream of listening and reading**. Students do not learn to write by writing; they learn to write by reading.

I do not worry about the silent student in level one, as long as that student can demonstrate that she understands the messages received in class. When we ask kids to output (write or speak) before they are ready, we risk invoking the monitor, that part of their brain that closely monitors output for correctness, choking their output and raising their affective filters. The monitor is helpful eventually, but first we want the language to flow freely and unconsciously.

> "A flood of input [comprehensible listening & reading] precedes a trickle of output."
>
> -Susie Gross

In class I do not explicitly correct student output until my level 3 students start writing essays, and even then I am careful. Krashen states that explicit correction is only useful in specific situations: mostly during the editing process when the student has the time to reflect. Researcher John Truscott famously argued that not only does grammar correction not work, but **it may even be harmful to students**. During conversation learners consciously attend to meaning, not structure. They rely on their unconscious understanding of the language to structure the way the language is put together. That unconscious understanding is built through much listening and reading.

All of this is to caution the language teacher against using fluency writing as a tool to "teach writing". Fluency writing is a technique that empowers learners by making them aware of the impact that all of the input has had. The texts produced by learners might also be used to lead teachers to reflect on the quality of input that they provide in class. However, a fluency write should never be graded for grammatical accuracy. That would be missing the point.

I assign a fluency write about once every three weeks starting three weeks into the school year. If you and your students are organized enough to keep them, they provide a convincing document of progress that will make most students and parents proud.

Routine fluency writing, when spaced out between several weeks so that improvement is perceptible, can lead students to reflect on their increased proficiency and thus develop intrinsic motivation to continue acquiring the language.

The process is simple: students write on a blank page as quickly as they can for between 5 to 10 minutes. Their goal is to write at least 100 words. The first time students are asked to write, many students may only produce 30 words in 10 minutes because they are worried about grammatical accuracy. When the time is finished have students count the number of words on the page. I usually exclude proper nouns from the count. Then have students close their eyes and raise their hands to indicate how many they have written. Start low, asking students to raise their hands if they wrote 30 or less words, then 30-50 words, 50-70 words, 70-90 words, more than 90 words. Marvel at the high counts. Since it is the first time your students have done the activity, give them a 50 word bonus to add to their count so that the students who only wrote 30 are boosted up to 80. Have them write that final number on the top of their paper; that is their grade. Obviously many will have over 100 with the bonus... the highest grade I record in my grade book is 100.

This process leads students to write with fluency and, with more input, their accuracy improves. You might think that students would just write unintelligible lists or copy random words posted on word walls, but if they have been exposed to Write and Discuss every day you will find that it is a lot easier to write simple sentences than scan the room for words. I occasionally get a new student from a different school system who writes a verb conjugation chart on their first fluency write, but that quickly is replaced by simple sentences. **It is wonderful to keep that first fluency write as a baseline to compare to future fluency writes.**

As a teacher new to this approach, these texts might help the observant teacher reflect on the input that they are providing in class. For instance, early in my career I realized that I was not using the first and second forms of verbs enough in class conversations. I was constantly using the third-person "he/she" forms, but I need to also talk about myself and address a specific student as "you", plus write those forms on the board so that students get broader exposure to how the Spanish language is put together. As a result I started to consciously use myself as a parallel character whenever we discussed student lives. If a student revealed that they played the guitar every Sunday at church, I would comment that I play the harmonica in my bathroom and my cat screams when I do that. All lies, but just a way to get the first person form into the conversation.

I would caution against looking too closely at these texts; some errors will not be corrected until students have received hundreds of hours of input. The research strongly suggests that the order of acquisition cannot be altered by focusing the input, so while you may use the verbs ser and estar in many comprehensible situations, students will fully acquire them later in their language journey. In fact, the intricacies of ser and estar are said to be among the latest language features fully acquired.

A few pieces of advice:

- You may be tempted to do a fluency write whenever your activity is losing steam… **avoid this temptation!** Look at the previous section on **bailout moves** and **extension activities** instead. I schedule a fluency write once every three weeks, sometimes once a month, so that there is observable growth between each text.

- The first few times you might want to schedule the fluency write to take place immediately after a long session of conversation. This will be easier for students because the language will still be sloshing through students' short-term memory and many students will write a summary of what you just spoke about. This is great for their self-confidence, **but eventually you will want to switch to schedule the fluency write on a Monday at the beginning of class**. You want to see what is in their long-term memory! Try doing it immediately after a class conversation for the first several fluency writes, and perhaps late October switch to Monday morning.

- I have Craig Klein's poster of characters posted on my wall (see the photo on page 35) and, of course, the Sweet 16 verbs. **For students who are truly "stuck", I tell them to copy one of the characters and then choose a verb to make a sentence.** These are just visual cues to give students ideas. Most often a student will write two or three simple sentences and then create their own sentences… but they just need a sentence starter.

- At first I do not require that students write about a specific theme or prompt. "Write about anything, but keep writing. Your grade is based on number of words written. It is okay to repeat phrases, just keep writing". Later, once everyone can easily write 100 words in 10 minutes, I may start giving specific prompts but only to serve as inspiration, never to require that they use specific vocabulary. In order to see what is truly acquired on an unconscious level **we do not want them pausing and editing their writing; instead we want a 'brain dump' of text.**

- Do not worry that in November there is a student writing 78 words and another writing 210 words. **People naturally develop at different rates**. As long as they are both putting an honest effort into the work, both deserve a decent grade.

On the following pages you will see a few sample fluency writes that were completed mid-year by **non-native, level 1 Spanish students**. Literally 5 months of conversation and they are writing like my 4th year students when I was a traditional teacher!

Spanish 1 non-native speaker
10 minute free write in class,
no access to resources other than sweet 16 verb wall and question words

Haley

Paula tenia una pesadilla muy malo. Paula va a la cama de Marcos y le dio Marcos la anillo. En la clasa Carolina y Victoria ve el anillo y dice «Esta Alfonzos» y Marcos dice «Mi hermana le dio a me». Carolina y Victoria va a la cama de Paula y se despierta a Paula y dice «Vien a al bosqu y le dio me donde tu vio el anillo.» y le dio tambien «Es una secreta de chicas» Fermin ayuda Maria. Maria es en la cama de Fermin cuando Jacinta viene a la puerta y dice «¡Fermin! Abre la puerta» Maria abre la ventana pero la ventana no puede ser abre. Fermin ve Jacinta cuando ella abre la puerta de su cama y Fermin corre y Jacinta no abre la puerta. Fermin ayuda Maria y Maria dice «Nadia tiene ayudame». Cuando Carolina, Victoria, y Paula va a la bosque Ivan viene tambien. Paula ve una flour blanca pero no puede tener porque la flour es muy alto. Paula ve una gnomo alto y dice el gnomo es buena.

Un Cuento de Ballena

137 words

Había un chico que escondió una ballena en el baño de su casa. Su mamá no sabía porque era ciega y cuando ella entraba el baño olía la ballena y pensaba que su hijo olía mal. El chico le gusta la ballena y es un secreto pero su mamá no sabía hay una ballena en el baño. Cuando su mamá entra el baño y le dijo, "¿Qué olía mal en el baño? Es tú?" Pero, él no quería por su mamá sabía una ballena en el baño. El le dijo, "No mamá, es la bascura en la papelera. No es mí." Y su mama es una ciega, ella cree que es la bascura. Día tras día, una ballena crecía mucho y es más grande por el baño. Un día, un chico tomó la ballena y ponerlo en la piscina. Es un lugar perfectamente por la ballena. En un otro día su mamá ciega, va afuera y le dijo, "¿Qué olía mal afuera? Es el mismo olor de baño." El le dijo, "Hay otra bascura afuera y olía mal." Pero, su mamá no cree. ¡Su mamá fui a piscina, y tocó una ballena! ¡Increíble!

Student Paired Retells

When I started my journey into this conversational approach to language acquisition, **paired retells** or "turn and talks" were a constant companion to the school day. I would present a new sentence in the story that we were creating, circle it repetitively by asking questions and making statements using language from that sentence, and then ask my students to turn to their partner and orally retell our story up to that moment.

Over the years, **paired retells slowly dropped out of my practice**. Terry Waltz famously declared paired retells to be the McDonald's of language acquisition: not the best nutrition for growing minds. The high-quality teacher-created language of our stories, such as a phrase like "a mi me gustan los coches", quickly turns into "Yo gusto coches, *do you* gusto?" in student-to-student conversation.

During a paired retell students give each other poor-quality input full of beginner mistakes... so why expose students to that?!! I was eager to make my classroom a more efficient laboratory where my students acquire language as quickly as possible, so I phased out the low-quality paired retells in favor of more high-quality input provided by me, the teacher.

If I am honest, I'll also point out that **paired retells had a place in my classroom management plan in those early days**. I could keep my students quiet and on task listening for short stretches of time as long as they knew that they'd have time for chaotic conversation in just a few minutes. While "turn and talk" pauses were great during my first few years in the classroom, they became less necessary as I developed the class management skills to maintain a quiet, respectful class in which one person speaks and everyone else listens.

I kept thinking about what Terry had said. How much class time did we spend on student-to-student conversation? Each "turn & talk" was quick, between 30-60 seconds per instance. I timed it one day; on that day we spent nearly 20% of our class period on student-to-student conversation!

I thought: Wouldn't my students acquire so much more if I could use those 10 minutes delivering more high-quality input instead of the low-quality input that they were currently giving each other?

Without the constant interruption of paired retells, we have gained more time to dive deeper into student interviews and learn more about the people in the classroom.

Some teachers might think that students learn to talk *by talking*, which is intuitive but not really how language acquisition works. **Talking is the *result*** of already having acquired language. When we have less paired retells, we have more time to acquire language effectively. Ultimately, I credit my students' incredible gains to the very efficient, effective use of class time described here in this book.

Yet I have to ask myself *what, if anything, have we lost by dropping paired retells from my language acquisition toolbox?*

Paired retells can be an empowering activity that leads students to recognize that they can speak more than they think. I remember having the same experience with fluency writes after taking five hours of CI German classes. A fluency write is another output activity that has a strong, positive impact on the learner's self-image as a language learner. Don't provide critical feedback; this isn't the time or place. Instead let students bask in the pride that the language is now flowing out of them.

Paired retells can also function as a sort of accountability measure. If you interview one student for five minutes and then, in pairs, the rest of the class cannot spend 30 seconds talking about that interview, then you know something is wrong. It could be that the teacher was not comprehensible, that there was too much new vocab and too little repetition, or it could be that students simply were not engaging to understand. They were not doing their 50%. When students know that they'll have to turn & talk in just a moment, it gives them an immediate reason to listen intently to the conversation.

I suspect that paired retells might also serve another purpose. Human conversations never naturally follow the "one person speaks, everyone else listens" rule. In a group of forty people, normally many small conversations develop. Otherwise, it is a presentation.

If you successfully follow the "one person speaks, everyone else listens" rule then some students may feel frustrated that they cannot always contribute their ideas to the whole class conversation; a "turn and talk" might give them more chance to be heard.

If we want to mimic a true conversation in large group settings, **perhaps "paired retell breaks" play a sociological function allowing everyone to claim some ownership of the whole class conversation.** If played right, a very short "turn and talk" moment might lead to greater engagement in the whole class "conversation".

Many teachers say that "blurting", "talking out of turn", and "side conversations" are their biggest classroom management issues. **I wonder if frequent paired retells might help these teachers transform their talkative classes into more focused classes with an outlet for talkative students.** The key is to clearly lay down a routine so that there is a clear time to talk to your pair, and a clear time to quietly engage with the whole group conversation.

Teaching can be like sailing in a storm; there are general principals to understand beforehand, but each teacher has to respond in the moment to the complex situation that each group of learners presents. I doubt that I myself will be including too many "turn & talk" moments in my future classes. I have so many other transition techniques that are good, acquisition-focused activities.

Yet, as I was discussing these thoughts about paired retells with experienced German teacher Robert Harrell recently, he commented that *not everything in an acquisition-based classroom is focused on acquisition*.

Developing a class culture in which all students feel seen and valued is a wise course of action, and you might find paired student retells to be a part of your plan to give all students a voice in your classroom.

Encouraging Student Voices

Conversational language teachers require frequent student responses in class so we can assess whether students understand us. It is such a struggle with silent classes whose main response is an empty gaze (or blank computer screen). Yet that lack of response may have been a trained response. Yes, I may have unwittingly trained my classes to be extra quiet.

At times I ask a question anticipating a specific choral response, and I follow that immediately with an open-ended question without any indicating to my students that this is a different type of question. There is no 'correct' answer. It is hardly surprising that students hesitate, unsure whether there is a 'correct' answer or if I am seeking creative responses. **When I do this, I am teaching them to remain quiet in their uncertainty.**

It is great when students are following me so well that they can instantly intuit the difference between a factual 'choral response' type question and a 'begging for creative details' type question. But what about the students that aren't following everything clear as water? What about the students who wonder if there is maybe a 'correct' detail that they missed. Of course they'll choose to remain silent rather than risk looking like a fool.

I want to ask questions so that my students are roaringly correct every time they open their mouths. **That is the kind of confidence I want to build.** When I ask questions that confuse them, I almost always step back and turn it into an either/or question so that they can choose the best option. **So why would I ask questions in such a way that plants doubt in the minds of my students?**

I've created several different routines to indicate to students whether I want a choral response or raised hands. I used to have a stop sign that I would raise whenever I wanted a choral response. I tried saying ¿clase? ¿clase? whenever I wanted a choral response. I myself have undermined both of these routines by not consistently using them. **Consistency is key to classroom management.** My silent classes are the price I pay for my lack of consistency!

Cécile Lainé shared her system so that students know what kind of response she is looking for when she asks a question.

Cécile Lainé
My system is:

I ask a question and raise my hands: ss know they have to raise their hand to answer.

I ask a question and I count to 3: students know they are answering chorally.

I ask a question and make a gesture with my hands (like "come"): students know they can blurt answers.

 · Reply · 1h · Edited   3

I like how having the teacher raising two hands in order to prompt students to raise one hand is so purposeful. I also like counting down, if only I can train myself to do this consistently. I *love* that Cécile has included an option for allowing students to blurt, because honestly that has its place in my class culture too.

A poster helps teach this class routine and, more importantly, maintain it as part of the class culture. **The poster helps remind me to perform this routine.** I recommend that the poster be written in English (unless you only teach heritage learners) so that you can silently point and pause when the rule is broken. All posters should be large enough to be seen from the back of the room. I would draw this on a huge sheet of butcher paper. The other English poster that I keep in my classroom is a banner stretching above the whiteboard that reads, "One person speaks, everyone listens".

Why English?! I think it is a novice teacher's mistake to fill their classroom with a scolding voice; experienced educators draw and maintain clear behavioral boundaries but rely on silent routines so as not to poison their relationships with students. I want my teacher voice to be consistently warm and inviting; I don't want to confuse students. Consistency is important. As much as possible I react to breaking of class rules silently. My silence is loud. I silently point and pause with a neutral gaze (neither smile nor frown, but rather relaxed facial muscles like I am bored), hand raised indicating the appropriate poster whenever the rule is broken. Slowly... I maintain my posture a few beats longer than socially comfortable. When I resume speaking, it is still a warm and inviting voice.

One advantage of adopting Cécile's system is that it builds in a tiny amount of wait time into the response, slowing down your instruction and giving students time to process the language. I recommend making an effort to adopt this system if you are like me and tend to forget routines when immersed in class conversation... it's worth it.

 raise your hand

 choral answer

 blurt

What does a beginners class look like?

Are you worried about grammatical accuracy? Focus on the **Basic Skills** presented in this section to make your teacher talk as comprehensible as it can be. Normally I say: *"stop worrying about grammatical accuracy because, with time and more input, everything will fall into place."* Accuracy is a characteristic of advanced learners. Beginners and intermediates needs lots of listening and reading, above all.

We know that most students need to listen and read *a lot* of the target language before being able to speak. **However, how do we best lead them to speaking?** Do we provide lots and lots of listening with comprehension checks and simply don't expect them to speak for a very long time (like Stephen Krashen & Beniko Mason)? Do we circle around one sentence and continue hammering variations of that one sentence until all students are speaking (like Blaine Ray)?

Both of these approaches work, but they are the extremes. I propose that a reasonable approach focuses on the Sweet Sixteen verbs to structure your class conversations. Let the highest frequency verbs of the target language guide the conversation, allowing for a truly student-centered experience while still limiting the language students hear. Find the balance so that students can experience some early success speaking in the target language.

This is the reason I start the school year with student interviews and card talks. These activities are **inherently interesting to students as they are student-centered, but the nature of the conversations make it easy to continuously loop back to the Sweet Sixteen verbs**. When I eventually move on to creating One Word Images and picture talks we are still pursuing a student-centered curriculum because it is the students' ideas and pictures that generate these conversations. I am still referring back to the Sweet 16 verbs as well. I am very gradually expanding their language through these activities, but I am even more dedicated to repeating the Sweet 16 in a variety of contexts so that my students firmly acquire these highest of high-frequency words.

Linguist Stephen Krashen has argued persuasively that the case for natural language use in the classroom is clear: students who hear and comprehend natural language acquire even the trickiest grammar concepts unconsciously while attending to the meaning. When I say to a student in class, "*quiero que seas feliz*" (I want you to be happy), students are not thinking about conjugations, rules of use of the subjunctive or change of subjects. Instead they are determined to solve the problem that a student has articulated because, after all, *we all want this student to be happy!* Every Tuesday our OWI character faces a problem that we solve. **When this happens frequently in class students hear the grammar enough to acquire it and be able to use it unconsciously, without hesitation.**

Here is a mental image created by a clever educator to explain why we need to repeat so much (if you know who developed this image please contact me so that I can rightly cite the person). You might imagine all of the not-fully acquired target language sloshing about in a learner's mind as if it were in a bucket. Every time the learner understands a phrase, you've added another drop to the bucket. Once the bucket overflows, then the learner can confidently speak. Here is the trick; the more vocabulary that you expose learners to, the bigger the bucket and therefore the longer it takes before the bucket overflows.

Students speak & write quicker in the target language if you provide a smaller bucket of language for them to process.

Don't get me wrong; students need huge amounts of input (listening & reading) before they are ready to output (speaking and writing). But **if we tightly control the language used in class so that there is very little new language every day** (i.e. a small bucket of input rather than a big lake) **students will move from listening to speaking quicker**.

I admire that Blaine Ray's TPRS 2.0 method provides the tiniest of language buckets so that students start speaking very quickly. Teachers who are trained in Blaine's method focus on one sentence at a time. My problem with this, however, is that if the teacher is directing the story, as amusing as it may be, it is not a truly student-centered class. It certainly is not a conversation. I have 30 students in my classroom and I want the class to be about their lives, generating language that is directly relevant to them.

The trick to teaching beginners in a conversational class is to remain interesting while introducing as little new language as possible... which is exactly why I begin my year with student interviews. If you are teaching beginners I suggest that you really limit your language in the first weeks of school so that everyone experiences some early success with output. This **early success is what impresses both students and parents and motivates students to become lifelong language learners**.

I limit my language by posting the Sweet 16 verbs and using those verbs to guide every step of our class conversations, every day. When a level 1 student reveals during an interview that she moved over the summer, I glance at my Sweet 16 verbs and use IR (to go) instead of MUDARSE (to move). **Simplifying is often not about speaking & writing shorter sentences, but rather re-using the high-frequency verbs that we already know**.

I also use whole language from the first day of school-- full sentences so that students are not just following a conversation but are hearing all of the verbs conjugated in the appropriate forms.

¿Tú tienes un perro? Yo (hand placed on my chest) no tengo perro. Tengo (hand placed on my chest) un gato. "Miau", dice (walk over and touch the dice poster) mi gato. Clase, ¿quién (walk over and touch ¿quién? on the interrogatives poster) tiene (walk over and touch the tiene poster)... ¿quién tiene un perro?	Do you have a dog? I (hand placed on my chest) do not have a dog. I have (hand placed on my chest) a cat. "Meow", says (walk over and touch the "says" poster) my cat. Class, who (walk over and touch who? on the interrogatives poster) has (walk over and touch the "has" poster)... who has a dog?

In my Japanese class recently we were talking about 'what we want in the near future'. My tutor wants to travel again. I tried my best to express how nice it is to have a garden in the backyard during the pandemic. I want to expand the garden this Spring. Reflecting on my statement, my Japanese teacher responded: そとにいかずに、そとにいけます。 Roughly, "you can go outside, without going outside". A beautiful phrase extolling the peace derived from a backyard garden in the midst of a pandemic.

I have to laugh though because, while I understood and appreciated her comment in the moment, watching the video of the lesson later makes me realize that it certainly did not appear so. I furrowed my brow, stared up at the ceiling struggling to respond and, when I finally spit something out, I said: きゅうりがだいすきです。 "I love cucumbers"!

Kaho, one of my Japanese iTalki tutors — Struggling to speak

It is okay if your students are not yet expressing complex statements that reflect higher-order thinking. The complexity of our spoken language is always several steps behind the complexity of what we can hear, read and understand. The only path for me to sound like a competent, clear-thinking adult in Japanese is to hear and read a lot more Japanese. Until then, I am stuck with my simple child-like observations. *I do like cucumbers!*

The better we get at the core skills of conversational teaching, the less we ask our students to speak. I don't want to waste class time forcing students to struggle with speaking. Understanding compelling messages will develop student speech much faster than speaking practice. **The more efficient and effective route is to focus like a laser on developing their listening comprehension.** As long as we remain comprehensible, the best path to rapid acquisition is a class full of rich hearing and reading opportunities with much less time dedicated to speaking and writing.

But please read the next section about advanced classes to understand how beginner classes prepare students for the upper levels.

What does an advanced class look like?

Teachers often ask me what CI looks like in upper-level classes. However, when we delve into the question, I sometimes realize that those teachers don't always understand what happens *in a lower-level CI class*.

For example, a teacher recently asked how to develop a rotating curriculum for levels 3 & 4 so that a small cohort of level 3 & 4 students can be scheduled in one section. The teacher wondered how to organize the grammar so that the level 4 students are exposed to advanced concepts without confusing the level 3 students.

My quick response is that students should be exposed to all of the grammar in level 1.

Okay, maybe that is a little too much.

My longer response is that lower-level students do need repetitive, easy language to facilitate rapid acquisition. **It makes sense to focus on simple language.** But, within the context of the class conversation, **students should also be exposed to natural grammar.**

Shelter vocabulary (such as by using the Sweet 16 verbs) so that you are using a limited number of words when you speak to students, but also don't stick to the present indicative when a native speaker would naturally use the subjunctive. Work to include prepositional phrases and transition words that lead to natural-sounding sentences. It is natural to speak in past tenses when asking about the past, even when discussing what happened yesterday. *Don't wait until level 2 to talk about what happened yesterday!*

On the next page I have included a transcript of a part of a student interview that was conducted in a level 1 class. You'll see that I am trying to **remain comprehensible and repetitive by asking questions to the audience & recycling language**, but I also **use natural grammar while remaining comprehensible**. With a transcript you don't see the speed of the conversation; you don't see how I pause between questions, stroll over to the question word posters and lay my hand on one before asking the question. If this were a rapid fire conversation it would have been far less comprehensible for level 1.

Some of the big differences between a level 1 class and a level 3 class are the speed of the conversation, the amount of scaffolds that I use to remain comprehensible, and the depth that I pursue topics. Since an advanced class moves faster, I ask more questions and we naturally get more information. In terms of grammar, in an advanced class I spend more time exploring the conversation and, as a result, we spend more class time using so-called "advanced grammar".

But first we need to appreciate how complex language emerges in a conversational class.

Even in a level 1 class, I am using the subjunctive. In natural conversation native Spanish speakers use the subjunctive in about 15% of sentences. 1 in 6 sentences! I'm not counting, but it is pointless to avoid the subjunctive. Just make it comprehensible.

The phrases on the right are translations of the Spanish included for teachers reading this book who do not speak Spanish. The phrases on the right are not a part of the class; presumably the students at this level understood what was being said.

Teacher: ¿Qué haces durante el fin de semana? (Teacher points at the question projected against white screen, where it was written in both Spanish & English)	**Teacher**: What do you do during the weekend?
Student X: I dance.	
Teacher: ¿Bailas?	**Teacher**: You dance?
Student X: Bailas.	**Student X**: You dance.
Teacher: AH! (write on board "bailo = I dance, bailas = you dance". Then points at "bailo" and says) Yo no bailo. ¿Y tú? ¿Bailas?	**Teacher**: I don't dance. And you? Do you dance?
Student X: Bailo.	**Student X**: I dance
Teacher: Clase, ¿quién baila?	**Teacher**: Class, who dances?
Class: (They say the student's name. If they didn't I would have pointed at the "quién = who" poster. If still no answer, I'd give them the answer and then ask again).	
Teacher: X, ¿quién no baila?	**Teacher**: X, who doesn't dance?
Student X: Usted.	**Student X**: You
Teacher: Correcto. ¿Bailas? Sí o no.	**Teacher**: Correct. Do you dance? Yes or no.
Student X: Sí.	**Student X**: Yes.
Teacher: ¿**Cuándo** bailas? (teacher points at "bailas = you dance")	**Teacher**: When do you dance?
Student X: on the weekend.	**Student X**: on the weekend

Teacher: el fin de semana (writes that on the board). Clase, X baila durante el fin de semana. Clase, ¿baila X en la clase de español?

Class: No.

Teacher: Correcto, X baila el sábado y el domingo, durante el fin de semana. No hay clase durante el fin de semana.

Teacher: X, ¿bailas **todo** el fin de semana (Writes todo = all)

Student X: Sí.

Teacher: ¿Tienes tarea?

Student X: Sí.

Teacher: ¿Cuándo haces tú (points at hace = does) la tarea?

Student X: Friday night. I have to do my homework before I can dance.

Teacher: Okay, tus padres... your parents (turning towards class) do we know that word yet? Padres are parents. (Writes on board padres = parents) Tus padres (point again at the board where it says parents) quieren (point at quiere = wants) que hagas la tarea. Clase, anybody know what I'm saying? (someone almost always will translate it immediately: "his parents want him to do his homework"). (Write on board: "tus padres quieren que hagas la tarea" and then, underneath, "your parents want you to do your homework").

Teacher: Clase, ¿quienes quieren que XXX haga la tarea?

Class: Parents

Teacher: the weekend. Class, X dances on weekends. Class, does X dance in Spanish class?

Class: No

Teacher: Correct, X dances on Saturday and Sunday, during the weekend. There is no class on weekends.

Teacher: X, do you dance all weekend?

Student X: Yes

Teacher: Do you have homework?

Student X: Yes

Teacher: When do you do your homework?

Teacher: Class, who wants X to do the homework?

Teacher: Los padres de X. (Holding one hand up) Los padres... quieren (point at quiere poster)... que (hold the other hand up) X haga la tarea... antes de bailar. Before dancing. Wow that was complex, let's write it all up on the board: "Los padres de X quieren que él haga la tarea antes de bailar." Can we do a choral translation here? Okay, 3, 2, 1...

Class: The parents of X want that he does his homework before dancing.

(The choral translation is awkward because students translate the words as I point at them. However, doing it that way allows any student to understand 100% of the phrase).

Teacher: ¿Quiero yo que X haga la tarea?

Students: ....?

Teacher: Sí, yo quiero que X haga la tarea. Todos sus profesores quieren que X haga la tarea.

That's the way we teachers are, we all want students to do their homework. Pero tú (looking at another student), ¿quieres que X haga la tarea? Sí o no. .

Student Z: I don't care.

Teacher: We have a good phrase for this! "Me da igual". It means, "I don't care". Me da igual. (Writes "Me da igual = I don't care" on the board).

Teacher: X's parents
The parents... want...
X to do his homework...
before dancing.

Teacher: Do I want X to do his homework?

Teacher: Yes, I want X to do his homework. All of his teachers want X to do his homework.

Do you want X to do his homework? Yes or no?

At the end of the class period, during the **Write & Discuss**, I returned to this and inserted the information into the W&D so that it got into their notes. There was more in the W&D and, since a W&D is a conversation bouncing between students and teacher, they did not bring up exactly what I wanted to include. So I made sure to tack it on the end. It looked like this:

A X le gusta bailar durante el fin de semana pero sus padres quieren que X haga la tarea antes de bailar. Señor Peto también quiere que X haga la tarea, pero a Z le da igual.	X likes to dance during the weekend but his parents want X to do his homework before dancing. Mr. Peto also wants X to do his homework, but Z doesn't care.

We may have done a choral translation of the W&D, but I would be satisfied if students can answer questions without actually using the grammar. They may answer in one or two word answers, demonstrating comprehension. The purpose of this is to expose them to the full grammar of the language without yet requiring them to produce grammatically correct sentences.

In class I will not say anything else about the subjunctive or the conjugations as long as they can understand. I will not expect them to produce the subjunctive. Not yet. With time they will develop a solid paradigm of the language because they were exposed to the full grammar in natural communication from the beginning. I will eventually give them more and more opportunities to produce the language, but in level one I am most concerned with developing a passive comprehension of natural language.

In both upper level and lower level classes I am likely to ask all sorts of questions:

"Si pudieras, ¿bailarías aquí en la clase de español?"	If you could, would you dance in Spanish class?
"¿Sabes bailar bachata? ¿Con quién lo has bailado?"	Do you know how to dance bachata? With whom have you danced (bachata)?
¿Bailabas de niño?	Did you used to dance as a kid?

In upper level classes I ask more of these questions, and we delve deeper into the answers, so the upper level students get a lot more exposure to "advanced grammar". The W&D will be longer too, because we can write quicker.

In the lower levels I tend to ask more questions in the present tense. Every time I use a new word or tense, I need to slowly scaffold it so that students understand. **It is useful to remember that with more complexity and more language, it will take longer before students start producing language.** So include natural grammar, but be judicious in lower levels.

If you studiously avoid "advanced grammar" in the lower levels, however, by level 3 or 4 students are not going to be able to quickly produce the advanced grammar that you are suddenly exposing them to. And that, by the way, includes the long, complex sentences that are a normal part of written Spanish. Get students used to reading a slightly more complex language in level 1 and, by level 3, they'll be writing and speaking with more complex language easily.

So... how are advanced classes different?!

In addition to simply exposing students to much more language in all its complexity, the upper-level classes expose students to a greater breadth of conversation topics. That is how I think we should organize our upper-level courses. Not in search of topics that will inspire students to use "si clauses" or some other advanced grammar, but rather in search of topics that inspire deeper conversations.

Those deeper conversations can emerge via the cultural presentations or delving deep into a topic brought up in class, but I'd like to propose **a path forward that retains the highly student-centered character of the lower level classes**. In my advanced classes, student choice is rooted in the independent reading program.

We do retain "anchor texts" as a common frame of reference for the whole class; commonly the anchor text is a television program or a film that we watch together and comment on in the last 20 minutes of most class periods.

However, the reading program is an essential foundation of a language class. In my classes, I seek to create **a place where we all talk about books**, rather than a class where we talk about the one book that we are forced to read.

Many CI teachers buy class sets of novels and read one novel at a time with their classes. *I think that is a mistake.* Honestly, I have never read a novel with a whole class and not gotten to that point where it feels stale, where the kids are resisting, and everybody is flipping pages to see how many are left. *Everyone*, including the teacher. That doesn't happen when students can choose their own novels.

A good midway position between whole class novels and pleasure reading is to offer lit groups where students choose one novel from a group of 5 or 6 and then read in small groups. But even better, I think, is to **do whole class reading of one scene and let**

students choose which books they'll continue reading in their pleasure reading sessions (pleasure reading is scheduled in my class to happen at the beginning of every class period). Many English teachers no longer read whole class novels for the same reason: students have their own interests and what we are trying to teach them is not that XXX book is a great piece of literature, but rather that reading in general opens doors to a much richer, enjoyable life. And yes, starting class with quiet reading is incredibly effective at settling down rowdy classes coming in from lunch.

The "one novel at a time that we all have to read whether we like it or not" approach teaches kids to hate reading, and unfortunately too many teachers fail to imagine otherwise. In fact, those teachers might not be readers themselves. **Developing LOVE OF READING is what I am trying to do with my pleasure reading program.** *It is also, by the way, a more powerful way to develop language.*

In class, during the 20-minute 2nd session in the "2 conversation" lesson plan, I like to present a scene, a single scene, from a different novel each time. I might just read in an animated voice if it is an easy read, or I might have student actors sit on stools to help dramatize the reading. I'll write and draw on the board to scaffold the text. I may even quickly explain the context in L1 so that we can get straight to the action. I do this twice a week. That means that I'll have time in a school year to present about 80 books. Last time I checked there were over 200 CI novels published in Spanish... we Spanish teachers are not lacking texts to read! French teachers have at least 75, which is enough to build a pleasure reading library.

Students never get bored of a class novel because we get a "taste" of it for a single period, and I get to touch upon many interests. For students who are interested in science fiction I can read a part of "Listos o no" by Adam Geidd without worrying about the 75% of my students who hate sci-fi. **It's 20 minutes of input, not 4 weeks of lesson plans.** My own two novels appeal to very different audiences: *Superburguesas* is a screwball comedy and *Meche y las ballenas* is about environmental activism. There are books that appeal to all sorts of readers, but I am convinced that **there is no ONE BOOK to please them all**.

Students browse books in many ways (please read the "browsing strategies section on page 125), but the twice weekly book talks that I have selected in class really is crucial to get students to look deeply into the class library for their pleasure reading sessions. Furthermore, when I am doing a read-aloud, I can scaffold the reading to my audience. Many teachers think of scaffolding as simplifying a reading for students, but I also love to use an easy reader to "scaffold up" the conversation. Adam Geidd's novel is actually a level one novel, but we can take one scene and then I'll talk about it at a level appropriate to the class so that the level 4 class is getting a lot of advanced language that I am making comprehensible, in the moment.

My experience is that it is perfectly fine for upper-level kids to read low level books, but there are also plenty of more advanced CI novels. Get a diversity of books. If you are just now building a new classroom library, start with simply book talking. This first year you might just talk about books and not have too many to actually get in the hands of students. Okay, you've got to start somewhere!

Start with the easiest to read and make your class conversations hit higher levels. But once you've got 50 books, you've got plenty of choices to start a pleasure reading program. I do the same process of book talks and presenting single scenes for my level 1 classes, but I focus on the easiest reads in my library so that level 1 students are ready to start pleasure reading in the second semester.

The crucial thing to aim for is to develop a class where you and your students talk about books, rather than a class where you are all forced to talk about "the one book".

Language Spoken at the speed of a native-speaker

Question: I understand that I am supposed to speak slowly and comprehensibly, but my level 4 students cannot understand when a native speaker speaks at a natural speed. When will my students finally understand language spoken quickly by native speakers?

Answer: This teacher has missed a crucial step in the "Basic Skills" section! The short answer is that **your LEVEL ONE students should understand language spoken at a natural speed**. *How?* Read on!

We have techniques to make ourselves comprehensible; we also have a set of techniques to improve the processing speed of our students. These techniques go hand in hand together.

The first observation we need to make is that **nobody acquires language that they do not understand**. Simply exposing students to videos of native speakers often does not help students learn to process native speed speech, and it causes a lot of frustration. Comprehension is everything; otherwise it's just noise. This is why **we speak slowly and comprehensibly**. But there is more to the story.

We speak slowly and, once students comprehend a new phrase, we want to get them to be able to process it at the speed of a native speaker. When you first define the new language chunk, write it on the board. You'll see students' eyes move towards the board and read the English. Now take five big steps away from the board. Use the new language again in a slightly different context and you'll see the heads of some students swivel from you towards the board again. They still need a scaffold to process the language, and of course they are still processing it slowly.

My advice is that you "park" on new phrases, especially those that contain one of the Sweet 16 verbs, so that students have to process it in multiple contexts. They get quicker the more they process the phrase, always in a slightly different context so that they have to pay attention to meaning. Classic TPRS teachers use a technique called "circling" in order to park on a phrase and lead their students to get so fast that they process without hesitation. I do a less rigorous version of the circling technique that I call "artful questioning" to achieve the same results.

In the first week of Spanish 1 when we learn that my student Jarod **has (tiene)** three dogs, I'll ask the class in Spanish: "Does he **have** three dogs or does he **have** four dogs?" I'll point and pause as I say the verb, nice and slowly, and follow up with several other questions using my question word posters: "Who **has** three dogs? Who **has** more than three dogs? (raise your hand please). I don't **have** any dogs, but I **have** a plant. How many dogs does Jarod **have**? Does Jarod **have** plants? Who **has** plants? (raise your hand please) Look class, Mary and Sara **have** plants!"

As I ask these questions, the pace of my speaking increases. I am nailing that one verb over and over again so that my students learn to process it at the speed of a native speaker. Their processing speed, as I measure from their hesitance as they respond, improves fairly quickly if I target one verb at a time. Tomorrow it will be slow again and we will repeat the process, but eventually they will not hesitate nor look up at the verb posters.

If you have to teach a curriculum with tremendous breadth of vocabulary your students might not get the repetition they need to develop lightening fast understanding of key, high-frequency words.

I urge teachers to seriously restrict the number of words that they consider essential. Start doing this process of artful questioning only with the Sweet 16 verbs in level 1, but do not restrict yourself to only speaking in one verb form, tense or mood.

In one class you might be talking about a student's dogs, in another it may be snakes, and in yet another class a student might reveal that she has her own home library of a hundred fantasy books. Is this a lot of vocabulary? Not necessarily, because in every class you'll be nailing the verb **"has"** so that *all students in all classes* process that verb and the other Sweet 16 verbs at the speed of a native speaker.

As students continue their language journey they'll get fast at processing the Sweet 16 verbs in many forms, tenses & moods. There will be less language that you have to explicitly slow down and park on. By level 4 (or even before) students will rarely need this technique and your classes will largely become fluid conversations spoken at a natural pace.

- The Reading Program -

Leading students to love reading

> **A pleasure reading program seeks to develop the love of reading.**
>
> Isn't this the most important mission we educators share? We want our students to be lifelong readers. However, teaching students *how* to read is not the same as teaching them to *love* reading.

Whole class reading may be better suited to teach kids *how* to read and certainly should be included in your classes, but self-selected pleasure reading exposes students to the kind of reading experiences that make them want more.

It might appear on first glance that both goals could be accomplished by teaching interesting whole class novels, but unfortunately **there is no single text that will excite every reader**. For example, when I present a short article on *Machu Picchu* for everyone to read, I am trying to instill in my students a sense of wonder and awe. Some students are impressed, but if I am honest with myself, many students are far more impressed with their social media feed. I try to make that whole class text activity short and sweet so that the reading experience is not terrible for those students not interested in *Machu Picchu*, but I know that the text will only excite some of my students.

There is no ONE perfect book that will delight every student, but there are many different perfect books that appeal to different students. Students need to find their perfect book that will turn them on to a lifetime of reading. This is the essence of a student-centered reading program.

For the students that are not delighted by *Machu Picchu*, I am trying to teach a few skills: strong readers can tolerate a few paragraphs that are not perfectly suited to their interests in order to understand the intent of the author; strong readers can read nonfiction texts for information and use that information to construct their own arguments. While these are important skills for our students, this is the "cod liver oil" of reading … not too tasty.

Pushing students to read hard texts is not an effective way to lead them to love reading.

Most students who develop strong reading skills do so through copious pleasure reading. If language learners are indeed reading a lot, they will only need a fine-tuning of their skills when they are advanced learners. We can do that through the editing process while learning to write essays and stories... in advanced classes.

This is what Stephen Krashen calls "the path of pleasure." We do not have to force hours upon hours of difficult texts on students in order to teach the skill that strong readers sometimes tolerate a difficult text. That can be taught through short whole class texts.

The goal of pleasure reading is to connect students with pleasurable reading.

Students may happen to enjoy reading about Machu Picchu in a pleasure reading context, but they are not forced to read about Machu Picchu, nor are they quizzed on the reading afterwards.

In order to develop a love of reading in our students, **do not risk mixing pleasure reading with the difficult texts that stretch their abilities**. Reserve your library of interesting novels for pleasure reading and use the short **Write & Discuss texts** that you create everyday with your classes to stretch their reading skills. Once they are ready, set aside a short session every day for students to read self-selected novels for pleasure. Easy reading will develop a love of reading.

When we prime students to enjoy their reading and then slip a little cod liver oil into the process, we ruin the taste of reading altogether. On the other hand, if we save our language learning novels for pleasure reading only and teach reading skills through short whole class texts, **students will strongly associate novels with pleasure**. It is a small adjustment to help lead non-readers over the bridge into the reading life.

If your district requires that you teach certain reading standards in your classes, address them through short whole class texts. But also cultivate the path of pleasure. **Allow students to gaze at your classroom library during whole class instruction and fantasize about escaping into a novel.**

That alone is a good reason to *not teach a whole class novel*.

Book Talks

In the section on advanced classes I describe how book talks shape my advanced classes (pg. 95). Shorter book talks are an important element in lower level classes too, especially at the beginning of the year as I introduce my library to my new students. My level 1 students don't get to choose books until January, but I am talking about the books from the first week of school. My level two and three students may start reading in the first week, but they still need browsing strategies so that they are exposed to the diversity of books in my library. **A near daily, one minute book talk is my strongest tool to sell my library.**

Usually after five or ten minutes of silent reading I will ask students to talk about their books in small groups for 60 seconds. They speak in their first language. The idea is to spread knowledge about the books. After a minute they pass their books towards the walls where the class librarians pick them up and return the books to their proper places. While the librarians are doing their job, **I present a book in very comprehensible Spanish.** Either I talk in general terms about what the book is about or I present one vivid scene, but this is often done by memory rather than reading aloud. I will use the whiteboard to illustrate what I am saying. The key is to talk about a book so that any student who is interested can follow up during independent reading sessions.

Brett Chonko in Virginia has brought the book talk to a higher level. When he starts the year with his Level 1 students, he will grab a book from his library and start the talk in English, adding Spanish words that they know. Within a few weeks the entire book talk is in Spanish, but all along he is "selling" his library so that students are browsing the books long before second semester, when they start to actually read them.

I have included a link to a video of Virginia teacher Teresa Torgoff giving a book talk to her French class. She speaks clearly about the book without giving away too many details, but sells the book to students who might be interested in a touching story that takes place in WWII. And she assures her students that it has a happy ending. Students who may have prejudged the book, perhaps assuming that the teddy bear on the cover indicates that the book is for children, now have a better understanding of what to expect and may be intrigued. **The purpose of a book talk is to intrigue!**

https://vimeo.com/369188911/a6524d0e4e

Whole Class Reading

Whole class reading dominates traditional classrooms. Traditionally texts in language classes are purpose-driven, designed to provide opportunities for students to practice an explicit set of vocabulary or a grammatical concept. It is of little wonder that students hate reading when the purpose of the text is to use 25 vocabulary words related to parts of a house or use the present perfect tense. A dry textbook paragraph that provides an overview description of a country is just as bleak. Utilitarian, soulless texts designed for language learning make an embarrassing genre; it is our profession's contribution to killing the love of reading. My general rule is that any text whose principal function is to "practice using the language" should be excluded from the classroom.

We need to re-envision classroom reading so that the texts we provide communicate a compelling message. When students read because they are interested, most of the work parsing the grammar of the language is completed unconsciously. I have seen this in my own study of Japanese through comprehensible conversation devoid of grammar explanation; at the end of each session we create a text based upon our conversation and, after several sessions, I have developed a fragile instinct for the grammar we have used. Research indicates that *compelling* reading is by far the most efficient way to acquire vocabulary and grammar.

The problem faced by teachers is that what is compelling to one student may be absurdly boring to the next. If compelling reading builds language skills best, how do we maximize the amount of compelling content for each student? A pleasure reading program addresses that key problem; the classroom library is stocked with level-appropriate texts on a diversity of topics so that every student can find something of interest to read. **The primary reason we do whole class reading is to develop our students' reading skills so that they can access the pleasure reading library.**

The foundation for students' reading ability is built through whole class reading. We can build that foundation in the first semester of instruction. Pleasure reading then becomes a more and more important component of the entire language acquisition program. We continue to present whole class reading activities in order to develop the cultural competence of students as well as to continue to support their reading skills. When we start pleasure reading with our students, we may spend only five minutes a day at the beginning of the class period but, over time, we expand to 10 minutes, then 15, even 20 when students have built their reading stamina. In the meantime we continue to expose them to short, whole class reading experiences.

How do we design whole class reading experiences that do not teach our students to hate reading? We write with our classes so that the texts are short, personalized, and highly comprehensible. **Write & Discuss is a powerful reading activity that I do every day, starting on the first day of instruction** (see page 61). This is the most common whole class reading activity that I do in my own classroom. It is a way to summarize the classroom conversation and develop a daily text through a community writing process.

Another technique that provides whole class texts is the creation of academic texts by the teacher such as the *maravillas* that I create for my own students. **Book talks** and **Reader's Theater** may be modified to produce whole class texts that provide many opportunities for the teacher to explicitly provide grammar explanations as needed. The **prepared readings that accompany specific Movie Talk lessons** are also excellent forms of whole class reading. These whole class reading activities are all:

1. short, completed within the class period
2. highly comprehensible
3. personalized to the class when possible
4. read along with the teacher who ensures that every phrase is transparent (often with a choral translation completing the reading)

All of these types of whole class reading support the pleasure reading program.

But you might insist on teaching a whole class novel anyways. Okay. In the following pages I will present two case studies of how to teach a whole class novel without filling your class with an endless parade of activities. The idea is to have a common class experience while maintaining elements of student choice.

Case study #1: Reading a lower level novel together

I have trouble maintaining enthusiasm for a whole class novel. Even if we start well, I am quickly reminded of **Donalyn Miller´s critique** of the practice: **a circus of lovingly prepared scaffolding activities limits time for actual reading.** Actual reading is what accounts for the incredible gains in language acquisition, not the skill-building activities surrounding the reading. Perhaps teachers who choose to teach whole class novel units (often structured by teachers guides) fear that the novel will not be comprehensible to students without their guidance. But look at it this way: in order to read a novel that is above their students reading ability, teachers are dramatically decreasing the time available to read in class. **The irony is that students who are fed a diet of incredibly easy reading in level 1 can eventually take on the level 3 novels easily, on their own.**

I wanted an approach to reading whole class novels that would allow my students to read at their own pace, but also provide the kind of scaffolding that is the hallmark of the whole class novel. I wanted my students who finish their class novel to be able to go on to an FVR selection so that everyone is maximizing the reading time we have available. I wanted a minimum of class time spent explaining the novel. In the past, when I taught whole class novels that students struggled with, I realized that my lessons teaching them how to read advanced texts does not make them into readers. Instead, it prepares students to confront complex texts, each year more and more difficult. It is easy pleasure reading, losing yourself in the action of a story and not having to stop to complete a written analysis... **that is what hooks a student on reading**.

If you want to spend less time *explaining* novels and more time actually *reading* them then it is crucial that you choose easy to read novels.

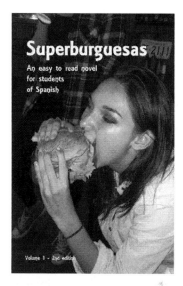

Struggling through one novel is far less effective for students than breezing through ten easy ones. Choose easy easy easy novels. I just finished reading my own novel, *Superburguesas*, with my Spanish 1 students in April (also in French). The first semester was dedicated to book talks. Students began independent reading in January, so they already had some experience picking extremely easy novels for their own reading. Several expert teachers with whom I have consulted place my novel within the reading abilities of 2nd semester Spanish 1 to 1st semester of Spanish 2. That means that Spanish 3 students can read it too, *easily*. We used many of the **free activities** that I have posted on my blog, but not in a traditional sequence. Although this teaching sequence took 5 weeks and 3 days to complete, **we dedicated only *seven days* of class time** to explaining the novel. Here is a description of how I did it.

Link to free activities: https://mygenerationofpolyglots.com/my-tprs-novels/

On a Wednesday I introduced chapter zero, using a **PowerPoint available in the free activities** to help us examine the concrete or shape poem in this very short chapter.

We also dedicated Thursday and Friday to whole class reading of chapter 1. **After those first three days reading chapters 0 and 1 together, I then let students enjoy the rest of the novel on their own during independent reading time**. Students finished at their own pace; the fast readers were able to choose new novels once they were finished but there was no effort to hurry anyone along. I wanted the first pass through the novel to be as low-stress and self-directed as possible. In the meantime, I offered a voluntary reading group once a week after school for kids that felt like they needed more structure. I had five regular participants, all kids who had transferred into our class midyear from traditional schools. Together we explicitly translated key passages together and I asked many simple questions based on what was on a particular page that we were reading.

On most days we started our class session with 10 minutes of independent reading. After three weeks most students had chosen a new book, so I spent the fourth week using the *Superburguesas* **comprehension quizzes** and **crossword puzzles** as brief warm-ups after independent reading. During this fourth week some students picked up *Superburguesas* again during FVR because those warm-ups must have made them realize that they needed to read the book a little closer. The warm-ups were just for a few minutes a day before our normally scheduled class (we frequently PQA about students lives, we also did several story-asking sessions, quite a few random movie talks and we have been watching episode 3 of *El Internado*).

At the end of the fourth week, I gave students **the chronology quiz available in the free activities** in which students have to label each sentence in the order that it happened in the book. I entered this grade into my online grade book so that all stakeholders (myself, parents and each student) would be well-aware of who needed special attention during the next week. I also attached a note to the assignment indicating that there would be a retake the following Friday and the highest of the two grades would become the permanent grade.

The next four days were dedicated largely to discussing and acting out scenes from a book that students had already read. Suspending independent reading for the week, we started each class session looking at **the word cloud for the chapter** we were going to review. When a student pointed to a word I (1) established meaning, (2) explained how it showed up in the chapter and (3) immediately connected the word to the students world.

For example, when a student pointed at the word *devolver,* I wrote on the board "*devolver* = to return a thing, like a book".

En capítulo 9, I said, *señor Marzo quiere que Rodney devuelva la pintura. No quiere matarlo, solo quiere que devuelva la pintura. ¿Quién necesita devolver la pintura? Rodney, claro. ¿Y quién quiere que la devuelva? Señor Marzo.* And then I asked what other things are often returned: kids called out *libros, ropa, comida mala. ¿Adónde voy para devolver un libro?,* I asked.	*In chapter 9,* I said, *Mr. Marzo wants Rodney to return the painting. He doesn't want to kill him, he just wants him to return the painting. Who needs to return the painting? Rodney, of course. And who wants him to return it? Mr. Marzo.* And then I asked what other things are often returned: kids called out *books, clothing, bad food. Where do I go to return a book,* I asked.

After looking at the word cloud I asked students to help create an oral summary of the chapter. I chose my favorite parts of the chapter for students to act out without having to hammer down every sentence. This was a whole class activity that led to a summary of the chapter written on the board. Students copied each chapter summary into their notebooks. We did 2-3 chapters per day and were finished by Thursday. On Friday students took the second assessment, a **fill in the blank assessment also available in the free materials.**

The last four days of instruction were intensive days of review, but **most of this unit was characterized by easy pleasure reading at the pace of the student.** I saw kids smiling while reading, but even more so once they were allowed to go back to choosing their own reading and could immerse themselves into their own interests. Yet I still had specific feedback on specific structures from the class novel, and I had time to make sure that they have been acquired. I much prefer starting the class with independent reading followed by our normal **Two Conversations**, but if I have to do a whole class novel then I think that this is a good approach.

If you attended my workshop and have access to the Master Class online, this book is available freely online for all of your students to access in the Master Class library.

Case Study #2: Reading a novel in an advanced class

Meche y las ballenas is a level 3 Spanish novel that is available for free for Master Class members and their students and is also available in paperback on the My Generation of Polyglots website. Before even opening the novel, **I introduce the setting of the novel by presenting the cultural presentation on the grey whale birthing lagoons in Baja California Sur**. You can download the PowerPoint presentation at the link below, but keep in mind that Apple computers and google docs sometimes strip the embedded videos from PPTs. It is best viewed using a PC and an edition of PowerPoint from 2013 or later:

tinyurl.com/4dckf5cn

I'll often do this the day before we start reading the novel. In my classes I try to limit almost any activity to 20 minutes or less, so this is the right amount of time to introduce the setting of the novel and then start reading the next day.

In general, I like to allow a lot of independent reading. If students choose, I allow them to read in small groups where they take turns reading a sentence aloud and can ask each other questions to verify comprehension. When they work in groups, **I encourage them to read the whole sentence first and not get bogged down by understanding every single word.**

However, **I always read the first chapter of the book together as a whole class experience when we are all reading the same novel in class.** For Meche, you might consider skipping the prologue if your students are level 3. The prologue was added at my beta readers request to clarify the direction of the novel's plot, but I think that the language of the first chapter is easier to read and a more inviting introduction. I usually start the novel on page 8, chapter 1.

We read the first chapter together, pausing while reading to ask many comprehension questions to the whole class (they respond together in chorus; I'm not singling out individual students). I go slowly, perhaps too slowly in the eyes of my students, so that everyone stays onboard. Then I talk about the three illustrations on those first two pages. This is important because **this novel is full of illustrations that we will talk about**. I am modelling the flow of how I expect our class conversations to be.

After we read chapter 1 (with discussion that is easily 15-20 minutes) we put the book down for the day. We go on to another activity, like a movie talk or the tv series that we are watching. **I think it is important when we read a book together that we do not overload students.** Let's wade into the book slowly.

After chapter 1 I tell students the minimum that they have to read each day and allow them to read at their own pace during the independent reading session at the beginning of the class period. Students can read beyond the daily goal and then eventually pick up their own pleasure reading, which my advanced and heritage learners often do. Slower readers (or readers who want to find out what happens next) read the eBooks outside of class so that they remain current.

Starting on the third day of reading we alter the flow of the class period. Normally we start class with up to 10 minutes of quiet reading, followed by the activities of the day and then finish the class with W&D and an exit quiz. **Once we start reading Meche, I start the class by post the illustrations from the previous days reading. In pairs the students discuss the illustrations.** I often give them 1-2 minutes, and then ask that they switch partners to discuss the illustrations again. They listen to each other and develop more to say about the illustrations. Ideally, I like to do this a third time, encouraging them to add transition words and more details to their comments. Then we discuss in whole group, calling on individual students if needed but **after so much paired discussion students are often ready to contribute by their own choice**.

There are so many illustrations in Meche that this is the main method we use to discuss the novel. Our whole group discussion sometimes moves beyond the illustrations, but we have a time set so that we do not spend more than 10 minutes on this initial discussion. **Knowing that we start class discussing the novel is strong motivation for everyone to keep up with the reading.** Now that everyone is caught up, we spend the next ten minutes silently reading. After our silent reading we have enough time to do one non-Meche activity, and then the W&D and exit quiz is usually about that second activity. For instance, my level 3 classes are watching a scene or two from the telenovela *Gran Hotel* every day after our reading session.

After students read chapter 5 we play an online game that I created to familiarize everyone with some of the vocabulary specific to the novel. The game also reinforces the geography of the novel:

https://www.purposegames.com/game/ballenas-grises-game

Every couple of chapters I might give a short, five question comprehension quiz. In general, we do **a fluency write** every 2-3 weeks (see page 74), so I might give a prompt for one of the fluency writes that asks students to respond to the novel in some way. I choose open-ended prompts such as "Describe Meche, her world and the problems she faces".

Finally, it is okay to stop reading a novel before everyone has finished it.

I try to get through at least chapter 21 so that we can discuss the images of the Japanese girl at the aquarium with her father. Some years we have read the entire novel, whereas other years I have announced that those who would like to continue reading Meche can do so. Everyone is now free to return to "free choice reading" during the 10-minute reading sessions at the beginning of class.

Build a Class Library

You should build the very lowest level readers yourself using the Write & Discuss texts created by your classes (see instructions and templates on page 61). These texts are uniquely comprehensible to your classes because they made them themselves! Rarely are they the homerun books that will turn a student onto a lifetime of reading, but you'll need extremely easy texts for students who insist that they cannot find anything that they understand. **The Write & Discuss pamphlets are a necessary step while you connect each student with a book that they enjoy.** Without this bottom rung of reading texts, your reading program will fall apart. Luckily, if you do this every week with every class, you'll develop a set of graded readers because the linguistic complexity will increase as you move further into the year. I staple the products of all classes for an entire week together into one pamphlet so that every student will find both familiar and unfamiliar texts in every packet.

https://vimeo.com/729998009/d17d03b116

It is vital that you have abundant student-created texts in order to serve the lowest level readers in your classes. After student-created texts, **the next largest part of your classroom library should be the specialized language learner novels designed for beginners.** For Spanish teachers, the selection of these books is good. (See CiReading.com for specific purchasing suggestions.) These books engage kids' imaginations and are designed with limited vocabulary to improve the comprehensibility of the text. I personally believe that acquisition is most effective when imaginations are engaged, which explains why boring textbook dialogues were never great reading. Nobody cared about those characters. That cannot be said for a novel like Esperanza, a gripping tale of life or death choices that can be read by students in their second semester. For languages other than Spanish, the selection is growing.

It may take years to build your class library. Don't be discouraged. Try to buy a few single copies of a few novels once a month and use them for book talks. After a year or two you'll have a small but functional class library that you know well.

Some readers—boys in particular—avoid novels almost completely, preferring magazines, atlases, and current events articles that I print out from websites such as NewsELA, Reading A to Z, El mundo en tus manos by Martina Bex, or Le Petit Journal

Francophone by Cécile Lainé. Take a look at the Spanish section of https://newsela.com (click on "Browse Content" on the top of the website and then scroll down the left margin until you find "Language: Spanish") and notice how you can simplify the language by changing the control buttons above the article. I like printing several NewsELA articles and stapling them together to form a "newspaper."

As you fill your library with easy-to-read language learner novels, **add a few illustrated nonfiction books to vary the text types available to your students**. Start with a few illustrated encyclopedias for children. DK and Scholastic are two publishers of highly visual, entertaining encyclopedic books. I usually have to search on Amazon.es (Amazon in Spain) to find a good diversity of books, but the breadth of topics is wide.

One popular title in my library is "Star Wars Los últimos Jedi. Diccionario Visual" (STAR WARS THE LAST JEDI: THE VISUAL DICTIONARY, translated into Spanish and published by DK). These books are anything but dry! Scholastic has a series called Explora tu mundo, which delves into descriptions of the natural world with titles focused on life in a rain forest, sharks, and other high-interest subjects. **These books are also full of cognates, contextualized with illustrations and often supported by students' pre-knowledge**.

My only concern is that I don't think these books engage students' imaginations in the same way that fiction does. Fiction requires more from the reader, and I suspect that the effort involved in creating a fictional world in the mind of the reader engages the brain more actively with the language. These nonfiction visual encyclopedias require less active engagement, and thus they may be a good bridge for reluctant readers. Advanced students may find them to be an enjoyable break between reading fiction. Students with a particular interest in the sciences may gravitate towards them. However, all of these students should continue to be encouraged to read fiction as well.

There are three buying mistakes that you should avoid when creating a library for first year language learners. The most costly mistake that I made was to buy children's books. Not only are they expensive, but they are also written for readers with thousands of hours of experience with the target language. A six-year-old reading a children's book in their native language has had thousands of hours more contact with the language than your students. These books exert a short-lived fascination among students based on nostalgia, but students quickly put them down. While their reading levels may be low, adolescents deserve reading that is compelling for their age level. Save children's books for kindergarten day. Borrow them from the local library rather than actually buying them. I do not want to dismiss the delights of childhood … it is just that these enticing books represent a bad cost-benefit ratio for the classroom teacher trying to build a useful classroom library.

The second costliest mistake that I made involved buying Spanish translations of popular English-language YA novels. What was I thinking!? I foolishly believed that students' pre-knowledge would scaffold the reading and make it comprehensible to diehard fans. The reality turned out to be different. Even if you have heritage learners in your classes, expensive volumes of Harry Potter exert a very limited appeal ... mostly to students who are already readers. While the novelty temporarily attracts the attention of diehard Potter fans, most students are at best thinking to themselves that they could read it in English instead.

Those books sit undisturbed in my library; even my advanced students avoid them. Certainly they are a bad purchasing decision for first year students.

The third costliest mistake that I made involved graphic novels that never made it to the bookshelves due to strong sexual themes or violence. Graphic novels are popular in Spain, and that is great, but **be sure to preview every graphic novel that you purchase**.

The Flow of an Independent Reading Session

I start each class period with reading. It calms the class and redirects their focus. This is a marvel for the last period of the day or the period right after lunch! My students are trained to get their book as they enter class, before the bell has rung, and we often keep the books under our chairs in case we need a five minute reading break. The exception is the first semester of level 1 classes, before students have developed the reading skills. In that case and for *any other class that does not yet have the skills to read independently*, I do a book talk to introduce them to the class library. See the section on book talks starting on page 102. By the time students are ready to read independently they are already well-aware of the books available and often have already decided which will be their first book.

As the last bell rings I am sitting on a stool up front, not at my computer. I take the book that I am reading off of the poster where is it fastened with Velcro at the front of the room. I pick up one of the bookmarks from the pile and I read a "good reading quote" from the back of the bookmark. At this point any latecomers have arrived and sit down immediately, not bothering with notes or excuses because I am reading.

With level 1 students we read for 5 to 10 minutes; if your kids can handle 7 minutes then only give them 5. **Several extremely short, frequent reading sessions spaced across the week are far better than one or two longer sessions.** Always add a word of encouragement. Some teachers quietly play baroque music to drown out incidental noise, but I always insist on absolute silence. In my view a teacher should be modeling the reading life and therefore the teacher should be reading. Some teachers like to conference during reading time, helping struggling readers find their homerun book or discussing reading with students. If you do this, it has to be so quiet that other students cannot even hear the murmuring of voices. Personally I think reading time is sacred; neither teacher nor student are allowed to do anything else.

When it is time to return the books I have all students pass their books to the side of the room where two student librarians take charge of placing the books back. My easiest to read books fastened to the wall with Velcro must be layered so that they do not splay out; replacing a rush of students with two student librarians makes the process quicker and limits damage to the books. The student librarians will be working on placing the books in their proper places for the next 5 minutes.

While the librarians are working I will allow students to speak in small groups about their books. This is a short, 1-2 minute activity that is best conducted in their first language in the lower levels because the goal is not to practice speaking, it is another browsing strategy to expose students to as many books as possible.

Then I will do a book talk for about 3 minutes which consists of me writing on the board, drawing, acting and doing whatever I can to intrigue students about one of the books in my library. At this point the librarians finish returning the books and we move on to the first conversation of the day.

Some classes I have librarians pick up the books about mid-way through the class so that we can hold on to our books as a bail-out move. **Don't use the books as a punishment if classes are misbehaving**; holding onto books as a bailout is a favorite at the end of the year when students are getting tired of hearing my voice and just want to retreat into a good story.

These essential truths about our 5 to 10 minutes of pleasure reading need to be emphasized so that student and teacher understand what is expected of them: (1**) easy reading is pleasure reading**, (2) **student choice is key**, (3) there is minimal to no accountability for the activity**, just find a book that is interesting** or at least "does not suck", and finally (4) **readers have permission to abandon a book** for any reason.

The Best Bookmarks

You'll want to be able to **keep track of students' reading habits in a non-intrusive manner**, without punishing the students who are already enjoying their independent reading by assigning reading logs. These bookmarks play a part in that system.

I used to use traditional bookmarks until Deanna Wanis, a Spanish teacher in Corona, California, showed me a much more effective system. The problem with traditional bookmarks is that they fall out when the next class comes in and opens up the books. There are multiple students reading any specific paperback over the course of the day. Kids get so frustrated when their bookmarks are constantly getting lost!

DeAnna's system uses **Clip-Rite Solid Clip-Tabs** from Staples (office supply store), which have paper clips built into the tab to fasten it securely to the page. She then attaches a photo of each student to the paper clip tab, which does not fall out. When the bookmarks are fastened into the book, **each student's face appears to be peeking out of the books**. It is adorable.

This system is useful because it is so easy for the teacher to check what everyone is reading. When I want to conference with a student, I track their reading for a few days before talking to them. Sometimes if I know that I plan to conference with a student in 3rd period, I'll be reading his book during 2nd period. That way I always appear knowledgeable about all of the books in my library.

During the conference I quietly ask about what happened previously in the book while other students are reading. Sometimes I'll also have the student orally translate a small section that he has already read so that I can track their reading accuracy. In fact, Virginia teacher Brett Chonko regularly conferences rather than reading on his own when students read and he reports that the one on one attention to reading accuracy has improved his students' reading confidence. He'll quietly work with one student at a time and make sure that they are translating verb conjugations accurately.

Another useful reason to have a system like this is **it becomes crystal-clear which books are read frequently and which books are not so successful in your library**. The frequently read books can be displayed on a "best-sellers" table. You can keep an eye on when they get frayed and need to be replaced. **The less read books may deserve a few extra book talks to introduce your students to them.**

Once you build a large class library, you'll want to separate the books into sections by theme. I still include copies of my "best-sellers" on the easiest to reach table, but I also have separate locations for sports, manga, animal books, non-fiction, the Orca Soundings books for my advanced readers, and a few other thematic areas.

I know that the Japanese *manga* translated into Spanish will have a limited readership, so I don't need to place them on the best-sellers table. Instead, I introduce the Japanese comic books during a book talk and my *otakus* (people obsessed with manga) gravitate to that area on their own.

And finally, the bookmarks look hilarious. **It brings a smile to my face every time I see my students faces peeking out of the books** in the class library.

What does intermediate reading look like?

It may seem like our job leads us to push students to read more and more difficult texts, as they can handle them. Yes, we should present increasingly challenging reading experiences **during whole class reading activities**. However, if we want students to get the most out of our **pleasure reading program** we should aim to increase their reading fluency-- the speed at which they can read comfortably.

A bountiful supply of very easy texts, well below a student's reading level, is the best tool for improving reading speed. Most students naturally gravitate towards easy to read texts. Feel good when your level four students choose a 'level 2 novel' for pleasure reading, knowing that you will expose them to more complicated texts in whole class activities. They may even be intrigued and pick up a more complex novel once you have read aloud a great scene, but let them choose their own pleasure reading texts.

By intermediate level most students are passing over class-created texts (i.e. the **illustrated Write & Discuss texts** that we create for students reading at the lowest levels) in favor of simple novels with longer plot lines and more developed characters. Students still seek a variety of text types, but they have developed increased stamina and tend to spend less time with texts such as children's encyclopedias.

Rather than worrying about students reading below their level, be concerned about the student who gravitates towards authentic texts that are far above their reading level.

My student Maddie came into my class every day and would make a beeline towards a hardcover, illustrated version of a Harry Potter novel that I kept behind my desk. She would fret over small rips in the paper jacket cover and spend our 10-minute pleasure reading session repairing the jacket with tape and lovingly glancing at the illustrations.

She was such a nice, cooperative student that **I did not recognize at the time that Maddie was failing to develop the skills that my other intermediate students were developing during free reading**: they were reading easy texts fluidly so that the rate at which they could read was quite fast. On the other hand, whenever Maddie took note of the text, she immersed herself in a difficult paragraph that prompted her to covertly check her iPhone and look up unknown vocabulary.

Maddie was learning to read slower, not faster. Rather than rushing down the current of the river of reading with the rest of the class, **she was learning to get caught up in every eddy and be distracted by irrelevant details on the riverbank.**

The principal characteristic of a pleasure reading library for intermediate levels continues to be a supply of highly comprehensible, easy-to-read texts. **Avoid the temptation of supplying increasingly difficult texts beyond novels designed specifically for language learning.** Increasingly complex texts should be presented during whole class reading contexts, such as when presenting a cultural presentation like the Spanish Maravillas.

The upper level language learning novels do expose students to complex language, within manageable bounds. Most of all, however, they provide good stories that students can get swept up in so that the language can be acquired as theory predicts: unconsciously.

If I could go back in time and get Maddie back in my classroom, **I would find a way of honoring her identity as a reader in her first language** (which she so clearly wanted me to notice) and then start exploring the themes that interest her. I would try to find her a home run, easy-to-read book among my library in Spanish.

One book that comes to mind is *El brazalete mágico* by Margarita Pérez García, the first book in a projected series of easy-to-read novels that takes place in a magical world in the lush tropical forests of Margarita's home country, Venezuela. In addition to being a novelist, Margarita is also a Spanish teacher. I once asked her about how she introduces her reading library to her intermediate students and she wrote the following lovely response:

> "When I introduce my library and the reading program with intermediate students, we all read first El Capibara con Botas [a Level 1 book]. I invite them to discover the genre, check the glossary and we discuss slow reading versus easy reading. How do they feel 'inside.' How close easy reading is to reading in their mother tongue.
>
> We discuss the flow, and the lack of pain, and the lack of distraction from unknown words pulling us out of the story. And then I 'set them free' to explore with one mission: read as much as you can, but read EASY and as you move up in the levels of the library try to preserve that feeling. Easy and loads."

Books I like to read with advanced heritage learners

If you have **advanced heritage learners of Spanish** in a classroom designed for second language learners, I think the best thing you can do with them is share a love of reading and good fiction. Yes, even if this is an upper level L2 class, the advanced heritage learners are in the wrong class! In this worst of situations, I give the heritage learners choices. They can hang out and enjoy class with the rest of the students (and are responsible for passing the daily exit quizzes) or they can grab a book and write a daily summary in place of the daily exit quiz.

I'd like to share eight titles that I love to offer to my **advanced heritage learners**. These books are probably more likely to appeal to students that Kim Potowski refers to as "homeland" Spanish students: those who spent a good part of their childhood in a Spanish-speaking country and have developed a native proficiency in Spanish. They may no longer use Spanish much beyond family situations, but they have a native 'feel' for the language. **These books *might not* be a good fit for heritage learners who spent their entire childhood here in the U.S., at least for independent reading.** These books are a bad fit for heritage learners that have a strong cultural connection to Spanish-speaking cultures, who have "heritage motivation", but whose language proficiency is weak.

These are the books I turn towards when, for example, I have a student who attended an elite school in Tijuana until she was 13, before moving to the States. If the student is reading independently, I like to have them keep a reading diary simply so that I can write notes after class and develop a conversation about the book. **The key is to keep the dialogue conversational-- you are sharing a good book, not quizzing.** Don't require long plot summaries-- just enough to keep the conversation flowing. This works best if you read the book too, even if you've read the book before, so that your comments are fresh. I read at night or right after school for about 20 minutes and that is usually enough to keep up with my student.

Keep in mind that I am a high school teacher who does not censor too much, so there will be scenes that may raise eyebrows. However, nothing that would be banned in, say, an English lit class. Nothing shockingly graphic. I always tell my students that they can skip scenes that make them uncomfortable or stop reading a book altogether.

I have included a description of the book (mostly from Amazon) and, when available, a link to a short video about the book that I share with students before reading. I want the student to realize that **we are tapping into books that native speakers love and cherish**.

Todas las hadas del reino (Laura Gallego García - fantasy) Camelia es un hada madrina que lleva trescientos años ayudando con gran eficacia a jóvenes doncellas y a aspirantes a héroe para que alcancen sus propios finales felices. Su magia y su ingenio nunca le han fallado, pero todo empieza a complicarse cuando le encomiendan a Simón, un mozo de cuadra que necesita su ayuda desesperadamente. Camelia ha solucionado casos más difíciles; pero, por algún motivo, con Simón las cosas comienzan a torcerse de forma inexplicable.

Video review from an excited reader in Spanish:

https://www.youtube.com/watch?v=lA9S-k2B2l8&t=309s

Transportes González e Hija (María Amparo Escandón) Libertad González, puesta en prisión por un crimen que no revelará inaugura el club de lectura semanal de la biblioteca, leyendo a sus compañeras de prisión de cualquier libro a su alcance, desde *Los tres mosqueteros* hasta *Guía Fodor's de puertos del Caribe.* La historia que surge, no tiene nada que ver con las palabras impresas en esas páginas. En su lugar, ella relata la historia de un ex profesor de literatura, prófugo del gobierno mexicano, que se reinventa como troquero de larga distancia en los Estados Unidos donde se enamora de la mujer que dará a luz a su única hija. Cuando repentinamente, Joaquín Gonzáles, se encuentra solo en la ruta con una bebita, nace la compañía *Transportes González e Hija.* Padre e hija hacen su hogar en la cabina del camión de 18 ruedas y comparten todo—aventuras, libros, comidas en los paraderos de camioneros y recuerdos de la mujer que fuera la madre de la chica — hasta que un día la niña se convierte en mujer y un encuentro fortuito con un hombre la provocan a rebelarse contra otro.

Video review in Spanish:

https://www.youtube.com/watch?v=nimi4LMURsE&t=11s

El libro de los americanos desconocidos (Cristina Henríquez) A moving book about a group of immigrants living in a building in Delaware. There is a scene with adolescent sexuality that will require a thoughtful discussion about consent. **Students love this book**. Video by author in English:

https://www.youtube.com/watch?v=bWFocdrecBE&t=33s

Caramelo (Sandra Cisneros) **Mike's comment: this is among my top three favorite books that I've ever read.** Every year, Ceyala "Lala" Reyes' family—aunts, uncles, mothers, fathers, and Lala's six older brothers—packs up three cars and, in a wild ride, drive from Chicago to the Little Grandfather and Awful Grandmother's house in Mexico City for the summer. Struggling to find a voice above the boom of her brothers and to understand her place on this side of the border and that, Lala is a shrewd observer of family life. But when she starts telling the Awful Grandmother's life story, seeking clues to how she got to be so awful, grandmother accuses Lala of exaggerating. Soon, a multigenerational family narrative turns into a whirlwind exploration of storytelling, lies, and life. Like the cherished rebozo, or shawl, that has been passed down through generations of Reyes women, *Caramelo* is alive with the vibrations of history, family, and love.

Short, insightful interview between the author and Jorge Ramos (in Spanish):

https://www.youtube.com/watch?v=r8qELDKV2CM

Rumbo al hermoso norte (Luis Alberto Urrea) Nineteen-year-old Nayeli works at a taco shop in her Mexican village and dreams about her father, who journeyed to the US to find work. Recently, it has dawned on her that he isn't the only man who has left town. In fact, there are almost no men in the village -- they've all gone north. While watching *The Magnificent Seven*, Nayeli decides to go north herself and recruit seven men -- her own "Siete Magníficos" -- to repopulate her hometown and protect it from the bandidos who plan on taking it over. Filled with unforgettable characters and prose as radiant as the Sinaloan sun, *Into the Beautiful North* is the story of an irresistible young woman's quest to find herself on both sides of the fence.

Long interview (in English) with author that I share after reading the book. This is an author who was born in Tijuana and raised in San Diego; his personal story interests my students in Southern California.

https://vimeo.com/41540037

La fruta del borrachero (Ingrid Rojas Contreras) Un debut fascinante situado en Colombia durante la violencia devastadora de los años 90 sobre una joven protegida y una empleada doméstica adolescente, quienes inician una improbable amistad que amenaza con deshacerlas a ambas.

La casa entre los cactus (Paul Pen) This is a fairly easy-to-read thriller by a Spanish author (yes, names don't always reveal who is a native speaker). My students have enjoyed this tale set in Baja California where many of my students have roots. Elmer y Rose han creado una familia perfecta entre los enormes cactus de un remoto paisaje desértico, un hogar lleno de amor para sus cinco hijas, todas con nombres de flor: Edelweiss, Iris, Melissa, Dahlia y Daisy. Pero la inesperada llegada de Rick, un excursionista en busca de refugio, revoluciona a las hermanas. Y cuando Elmer y Rose descubren que el muchacho no es quien dice ser, el enfrentamiento que librarán -una lucha entre la verdad y la mentira, la justicia y el crimen- destapará terribles secretos que cambiarán para siempre la vida de todos ellos.

Author interview (from a country where authors are rock stars):

https://www.youtube.com/watch?v=QJcLCjQJcZk

Huesos de lagartija (Federico Navarrez) Engaging novel about the Conquest from the perspective of an indigenous priest, written for adolescents. Frequently read in Mexican schools. I think I would send them to the following link after they have read the book as the review isn't so much a book trailer:

reseña: **https://www.youtube.com/watch?v=19KgHi0Kt-s**

Browsing Strategies

A browsing strategy is any activity that gets your students more familiar with the books in your classroom library. This is a crucial activity for any pleasure reading program because non-readers generally don't know how to browse— they will just grab the first book they see and, since it probably will not be a match to their interests, that will confirm their self-belief that they hate reading. Book talks, Reader's Theater, and CALP lessons related to a book in your library are much more effective ways to get students interested in what you have to offer. Heck, when a student interview reminds me of a book in my library I take the opportunity to advertise that book. So let's take a look at some of these browsing strategies.

Book talks have already been discussed as an essential, nearly everyday activity. Review this on page 102 and watch the video of Teresa Torgoff doing a book talk in her French class.

Speed Book Dating: This is a one time activity in my classroom, completed on one of the first days of school for level 2 or above, or on the first day of Winter semester for my level 1 students who start the independent reading component of the pleasure reading program in January. I simply want to get several books in the hands of students.

Students who have not grown up with books have never browsed; they just grab the first book within reach. This activity teaches students to read the back cover of the book, glance through the illustrations and evaluate the book in very general terms. In the past I have returned their browsing sheets with the expectation that they will refer to them when deciding what to read next; that never happens! **The value of this activity is truly in getting students to understand that they should not settle on the first book to fall into their hands.** The Speed Book Dating form is reproduced on the next page. Collect them after the activity in case you need to suggest books to a student.

Reading aloud to students is a powerful technique that should be done at all levels. While a book talk is simply talking in a spontaneous manner about a book, a read aloud is actually reading from a book. I usually chose the scene carefully before class, practice how I am going to make it comprehensible and intriguing to students, and save my place in the book with a sticky note. Often I will explain in English what happened in the book before the scene that I am going to read. Sometimes I will put the book under a doc cam and project it against a white screen, especially it is a graphic novel.

Read alouds help students browse your library, models good reading skills, and is a great way to scaffold a text that might be a little too difficult for some of your students. Better yet, these are great techniques to perfect while you are still building your library.

Speed Book Dating

Student name:

title	things you noticed	do you want to try it out?
		yes or no
		yes or no
		yes or no
		yes or no
		yes or no
		yes or no
		yes or no

Once you start reading aloud a scene from a novel, do not feel like you have to finish it; none of these techniques requires you to read the entire text. In fact, you do not even have to start at the beginning. **I like to simply choose a favorite scene and give my students a taste of the novel** so that, if they choose, they can pick it up during independent reading time. It is important to note that read alouds can begin with any scene in the book. In fact, the teacher can do several read alouds throughout the year based on any one book. **Do not worry about revealing key plot twists; like a good joke or song, a good book can be revisited frequently**.

Kindergarten reading is generally used with colorful children's books. These books are actually inappropriate for second language (L2) independent reading at this level. They are designed for children with thousands of hours of contact with the language moving from fluency to literacy. Instead, we use these to prompt a cozy storytelling session. **If you have ever read a book to a two-year-old, you probably did not read the text as written. You may not have even followed the plot, instead relying on the colorful images to narrate and retain the child's interest.** Gather your students in a circle, pass out a bag of pretzels and simply try talking about the book in comprehensible language. I like to place the illustrations under a document camera and project the image against a white screen so that all students can see the images easily.

Reader's Theater is a technique is often used when teaching a whole class novel, but there is no reason not to use it as a way to advertise a book. It requires a little bit of planning. Before class I read a scene from a book with potential for a lot of dialogue and a lot of dramatic tension. Then I will rewrite the scene as a dialogue-only script.

On the next page I created a short reader's theater dialogue for Bryan Kandel's novel, *Sobrevivientes*. This often involves me adding lines, even adding lines for characters who do not have dialogue in the book in order to flesh out how each character is feeling. I add stage instructions in English to help clarify what I want my actors to do (although I always have them sitting on stools in front of the room as if they were doing a stage reading for a drama troupe). I print out a copy for each actor, large font.

When we start, I set the scene in Spanish, using the board to draw pictures. The fun part of Reader's Theater, however, is coaching your student-actors to perform the scene in a variety of ways. Ask a character to repeat a line in several different ways: first sad, then excited, then angry. After performing an action, ask students to do it again in slow motion. End by recording the final version of the scene on video so that later in the semester you can play it again. Always have a copy of the book front and center so that students associate the theater production with the book; the recorded version should present the book as a book commercial that you can use for years to come.

Once again, **the purpose of the activity is to give students a taste of the book so that, if interested, they can follow up during independent reading session**.

[Actor who plays Nando holds up the book and announces, "A scene from *Sobrevivientes* by Bryan Kandel"]

Roberto: Hermanos, sin comer vamos a morir. Hay 18 cuerpos. Necesitamos comer los cuerpos. [rubs belly like hungry]

Carlitos: ¿El canibalismo? Prefiero morir.

Nando: Entonces moriremos. No hay otra opción.

Roberto: Tenemos que sobrevivir.

Carlitos: ¿Por qué? Estamos perdidos en Los Andes. Nadie nos busca.

Nando: Tengo una familia. No me quiero morir. Quiero vivir.

Carlitos: Entre los muertos está mi hermana y mi madre. Son tus amigos.

Roberto: Eran nuestros amigos. Ya no son, solo hay cuerpos. Carne.

Gallery Walks: Pleasure reading programs work best when there is no accountability and students are simply reading for pleasure, but how do you lead students from a toxic culture of fake reading to a culture of reading for fun? This browsing strategy appears like an assessment to some students, but in class it quickly transforms into an exciting class browsing session. I plan these on the last Friday of every month.

I have a very particular way that I organize gallery walks designed to celebrate reading achievements. I do not want to assign any burdensome projects, and creating a poster outside of class can indeed be a burden. **Gallery walk days are announced ahead of time so that students will have time to reflect on the reading they have done in the past month.** On Monday I announce to students, "We are going to have a gallery walk on Friday, so start thinking about the different books you have read over the last month. Take a moment during our pleasure reading sessions to collect those books to review and reread." On Thursday I ask students to make a list of texts that they have read during our pleasure reading sessions. That list will be taped on the back of the poster that they make for the gallery walk.

On Thursday after school I remove the One Word Images and other posters from my walls to leave space for the gallery walk posters. By the end of the day my walls will be covered with several layers of student posters. **In each class students take a large piece of butcher paper and spend 20 minutes creating a poster advertising one book that they read in the last month.** Like a One Word Image, the posters typically have the image of one character surrounded by small images that depict important characteristics, objects or scenes related to the character. In order to make crisp portraits I tell students to use one marker to create the outlines of the images and then quickly fill in the images with crayons. No white paper may remain exposed; all of the paper must be covered with illustrations. The title of the book is the only written words allowed. Hands move quickly to finish within 20 minutes. After 20 minutes all crayons are put away. Don't let perfectionists drag on or you won't have time to finish the activity.

Posters are then taped to all four walls of the classroom. **Student names face outwards, but their lists of books read are taped to the back so that the breadth of their reading during the last month remains a secret between student and teacher.** A secret: I don't really take the time to look at these lists when I remove the posters at the end of the day, but it adds to the 'feeling of accountability' that motivates some students.

We then present one wall at a time: students stand in front of their posters and the rest of the class forms small groups of one, two, or three observers in front of the student presenting their posters. If you have shorter periods you might have two walls present at a time. My Level 1 students present their posters to their peers in the language of their choice, but by Level 3 my students talk about their posters and books in the target language. Each presentation lasts one minute, then groups rotate to another poster. **Each**

wall presents five times, for a minute each time, so every student actually completes five small group presentations before we rotate to the next wall.

The presentations often start with concrete descriptions, but encourage students to describe a scene from the book that they really enjoyed. This social interaction is an important browsing activity for the student observers and helps feature the class as a community of readers. Having every student spend five minutes in front of a poster they created, talking about a book that they have read, invokes the "pride of accomplishment" that some students yearn for without requiring studying or activities that turns the reading experience into "work".

Book Walls
The social dynamic of knowing what peers enjoy reading can be harnessed to become a powerful, passive browsing strategy. Place the name of each book read in your library on a butcher paper hung on back wall. Allow students to draw a colored star next to the book title when they finish the book. I have used green="loved it", yellow="it was okay", and red="not for me, but maybe you'll like it". Students looking for a new book can glance at the book wall and immediately see what is popular.

An important note: I never have students write their name to indicate that they have read a book. It leads to competition and fake reading.

The text type challenge
is a way to encourage students to experience a wide variety of texts from your classroom library. **Each student receives a list of the various text types that appear in your library** (see example on next page) and are encouraged to add at least one title from each section to their list of books read. I would not advertise this as an assignment so that students still feel free to choose their own books. Instead, this is a challenge! If you limit it to a certain month, like calling it the "February Text Type Challenge", the activity can inject a little excitement into your reading program during a hard part of the year.

Infographics
that allude to content knowledge that students have learned about in other classes can be a great hook to interest students in our library. For example, when I preview my novel *Superburguesas,* I use an infographic that I found on the internet about how infections are spread when people do not regularly wash their hands.

Before class I project the image against a large piece of white butcher paper and I trace it lightly with a pencil. The pleasure is in revealing the drawing using marker in class. While we discuss hand washing in Spanish, I trace over the illustration of the hand. Then I overemphasize the creepiness of the comical illustrations of common pathogens found on unwashed hands, especially noting the ones that cause diarrhea and other unpleasant symptoms.

Text Type Challenge

Read a book from as many categories possible and write title below once finished. Books can only be listed once.

Newspaper article	Class-created text	Hard cover children's book
Novel less than 50 pages	Novel 50-99 pages	Novel 100 or more pages
Japanese manga	Graphic novel or comics (not Japanese)	An article from a children's encyclopedia
Non-fiction sports	Non-fiction animals	A-Z reader

Student name: _____

Bringing the conversation back to the book, I describe the character who does not wash his hands when he works at a fast-food hamburger restaurant. Slowly revealing the infographic while discussing it in easy, comprehensible language adds great dramatic tension to the activity. Infographics are a great way to introduce high-interest content to learners, devoid of burdensome follow-up activities.

Impromptu book advertisements: At the very beginning of the year when a student interview reveals that someone in my class likes baseball, you had better believe that I will be backing up towards the table with my sports books simply to hold up the books that I have about baseball players. Impromptu book advertisements are easy to include in your classes in an organic way, as long as you are thinking about the books that you have.

Before class, stroll around your library and consider the themes so that you connect students with books. A student who expresses that the environment is important to her, or even professes enjoying hiking, might like *Juliana*, a fictional novel about a real cave complex in Spain that houses hundreds of bats. She may not find the novel if you do not point the way. Heritage learners of Spanish often enjoy novels set in the country where their family members are from. A student interested in fashion might enjoy *El último viaje* by A.C. Quintero. An advanced student who is an avid cyclist will surely enjoy *El cóndor de los Andes* by Adriana Ramírez. An intermediate student who talks about her sister may not bother to browse your collection of graphic novels, but be thrilled when you point her towards a copy of *Hermanas* by Raina Telgemeier. **A great time to introduce a new book is when the theme comes up organically, during a student interview.**

Book Trailers : A final post-reading activity that requires some work outside of class is a book trailer. Once per year I offer these as one of the possible projects that students can do and I always provide other options for students who are not adept at video editing or who simply cannot collaborate with peers outside of school. Writing an illustrated short story is a comparable alternative.

If you are considering assigning these as an end of school year project, perhaps it will be more rewarding to assign them in January or February when students do not have to manage the weight of final exams and end of the year projects from their other classes.

In any case, provide direction so that this project can be completed efficiently. I give students a set of directions with a timeline so that they complete it over a weekend without being perfectionists. First, on a Friday, plan out a set of scenes and describe them on paper including ideas about where the camera will be, how characters will move through the scene, and narration. If there is dialogue, I like to preview it so that the book trailer is usable with other classes.

On Saturday, students film each scene as written. Tell them not to be perfectionists, just film it and move on.

On Sunday, have one person edit the scenes using a program like Shotcut (or many students can do this on their phones). Stitch the scenes together, and add music and narration and any post-production additions such as animated transitions.

A book trailer should not last longer than four minutes. I ask that book trailers are captioned so that they are easier for next year's students to understand. When done well, book trailers can be later shown to help students browse your classroom library. **The two minute book trailer below is an excellent model to show beforehand** so that students understand that they do not have to tell the story. They just want to intrigue viewers so that the viewers read the book.

Superburguesas trailer: http://bit.ly/2LyLNGb

Powerful Display of a Classroom Library

There are several concepts that you should keep in mind when organizing your classroom library. Two of the most common organizing concepts– (1) creating a visually pleasing space and (2) creating a extremely clean, organized space– are actually not the most important concepts to consider.

Children feel comfortable in a visually appealing space, and many adults feel comfortable in a very orderly space; I understand why these concepts are often prioritized. Yet a beautiful reading nook with few books is nothing but a hangout space. An orderly selection of containers of books is *unbrowse-able* and undermines the reason you are building a reading program in the first place. The question behind the organization of a classroom library should be, "how easy is it to browse?".

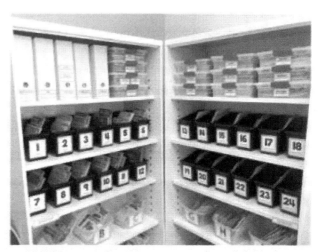

A highly organized library may be intimidating and impossible to browse for your students.

Browsability is an essential characteristic of an effective classroom library. As your library grows, think closely about how to display the books so that students can easily find their personal homerun book.

I first identify the most accessible space in my classroom to display the easiest, most read books. In my classroom, that is a large wall space to the right as students enter the room. I have attached Velcro strips to the wall where I fasten these highly readable books facing cover outward. This is the "easiest to grab a book" space. I place books like El ratón Pablito here, an easy read that is also pleasing to most students. A book like Vida y muerte en la Mara Salvatrucha also hangs on this wall, not because it is the easiest but because it is one of the most popular books among students, with extremely attractive cover art. I want that book to entice students. I want students to admire the artwork and long to read that book.

Another high traffic location in my classroom is along several tables along the far wall, pushed up against the windows. Students place their book bags under these tables at the beginning of the period, so they all cross the room and pass by these tables. On top of these tables I place a selection of different kinds of popular books. The idea is to encourage students to stumble upon a text type that they might not normally pick on their own. I own perhaps two dozen animal encyclopedias, but I only place two or three of the most popular on these tables. Likewise, only a few highly popular (and easy-to-read) graphic novels rotate through this collection of books, as well as the rest of my language learner novels. Since I usually buy the language learner novels in groups of five copies at a time, students who want to read the same novel as their friends often browse this table. There is no prohibition of impromptu lit circles in an independent choice reading program!

Once I have filled the two highest accessible locations with the best books in my collection, it is time to create specialized sections so that students can search out a particular kind of book. In the back of my room I have a table with manga and graphic novels, placed cover-up to highlight the cover art, and another table dedicated to sports. There are also two bookcases against the back wall. Each shelf is labeled with a large sign (thick letters about 4 inches high) with sections such as ANIMALS, CHILDREN'S ENCYCLOPEDIAS, and EASY AUTHENTIC READING, which contains titles such as Diary of a Wimpy Kid, the Goosebumps series, and other middle school staples. The easy authentic reading section services heritage learners placed in my Level 1 class; if you do not have that demographic in your classes, then those kind of books will be too incomprehensible to Level 1 students.

Once I have hundreds of student-created pamphlets (two or three months into the school year), I staple them together into groups of five or ten and stack them in the back of the room for students to grab a handful at a time. I have also combined Velcro with Styrofoam presentation boards to create light, mobile displays that hold up to 20 of these pamphlets. The presentation boards can be stored easily and pulled out at the beginning of class so that they lean against the ledge in the whiteboard.

There are several more spaces to highlight a rotating selection of interesting books so that the book selection always appears "fresh." In my classroom these books are mostly fastened with Velcro to a space in the front of the room where students will gaze during class when (incredibly) my teaching is not maintaining their interest. There is a high, visible space up front where I hang the book that the teacher is currently reading. The space is labeled, "My teacher reads, too." There is a small space for recent acquisitions, as well as another space reserved for books that have recently been the subject of a book talk in class. Finally, I have several plate easels placed on top of a filing cabinet to display a rotating selection of extraordinary books (i.e., "most popular," a holiday themed book, or a student highlighted book).

Wire and clothespins run along the front board from which I hang current news selections printed off from NewsELA.com or El mundo en tus manos by Martina Bex. I often staple several articles together to create a little heft so that the articles do not bend over. It is a nice way to create a fresh display every week and the photos often supply interesting conversation topics in class.

Should teachers display or label books by reading level? The argument is that students enjoy books that they can understand; making the books easier to identify by level will help students quickly locate an appropriate book. I think, however, that labeling books by level only leads students to compete against each other and does little to teach them how real readers browse for pleasure reading. I would rather a student bring three or four books that look good back to her seat and evaluate them by glancing through the first few pages than never opening the cover at all.

An attractive physical space to display your library does not have to break the bank. You do want to display the cover art of as many of the books as possible, however. Several bookcases showing only the spines of the books may appear clean and orderly, but it is nearly impossible to browse. Consider how bookstores entice customers to browse; the most browsed books are lying face-up on tables. You can use revolving racks, rain-gutter shelves, or Velcro fastened to walls to display books facing cover-out.

Some teachers use labeled plastic tubs to hold their books because the tubs are orderly and aesthetically pleasing; be sure that students can quickly evaluate what is in the tub or you risk making the library unbrowsable. Likewise, a cute Pinterest-worthy reading nook complete with sofas and adorable throw rugs is not necessary to create an environment conducive to reading; simply consider where eyes and legs naturally traverse the room in order to encourage browsing.

Reading Activities & Assessments

If you have been teaching for a few years you probably have highly developed skills to ensure that students actually do the reading. In workshops across the country, whenever we speak about reading, teachers immediately ask me about reading compliance measures: reading logs, projects, all of those products that demonstrate that students have done the reading.

In this section I am going to encourage you to distrust those instincts. What I am concerned with here is what teachers are really struggling with: **how to transition students from the punitive compliance approach to reading that is common in many classrooms so that students embrace the pleasure-based approach** advocated by Stephen Krashen.

Students are familiar with punitive compliance approaches to reading. **They have been trained to play the game in all of their other classes and reading has become a task to undermine**. Teachers respond by finding ways to ensure reading compliance, such as quizzes, reading guides, writing assignments and random (humiliating) in-class comprehension questions. **Our students are immersed in a punitive reading culture that rouses their counter will; is it any wonder that they huddle before class discussing the reading with the one kid who actually did it**, that they send text messages to students in other sections about "surprise quizzes", that they copy answers to reading guides in the hallways during morning break and that they despise the astute teachers who also manage to "play the game well"?

Undermining the teacher's attempts to enforce reading compliance is *"the game"* and, I think, one of the reasons adolescents report that they hate reading. The so-called good students may read due to an external motivator (grades, desire to impress an adult), but research on external motivators indicates that they actually decrease internal motivation. That is to say, **reading compliance assignments are unlikely to motivate compliant or non-compliant students to become lifelong readers**.

By setting up a pleasure reading program, **we are attempting to step outside of this game**, coaxing students to abandon what is truly a non-reading culture and nudging them to discover a home-run book... the kind of reading experience that is so satisfying that it opens a new world. How naive we must seem to those calculating students who have spent their lives perfecting the game! How silly we must seem! How easy to fool!

When I start my pleasure reading program, I very briefly describe in L1 why we are spending 5-10 minutes at the beginning of the class on independent reading. I have several browsing strategies to get multiple books in their hands in the first few days before they commit to any book. Students are allowed to change books until they find one that is "not too bad", they are always allowed to abandon a book, and they are never quizzed on their independent reading. I demand a silent room while we read, and then I sit with them and read. Afterwards we often spend a brief moment talking about our books in L1 in small groups (this is both a documented way to add pleasure to the reading process as well as a browsing strategy) and I often do comprehensible L2 book talks describing a favorite scene from books in the classroom library (another browsing strategy).

Krashen states that studies have shown that **very few students are merely staring into space with glazed eyes during reading period**, yet for us classroom teachers it is a subject of heated discussion. Are they really reading? What can we do to make sure? *That kid certainly is not reading.* The handful that I know are certainly not reading define the entire class in my mind, and it frustrates me. My heritage learners in particular, the ones who gain most from easy pleasure reading, seem to be among the best at faking it unless they think there is going to be real accountability. I need to perfect this bridge between our current reality of the game and that wonderful future when each student has discovered a home-run book. **My role as a teacher is to connect students with a home-run book so that they become readers**. My instincts and my training as a teacher, however, constantly intrude and push me towards reading compliance measures. I am aware of what is happening in my classroom… I am actually pretty good at the game. **But winning the game is counter-productive**; I need to short-circuit the logic of the game.

This is what I would like to propose here: (1**) teaching a student to read and developing discrete reading skills is different from** (2) **leading a student to love reading**. Educators must be very clear that (1) does not lead to (2). The first can be done through brute force such as assigning reading journals, essays, comprehension quizzes, "minimally intrusive" post-reading paragraphs, graphic organizers, rubrics designed to encourage students to reflect on either the reading or the act of reading, assigned discussions in pairs after reading or assigned book talks. **The second, however, can only be accomplished through the path of pleasure.** If a post-reading discussion is pleasurable, if writing a reaction to a book is pleasurable (for instance, doing so voluntarily on Goodreads.com) or reading about other students reactions to the reading is pleasurable, then the activity will contribute to the greater goal of developing love of reading. If it is not pleasurable, then it plays into the dynamic of the game.

How, then, can we successfully confront the toxic culture of non-reading which is expressed by the game? I have an idea, and this once again is inspired straight from a conference talk given by Krashen. At NTPRS 2015 Dr. K spoke about the process of becoming a reader and he observed that, **before pleasure reading, almost all lifelong readers were read to**. I am not talking about being forced to read aloud in class or having the teacher read a boring text aloud. I am talking about an essential kindergarten reading activity that is fun and should not have been dropped neither in middle school nor even in high school. Readers tend to have had parents or older siblings who read pleasure reading texts to them. Being read to is not the only step to transform a person into a reader (they will then need access to highly-compelling reading), but most readers report that they were once read to. **I suspect that most of our students have not had enough experience being read to in pleasurable, read-aloud settings.**

Here is the key idea in this section on accountability: **I wonder what would happen if teachers rewired their brains so that, when we witness a non-compliant student during silent reading period, we reacted differently.**

Rather than reach for a reading compliance strategy, what if we were to think to ourselves, "I have got to do more read-alouds"? I am suggesting that not only would more pleasurable read-alouds move the student further down the road towards becoming a reader, but we would also short-circuit the logic of the game.

In the short run I will sit next to that student, engage in a conversation about reading, try to find a better book for him, try to make a connection during a read-aloud, but what I will not do is allow my frustration to perpetuate the dynamic of the game. That is a win/win for all of my students, especially the ones that are actually finding good books and are beginning to think that maybe this class is different.

Jen Schongalla told me about one of her nephews who described the pleasure reading program in his elementary school. He said to her:

> *"All the free reading books were labeled with colored stickers according to the level. I would pick a book, open it at my desk and just sit and think. I'd look around to see what level everyone was on, pick books that were 1-2 levels higher and just sit there. I never read during free reading until I discovered Calvin and Hobbes. Then I was hooked and read the whole series. Around 5th grade they evaluated our reading level and I was told I was reading at a college level."*

Did he really "discover" *Calvin and Hobbes* on his own? What strikes me about his recollection is what we can infer to be in the background: a patient teacher who was working hard to connect a non-compliant kid with his home run book.

Encouraging students to become lifelong readers

We now recognize that our goal of our pleasure reading program ***is not to verify that students did the reading***, but rather lead them to discover their own home run book. A home run book is such a pleasurable reading experience that the fruits of the reading life have been tasted.

I think **we have enough reading activities among the browsing activities listed in the section starting on page 125**. Even the activities like Gallery Walks that feel like assessments eventually play into a different dynamic. **We can still assess reading skills based on our whole class readings**, but let's develop students who love reading in our pleasure reading sessions.

If we do not have books in our library that our students find compelling, then we will never truly open the door to the full reading life. Students will know how to read, but they will not be readers. Oregon French teacher Tina Hargaden has a wonderfully blunt reaction when she sees a student uninterested in a book during silent reading period. Rather than sending death stares or sternly mouthing commands like "READ!" across the silent room, she simply approaches and whispers, "looks like your book sucks, let's find you one that doesn't suck too bad". **No need to blame the student for being off-task, no need to make this into a discipline issue; simply bring over a few more books and guide the student to browse more.**

Let me also describe an alternative to my approach, which is adding more read-alouds when students are fake reading. **Brett Chonko**, the Virginia Spanish teacher who has such a great approach to book talks**, has a slightly different approach to pleasure reading**. We agree on many things: he has a large library and is committed to connecting his students to books that fit their personal interests and reading levels. **However, during the reading session he does not read with his students. Instead he walks around and conferences with just a few every day.** By the end of every month he has circled the room and privately conferenced with all students.

Brett found that pleasure reading works for students who are already readers in their first language, but he was frustrated that his least proficient readers continued to fake read when not assessed. **He added one simple requirement to his pleasure reading program: *all students will be able to translate what they have read when asked in private conference with the teacher.*** Brett circles and spot checks, sitting with a student and asking her to translate from the page she just read. Brett reports that this tweak encourages less-proficient readers to choose easier books that they can read without hesitation—exactly what we want from a pleasure reading program! Note that **what Brett does in his class develops relationships with his readers in a way that a reading comprehension quiz does not.**

Boys Reading

You may have observed some patterns among students that help you differentiate reading instruction. **In class many teachers look for the soft skills that lead to better reading skills**: ability to choose an appropriate text quickly, ability to sit quietly, ability to focus or 'reading stamina', ability to avoid distractions. All of this tends to confirm to teachers that, *in general*, girls appear to be better readers than boys.

I want to unpack some problems with how we may be approaching this issue. Yes, by the way, it appears that adolescent boys ARE *on average* less proficient readers and girls DO read for pleasure more than boys, *on average*. If you have a class full of fourteen year old boys engaging in classic reading avoidance while the girls are quietly reading, your class is not unique.

What we do with this data defines us. Very few teachers would point to all of the observable steps that boys could have taken *but are not taking* and simply declare, "I've done my job!" We all feel the frustration, but that is a gatekeeper approach that simply observes and penalizes.

When I was a less experienced teacher I might have sought to make the reading process even more clear and document every time a child fails to model good reading skills. Imagine posting their names on reading ladders so that every child knows exactly 'where they are' and what they need to do to improve. **This is a perfectly logical approach to the mind of a technocrat but cringe-worthy to those of us who spend a lot of time with children.** I can destroy a child's self-esteem even without assigning dunce caps to the lowest achievers.

Here are some concrete steps you can take to make reading more pleasurable for all students, but especially attending to the needs of boys:

(1) **Unpack the social cues that lead us to misinterpret the reading experience.** A girl who flashes a smile when I sit next to her to conference during reading and a boy who rolls his eyes may be pursuing the same objective: "*get the teacher to move on quickly and leave me alone*". The theatrical roll of the eyes might be for the amusement of his peers, but a boy who craves the social approval of his peers has just revealed what he wants most. You'd be crazy to react with disapproval! React with contagious positivity because that scene he just made is likely not about you.

(2) **Take seriously the genres that your students are interested in.** If you have a set of motorhead magazines in the target language that your boys grab for pleasure reading, consider spending a book talk exploring them. Same with the encyclopedias of athletes. Sports journalism and the art of writing about automobiles deserves to be lifted up as

serious, important pursuits. **When a reluctant reader perceives that their reading choices are not 'high-prestige texts', they are left in a no-win situation: read what they like and remain a problem to be solved, or read the high prestige texts and hate the reading experience.**

One of the big take-home points of a study by Theresa Cremini is that **boys find it difficult to escape the label of deficit readers, even when they struggle to gain the teacher's respect**. A student who has a pleasurable conversation about books when conferencing with the teacher has a different experience than a student who senses that they are 'a problem to be solved'. While pleasure reading should be about pleasure, we can use our book conversations to counter the negative self-perceptions that our students hold by valuing their choices as readers.

(3) **Stop limiting your student's selection of pleasure reading material** (within reason, of course). I recently came across a teacher who claimed that her middle school students only like realistic fiction and hate fantasy, and so she removed books with 'unbelievable' plots. I suspect she was reacting to criticism received by students in class. Most probably these were highly vocal students who were forced to all read the same class novel. That is why in my class whole class texts are all short stories and short texts that can be read in one class session... ideally any whole class text will not drag on.

However, by removing fantasy she limited selection for a quiet minority of students who are looking for their homerun book to hook them on a lifetime of reading. **I think we need MORE CI books with dragons and zombie pirates, even though those plots are not for everyone.**

(4) **Novels, in my opinion, should be mostly reserved for choice (pleasure) reading.** A whole class 'forced march' through a single novel inspires adolescent rebellion. You may be engineering a teaching situation that lures boys into a non-readers camp.

When students are required to develop a serious, ongoing relationship with a text, they should at least have some say about which text they choose. Instead of a whole class novel, substitute a daily Write & Discuss class-created text to be the communal whole class text. You can plan to include whatever textual elements that you need to focus on in class, but the topic of the W&D should be of interest to the whole class.

Trouble-shooting a Reading Program

How to address negative attitudes towards reading? I never say the phrase "Free Voluntary Reading" to my students. I call it reading; I tell them that they need to find a text that is not too bad. Of course I know that I am trying to connect them with a compelling read. There is no discussion, pleading or rewards. Reading is an expectation in school, I will help you find a book that is not too painful.

"My students struggle with the books that I have". Make more class-created texts and do more read-alouds to scaffold the reading experience. If you have plenty of appropriate texts, you may need to incorporate more browsing strategies so that they find the books and reconsider how your library is organized so that it is easier to browse.

"My students never finish any book". Abandoning a book is okay, but you do not want them to abandon *every* book they ever try to read. Focus on the reading environment; is it silent and free from distractions? Are there enough appropriately-leveled books available? Is there a big diversity of themes and text types available? If not, do more read-alouds while you are building your library.

"They always want to browse during reading time". Give them a pile of books, preferably different text types, and do not let them get out of their seat during reading period. No bathroom passes, no discussion about anything regardless of how important. This has to apply to the teacher to: no grading, no taking attendance.

"I have a kid who is always looking around instead of reading". Long term plan is to try to connect him with a homerun book. However, David Ganahl from Centennial HS in Corona, California shares a marvelous short term plan. Give him a class seating chart and tell him that you have a hard time tracking who is reading and who is just looking around. Ask him if he would mind just spending the next 10 minutes watching class and mark a check whenever someone looks up. Now go read your book and thank him when reading period is done. The following day pass the same chart to someone else with the same instructions. Watch his face when he notices that someone else has the chart!

Encouragement & Good Reading Quotes

When it comes to independent reading programs, I think that **appropriate encouragement goes much further than policing students**. In fact, finding *the right* ways to encourage students to read is one of the research-based essential characteristics of a successful independent reading program according to Janet Pilgreen, a researcher who completed a large comparison of successful and less-than-successful reading programs around Los Angeles. I do not ever congratulate my students for reading independently... that just seems patronizing to me. I do let students in on the secret, however, by sharing the theory and research behind pleasure reading in bite-sized observations in class.

Effective browsing strategies can do double-duty to provide the type of situations that encourage students to read more. The "gallery walk" activity described in the video in the browsing strategies essay initially feels like accountability to students, but in my classes students emerge energized from these structured small group conversations. With so many great ideas for future reading and feeling empowered after passing on their own opinions, students have received meaningful encouragement from peers to keep reading. For many adolescents, **building in peer encouragement is more effective than direct teacher to student encouragement**.

Ideally you want to develop a group of student allies who can articulate and defend the practice of pleasure reading. One of my best allies was a student named Kiera who would respond to student complaints before I was even aware of the disturbance. At the beginning of class, when we read quietly for 10 minutes, if a student began to mouth the phrase, "Reading again?!", Kiera was already repeating my stock retort: "**We acquire languages most efficiently through pleasure reading**."

Sure, there was a gentle dose of jest as she imitated even the rhythm of my response, but she managed to police the class with such deft good humor that I did not mind at all.

I have made it easy for teachers to pass on good research by curating a set of good reading quotes. I often read one of the following quotes to students before our reading session in order to emphasize that this activity is not a waste of time. This is not a result of their teacher failing to plan a lesson: it is firmly supported in research.

Having a place where the quote is posted, perhaps a reading quote of the week, seems to have a bigger impact than simply reading the quote.

"**Because repetition is so important for learning, it is good to read a book you have already read before.**"   — Linguist *Paul Nation*

"Nothing does more for language development than reading—it builds vocabulary, spelling, awareness of syntax and morphology, and so much more, all in a way that goes deep into the part of the brain where language is processed."

—*Connie Nelson Navarro*

"Many studies confirm that those who read more write better… it is reading, not instruction, that helps us develop a good writing style."

—*Stephen Krashen*

"Picking up word meanings by reading is ten times faster than intensive vocabulary instruction."

—*Stephen Krashen*

"The best way to improve in a foreign language is to do a great deal of comprehensible, interesting reading. The case for self-selected reading for pleasure is overwhelming."

—*Beniko Mason*

"We can learn grammar through listening and reading. When we repeatedly meet grammatical constructions in our reading and listening, we learn them without having to give them much, if any, deliberate attention."

—*Paul Nation*

"Common sense should tell us that reading is the ultimate weapon—destroying ignorance, poverty and despair before they can destroy us. A nation that doesn't read much doesn't know much … the challenge, therefore, is to convince future generations of children that carrying a book is more rewarding than carrying guns."

—*Jim Trelease*

"If your language course does not provide large amounts of reading and listening at the right level for you, then you are missing a very important opportunity for learning."

—*Paul Nation*

- Student Voice Activities -

> This is the first of two modules that present the main activities done each day in our classes.
>
> **All of the activities in the 'Student Voices' module seek to make students the center of our curriculum.**

The teacher, who models the target language best, physically remains in the front of the classroom, or to the side if that is your preferred perch, but someplace where students can observe our point & pauses and where we can easily write on a board to clarify.

However **it is student-generated ideas and information obtained by students that determine what is said, what is important to review, and what shows up on the exit quizzes each day.**

Learning about their peers is key to success in our classes.

Students cannot ignore each other and just study a vocabulary list. Discovering something new about each other or collaborating together to imagine an original character or story is what drives the class forward.

You might ask yourself, "but when will students learn the vocabulary that my department has prioritized in our essential learnings documents?"

Firstly, the highest-frequency vocabulary will emerge naturally in context because it is indeed *highly-frequent*. If you are conducting student interviews you should never have to worry about formally introducing the verb *tener* (to have), for example, nor should you burn class time on conjugation charts or grammar discussions. Use the language in context and be sure that it appears in the Write & Discuss summary you create at the end of class. Over time, it will be thoroughly acquired.

Secondly, you can introduce any vocabulary, grammatical or thematic topic through these activities. It may be a drag on engagement if you conduct a card talk about parts of the house, but if you are absolutely forced to teach content that does not engage students it is even more important to personalize the conversation.

Picture Talk from Student Pictures

The "Student Voices" module focuses on activities that are easily personalized and make our students the stars of our curriculum. Using student pictures as the basis of "*Picture Talk*" develops CI skills that are the foundation of so many other techniques, such as *One Word Images*, *Movie Talks* and *Maravillas*. This is a wonderful activity to use in the first few weeks of school, and to keep pulling out throughout the year. Let's explore a few ways to do a very comprehensible *Picture Talk* that focuses on student lives:

If you can get students to send you photos, you have a virtually inexhaustible source of Picture Talk activities. You can simply ask students to bring in a photo from home, which is how I do it in my classroom. If your school allows you to access Twitter, establish a class hashtag for students who post photos of their home life on Twitter. Make your hashtag specific enough to your class, such as #PetoPer1, and be sure to establish guidelines on school appropriate photos. BEFORE class you simply save ONE photo (never pull up a live Twitter feed displayed in class) and then, in class, describe it using all of our basic skills to remain comprehensible.

Look at the Sweet 16 verbs that you have posted and try to rely on them as you think of things to say. Start with the word "there is", point and pause at the verb in the target language, and then point at something in the photo and name it in Spanish. You can move beyond simply "there is", but move slowly and deliberately. Speak slowly, your students are probably processing the language even slower than you are moving, so take your time slowly strolling over to the verb poster, reaching up to touch it as you say the word and make eye contact with your class, then slowly walking back to the photo to touch whatever you are referring to in the photo. Write on the board instead of code switching (i.e. speak only the target language, but write in English). Ask the student Artful Questions to learn more about the people and place in the photo. Fill a board with notes as you try to use as many question words as you can. Go back and review for your students so that they have the opportunity to hear the language again. Ask the class questions and demand a choral response. Verify with individual students, allowing either English or the target language.

Resist the urge to flip through other photos, even though students may be begging you to show their photo too. On one hand, you want to train students to focus on the input, but on the other hand you also want to inspire them to submit interesting photos so that you will choose their photo next time. Tell them you only have time for one today, and you will choose another tomorrow. Try to spend at least five to ten minutes on that one photo. End with a Write & Discuss activity, and then have students copy the text about their classmate's photo. There is no stronger way of declaring that the students are the curriculum than by putting that text in everyone's notebook, except perhaps by the ending the class with an exit quiz about that student's photo. Definitely do that, allowing students to take out their notebooks right before the quiz and let them review. This teaches them not only to pay attention to the class discussion, but also to faithfully copy the W&D.

A few suggestions:

- Require that the student appears in the photo! A photo of a dog, a house or a bedroom is inevitably easier to personalize and talk about if the student appears in the photo. You also are developing class bonds as students see each other in a context beyond the classroom.

- At the beginning of the year I often do W&D after every activity, but as the year progresses I start simply doing it at the end of class to summarize the entire period.

- Never pull up a live Twitter account on the projector to find the photo while the class is watching… this will inspire a clever student to post inappropriate photos with the class hashtag.

- If you are forced to use a thematic curriculum, this is a great way to personalize each unit. Every weekend you can challenge students to post their home photos based on the theme of the unit. At the beginning of my career I was forced to teach a horrible mini-unit on different kinds of fabric; it would have been a lot easier if I had challenged students to take photos of themselves wearing as many kinds of fabric as possible.

Student illustrations are also great pictures to use for Picture Talk. A doc cam is one of the essential pieces of technology for a student-centered class. Ask students to quickly illustrate something using stick figures… the people they live with, where they live, their favorite place to hang out, their favorite food. The possibilities are endless. You can use their illustrations to improvise a complete lesson or a simple warm-up activity. This is a wonderful activity for the beginning of the school year, but don't stop there. In January ask students to illustrate one day of their Winter break, if your school requires that you cover certain tenses such as the conditional, ask students to illustrate where they would like to go during the summer, to focus on the future tense ask them to illustrate their best prediction of what they will be doing in ten years, and if you have to teach a lesson focusing on uses of the

A doc cam is an indispensable tool in a student-centered classroom.

subjunctive ask them to illustrate what their parents do NOT want them to do (school appropriate, of course).

Give students five minutes to quickly make sketches– don't let the drawing part burn too much of precious class time. Then follow the process outlined above: point & pause, use your high-frequency verb posters, ask artful questions of the entire class requiring choral responses, speak slowly while touching the posters, write on the board and follow it up with a W&D.

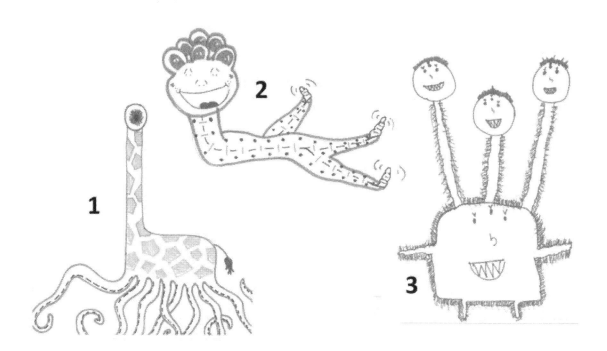

When you start talking about student drawings, don't just describe what you see. Use the Sweet 16 verbs to delve further: What does it DO with this part? Who HAS four heads? Why IS it so happy? What does he SEE with that big eye?

In my own classes I have a student volunteer sitting at my desk who controls my computer, and the doc camera is on the desk next to the computer. That student handles the papers while I remain at the front of the room pointing to the projected image on the screen. Everything runs so much smoother if you have a computer kid who operates the technology of the classroom. Hiring that class job is one of my first priorities of the new school year.

Finally, if you think that simply holding up a piece of paper for students thirty feet away to squint at is "good enough", you really need to experience the student engagement when their drawings are projected to be 6 feet high. If you don't have a doc cam, there are ways to connect an iPad or even a smart phone to a projector to serve the same purpose as a doc cam.

Card Talk

Card Talk is a way to learn about your students. This constitutes the majority of my class time during the first two weeks. Students illustrate something they like to do and then place the card in front of them, allowing the teacher to improvise personalized CI. But Card Talk is not just for the first days of school; ask them to illustrate something they want to do someday, something weird they have seen or done, their favorite outfit, an imaginary pet that they would like to have… the possibilities are endless. Then walk about the room and talk about their pictures, holding up the picture for everyone to see. Compare students, ask them follow up questions using a variety of interrogative words, verify by asking comprehension questions to the entire class, write on the board and follow up with a **Write & Discuss.**

I want to stress that Card talk does not have to be limited to "what do you like to do". Ask students to quickly illustrate what they did over the weekend or Winter break, where they would like to go during the summer, ask them to illustrate their best prediction of what they will be doing in ten years or something that their parents do NOT want them to do (school appropriate, of course). You can feature advanced grammar in a comprehensible, communicative context by choosing the right picture prompt.

You do not have to explicitly pre-teach advanced grammatical structures as long as students fully understand the prompt. This activity can invite very rich CI. Do

> **MANAGING CARD TALK**
>
> If you feel restless, roaming the classroom too quickly, then stop and delve deep with one student. Pick up their card, make a statement, write that on the board, and then stay with that student. Look at your list of question words and ask a variety of questions. Don't worry that the questions are obvious, or silly. He likes to play guitar? Where does he play the guitar? How many times per week? With whom? What kind of music? Once finished, write it all on the board.

not expect your students speaking or writing to immediately mirror the complex phrases you are saying. Most will respond simply. However if you do not restrict the complexity of your language while still remaining comprehensible, students will naturally develop a grammatical paradigm of the target language without any grammar instruction. In time they will start speaking and writing with the complex language that they have been hearing and reading.

Writing the prompt on the board in the target language with an English translation is a perfectly fine way to maintain comprehensibility. Remember to end the activity with a quick **Write & Discuss** activity and, if it is the beginning of the year, even consider giving an **oral or written exit quiz** to get hard data on whether your students truly understood you while also holding them accountable to attending to the class conversation.

Some teachers use *Card Talk* in the same way that I use *Student Interviews*; they use the cards to delve deep and get to know one student at a time. Those teachers typically ask their students to hold on to their cards to use for a week or two of classes.

> Card Talk is the perfect ZERO PREP, highly student-centered activity. The only thing you need is a stack of blank notecards.

I tend to use card talk more as a tool to do student surveys. I quickly move among the students and find commonalities. If I find one person who has depicted X, I will often ask how many other people have made a picture of X. then I count them and say "__ people in this class made a picture of ___!". Then I may draw a simple pie chart on the board to reinforce the idea that, for example, 40% of my students like soccer.

Using card talk as a student survey is especially effective if you know that you'd like to talk about a specific theme. I have a *maravilla* cultural presentation about a ballet teacher in Lima. Earlier in the class, before starting the *maravilla*, I might schedule a card talk in which I ask students to illustrate what they do on Saturday morning (knowing that I have several students who attend an extracurricular dance academy on Saturday mornings).

We start by observing all of the different responses. With a survey I will note that most students made a picture of themselves sleeping in bed, but some are at football practice, one is at the beach, another is with her family and… *"look at this class, three students are dancing. Where do you dance? Do you all dance together? How long do you dance? Do you dance ballet? Do you have a ballet teacher? How many people are in the class"*.

If I am mistaken and nobody illustrates themselves dancing, I can simply state, "wow, nobody dances?!" or I can even tell them that I like to dance ballet every Saturday morning. It does not have to be true! This is a natural conversation that leads organically into the cultural presentation that I had already planned to present to the class. However, be sure to spend time discussing everyone's cards. You don't want an activity designed to generate student ideas to be perceived as a cheap way to get your words into the classroom. I call that the Kanye West "I'm going to let you talk but first I've got some things to say" approach that will embitter some students who'll conclude that you don't really care what they do, that it is a ruse to talk about the teacher and the teacher's presentation.

Troubleshooting Q & A

Teacher: *My class gets really bored when I try to do card talk. How do I spice it up?*

Mike: Stop trying to be interesting to all students; use card talk to have a conversation with ONE student while everyone listens. Train your students to listen to the one conversation. Real life conversations aren't all laughter, shock and surprise. Ignore the energy for now, you're not a talk show host. Instead focus on making a connection: "You like cereal? I like cereal! I eat cereal for dinner. Do you eat cereal for dinner?"

When you feel like the energy is pushing you to move on, stay with that student and drill deep. Make a connection. Then give an exit quiz so the whole class is accountable.

Card Talk Database

It is great if you can get kids to keep their cards and you reuse the same cards for several sessions of card talk, but I just cannot be so organized. Each time I do card talk I pass out the largest size flash card I can buy and choose a different prompt from the list below. Notice that the prompts all feature Sweet 16 verbs. Some are a bit weird, but the purpose is to get a lot of repetitions of high frequency verbs. I write the prompt on the board in both the target language and English. Students have five minutes to illustrate. AVOID making fun of badly-drawn illustrations, even if it feels funny, because students will stop putting effort into their drawings. **Remember to only allow 5 minutes for drawing, then all markers, crayons and pencils need to be placed on the floor & all students should be listening, not drawing.**

1. Draw the people you live with. Stick figures are fine.

2. Draw something that you **gave** away as a present.

3. Draw someone who **tells** you what to do. Stick figures are fine.

4. Draw the place where you feel best.

5. Draw an image of what you **do** in your free time.

6. Draw something that you **can** do alone.

7. Draw something that you **put** in your bag / purse most days.

8. Draw something you **want** to have in the future.

9. Draw an image of a person, place or thing that you want **to know** more about.

10. Draw an image of how you would **leave** your house if you could not leave through the door.

11. Draw an image of a pet you either **have** or would like to have.

12. Draw an image of what you'd **bring** with you if you were moving and only allowed to bring ONE thing with you.

13. Draw an image of where you would like **to go** on a school trip.

14. Draw an image of what you **can see** from your window at home.

15. Draw an image of something that makes some noise (use the word '**hear**' when describing the images).

16. Draw an event that is going to happen soon.

17. Draw something that **makes** you happy.

18. Draw something you have seen someone **put** in their nose.

19. Draw a person that has a job that you think is cool.

20. Draw a monster from another universe.

Student Interviews

A student interview at the beginning of the year often includes code-switching. I ask questions and students often respond in English, which I then rephrase into the target language.

I conduct an interview on the very first day of classes. It is simple: I just have a power point slide behind the student with **the question both in the target language and English**. The student turns around to read the question, while I am able to speak Spanish the entire time. I ask many comprehension questions for the entire class to answer with a choral response. This is the perfect activity to train students that their job in class is to listen to the one class conversation and focus on the content of the conversation, not the form. As long as students can understand, they will acquire. **After a week of this all of the interrogative words will be thoroughly acquired by almost all of your students.**

https://vimeo.com/730380690/0863106d04

Watch a Student Interview in a first day of Portuguese class that I conducted in Michigan (0:00 to 12:08), followed by teacher talk (12:08-13:06), Write & Discuss (13:06-17:33), more teacher talk (17:33-19:28) & then finishing with a Review Of The Text (19:28-23:00) and finally an Oral Exit Quiz (23:00-28:00).

The most important thing that you are doing is learning about your students. Simply speak the target language, pointing at the questions. Translate student answers and ask the class easy comprehension questions. Write on the board when necessary. End the activity with a Write & Discuss.

I use the same power point throughout the week and switch to a new set of questions the following week so that students experience both repetition and variety. The questions I ask use a variety of question words and Sweet 16 verbs. I often use the same power point with the same questions for all levels, especially at the beginning of the year. In upper levels the conversation will often flow more naturally in unexpected directions, but I want to remain comprehensible… especially to students who have switched into our school and have not had conversational classes before.

EXPERT TIP: Keep the entire class W&D texts on one google doc that you project against the screen. Throughout the semester as you interview new students you can go back and compare information to previous interviews and even ask follow-up questions to students that were interviewed before. This ongoing document will help build a class community that will be a useful source of information for midterm exams.

But how do I keep the rest of the students engaged when I am interviewing?

It's true that some students will disengage if you spend 10 minutes talking about another student! For that reason, (1) it is very important that you have a system in place so that you **always have time for an exit quiz**. I have a student job called the timer who announces when we have run out of time. **Student helpers who track time management are crucial** so that I don't get sucked into a conversation because we need to complete the W&D and the exit quiz every day. (2) During the interview, be sure to **ask choral response questions** of the student audience. When you learn that a student was born in a town 30 miles away, turn and ask the whole class where she was born, ask if anyone else used to live in that town, point and pause at the students who have connections with the student interview. (3**) If the audience is not responding to choral responses** but you know that they know the answers, start asking individual students the same questions and then ask the same question to the whole group. I'll then comment that I thought they didn't know the answer.

Keep everyone engaged by keeping them on their toes!

Teachers sometimes erroneously assume that student interviews are only conducted with beginners to elicit 'getting to know you' vocabulary. I think that **student interviews are a life-skill that we should conduct at all levels.** These are the interpersonal skills that our students will be honing even in upper levels. Some teachers may presume that we need special, advanced questions for our advanced students. Once again, no! I actually use the same set of questions with all levels. **The differentiation comes with how we conduct the interview, how we ask follow-up questions and how often we are compelled to write on the board to scaffold the interview for our audience.** I have also found that advanced classes need less checking in, whereas when I interview a beginner I am often checking in with the non-interviewed students.

A LIST OF INTERVIEW QUESTIONS

Ask the same 5 questions all week long. Feel free to delve deep and ask follow-up questions... when a student indicates that they have a pet, ask them what kind. Get to know the student being interviewed. The following week ask 5 different questions.

1. What are you afraid of?
2. At what time do you wake up? At what time do you go to bed?
3. What do you like to do outside of school?
4. Where do you live?
5. Do you have a pet?

1. What makes you angry?
2. What makes you want to work hard?
3. If you were a superhero, what would be your superpower?
4. What do you like least about your classes?
5. Who is your hero?

1. Where would you go if you could go anywhere in the world?
2. How many siblings do you have?
3. Do you have to do chores at home?
4. Who do you talk to when you need advice?
5. If you could only eat one thing, what would it be?

1. Do you like surprises?
2. Which do you prefer: playing a game, watching a movie or reading a book?
3. Who would you choose to be with if you had to choose one person to be with on a deserted island?
4. Do you have a hobby?
5. What annoys you most?

1. Imagine five years into the future: What do you want to be doing?
2. What is the best gift you have ever received?
3. If you could go back in time, which year would you visit?
4. Where do you go when you are sad?
5. How many pillows do you sleep with? Are there stuffed animals on your bed?

1. If you were a wild animal, which animal would you be?
2. Is your room clean or messy?
3. Do you like roller coasters?
4. What job do you want to do in the future?
5. Where would you prefer to go on vacation: Alaska or Hawaii?

1. Name one thing that you do every day.
2. Where do you want to live when you are older?
3. Who do you like to go shopping with?
4. What do you like to do on a rainy day?
5. Do you have a job outside of school?

1. Who do you talk to every day?
2. How many hours do you sleep each night?
3. What is the worst food you have ever eaten?
4. Which do you prefer: coffee, tea, juice or water?
5. Where do like to go to enjoy yourself?

1. Who normally makes dinner in your house?
2. Name one thing that is in your bag right now.
3. Do you want a tattoo?
4. Do your parents/guardians let you stay out late?
5. Who knows your secrets?

Calendar Talk

Calendar Talk is NOT about presenting vocabulary related to the calendar. Instead, it is about discussing **major and minor life events that your students are experiencing and** being able to recycle those conversations while looking at a calendar. Avoid topics such as the weather and dates. Instead hone in on life events.

First watch this demonstration of Calendar Talk that I did in a workshop in Colorado. This is a first day of a Portuguese class, so there is a lot more code-switching from English to

https://vimeo.com/730413075/ae0d38fd9e
Calendar Talk is a powerful beginning of class routine

Portuguese than you would see even two weeks into the school year. Also, since it took place in a workshop, I did not have my permanent posters up but rather a limited selection of verbs posted directly on the power point side.

In my real classes **I would draw out a monthly calendar on a big piece of butcher paper** that would be taped to the wall. Every class has their own calendar because I will be making notes about what students are doing throughout the month. One student job is the student who comes in and moves the class calendar from the wall to the board in front of the class. On the next page is a sketch of how the class calendars are organized.

I recommend that you **take the time to calmly draw the calendar for each class during the class period** at the beginning of the month. Creating something live with your students is so powerful and this simple process will expose them to names of months, days and even names of holidays in a nice, relaxed manner. Better yet, a hand-drawn calendar on butcher paper will be larger than any calendar that you buy at an office supply store.

Having the whole month to glance at is invaluable for the purpose of class discussion. It could be that at the very beginning there is not much written, but quickly you will have an excuse to write birthdays and other dates that are important to students. Then, perhaps a week later when you observe one student's birthday you can go back and mention the birthday that happened last week. **This recycling is powerful**; when one student mentions in calendar talk that he is going to his grandmother's house over the weekend, glance back and note whenever another student visited a family member. **You can routinely talk about chores or after school activities**, referring back to the calendar to ask for updates about the school play or a football game. I don't have a good memory, but **the calendar is a crutch so that I can check in on students' lives in a natural, spontaneous class conversation**.

You will certainly want to post every students' birthday... I check their records and write in these dates on the first of the month. At the beginning of the week I ask students who participate in band, sports, and any clubs about events happening that week. **I want to get everyone on the calendar at some point in the month**, so I may refer back to a student interview in order to write what someone is doing during the weekend. Basically, there are no rules; anything can be written on the calendar and then referred to later in the month.

Calendar Talk may start out lame on the first few days when you are fishing for things to write. Fight the urge to give up!! After a week or so it builds into a great community-building activity and students are often excited to get their names on the calendar.

One Word Images

What is an OWI?

The creation of a One Word Image (OWI) **is a central technique tapping into student's creativity**. Invented by Ben Slavic, it is a activity that encourages students to enter a state of flow where they are so intent on the message being communicated that they seem to forget that they are listening to a second language. We become so immersed in the character and story being created that we acquire the language unconsciously, just as Krashen predicts. **There are few classroom activities as beautiful as creating a OWI.** I recommend taking the time to truly master this technique and cover your classroom walls with the student drawings created.

Watch video demonstrations from a workshop in Savanah, GA

(1) First day creation of basic OWI

https://videopress.com/v/3uYt59Jb

(2) Second day 'story' based on OWI
https://mygenerationofpolyglots.com/wp-content/uploads/2019/03/Bunny-Spears-story.mp4

Before getting started you will need an easel with a large piece of butcher paper angled away from the class **so that you can see the drawing being made by your student artists but the class cannot.** Choose two students to be the class artists: the first will use a thick black marker to create the outline of the character and add details. The second has a box of crayons to fill in all shapes with color. Instruct your artists to make the image large, but do not write any words with the exception of the character's name. When I do this activity in online Zoom classes I ask every student to draw and I take a screen shot when they all hold up their illustrations together at the end of the session.

Stand in front of the class and tell them in English that today you will all collaborate to create a character together. Before we get started, we need an inanimate object that we will fill with life with our own creativity. Students are often reluctant at first so I like to mention that I am partial to talking food, but it could be anything as long as it comes from our own minds. No Sponge Bob because that is a character that someone else imagined.

Allow your students to make suggestions and **wait until you hear an idea that you like**, or alternatively point vaguely towards the back and say your own suggestion as if you were repeating something said by a quiet student. "Cucumber, yes! Our character is a cucumber!"

Turn to your artists and **caution them not to start drawing**. We need a few details before they can put pen to paper.

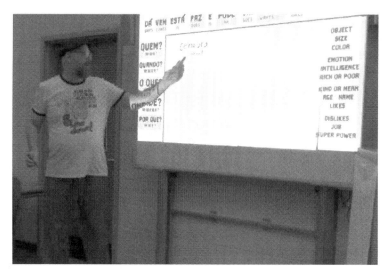

Point at and repeat the word

Continuing with our example, **write the word "cucumber" on the board in the target language**. If I were teaching Spanish I would write the word "pepino" and then say it

aloud slowly, savoring the sound. I repeat the word, now with a lower voice, and three times again with a quick, high-pitched voice. The purpose is to allow students to hear the word many times.

Then I ask students to imagine our pepino. **I physically lift the pepino off of the board, carrying it in two arms, and plop the imaginary character down onto the stool** at the front of the room. Express amazement, putting hand to cheek and cry out, "¡Qué pepino!"

Ask students if they can see the pepino. Offer to reseat students in the back so that they can get a good view. The purpose of this theater, conducted in either English or the target language as long as they can understand, is to encourage students to suspend disbelief. **We want them**

164

focusing on the theater, not the language. Language is acquired best when the message is the primary objective and the learner does not pause to consider how the language is put together.

Now, still looking at the empty stool where the imaginary pepino is resting, ask students in the target language whether the pepino is big (widely opening your arms and raising the volume of your voice but lowering the tone to as close to bass as you can) or is it small (clasping fingers together and speaking quietly but with a high pitch). ¿Es grande… o es pequeño? **Let students respond in the language they feel comfortable**. Spread your arms wider and ask, "¿es enorme? O… ", tightly clasping fingers together as if trying to keep water from escaping, ask, "¿es microscópico?". Is it enorme or microscopic?

Once your students have chosen (or if they are all shouting different answers try the 'point to the back' trick again, nod and say whichever response you wish as if you were agreeing with some imaginary student in the back of the room), then take a moment to review. **Announce in an astounded voice, "clase, hay un pepino microscópico aquí",** gesturing towards the empty stool. ["Class, there is a microscopic cucumber here"]. Glance at your artists to make sure that they have not started drawing yet. Ask another question, "clase, ¿es pequeño?" "No, claro que no… ¡es microscópico!" Turn to a student who is not expressing marvel and ask, "Bobby, ¿ves…", **make the gesture of two fingers moving away from your eyes that you use to communicate the concept of to see**, "¿ves el pepino microscópico?" ["Do you see the microscopic cucumber?"]

Express amazement at the size of the character.

If Bobby says that no, he does not see the microscopic cucumber, then move him to the front so he can get a better view. If he says yes, ask him what color it is. ¿De qué color es el pepino? You don't need a response, wait a beat and then turn to the whole class and repeat the question. If Bobby does not answer yes or no, go to the board and write the word ¿ves? followed by do you see? and ask the question again. **If a student is being petulant and refusing to answer, smile and act as if you are assuming that he simply does not understand. You are there to make sure everyone understands.** Thank him for helping you.

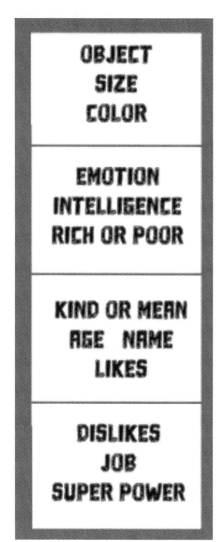

Once these first three characteristics are created the artists can now start illustrating. They should continue to listen and add details to the drawing as the class further develops the character. Keep the easel facing away from the class and observe to make sure they get it right. I tell my artists to work quickly; the entire process will not take more than twenty minutes. **Check to make sure that the illustrations are school-appropriate.**

I have a list of characteristics that is displayed in English beside my white board so that students can anticipate the questions that I will ask. **This allows me to stay in the target language and encourages their creativity**, as they glance at the list and come up with ideas while I am busy speaking slowly and deliberately. I often only cover 5 or 6 characteristics for each OWI, knowing that we are likely to add new details once we make a story with the character. Here is a list of possible characteristics: Is it sad or happy? Smart or dumb? Rich or poor? Kind or mean? How old is it? What is its name? What does it like to do? What does it dislike? What is its job? What is its superpower? You can download the posters in English to guide the OWIs by following this link:

https://mygenerationofpolyglots.com/wp-content/uploads/2018/04/OWI-characteristics.pdf

After each characteristic, be sure to go back and review in the target language, rearranging the order of the characteristics. Ask questions. In Spanish I say, "wow, we have a very old, blue cucumber that likes to ski! Class, is he purple? No, he is not purple, he is blue. Blue and very old. How old is he? Is he 100 years old?" Keep them processing the language!

At this point the artists are busy drawing. I continue through the characteristics listed on the board, but I do not worry about covering all of them. **We contemplate answers that are compelling, sometimes exploring the ideas in both the target language and English as we imagine the character and sometimes skipping over a characteristic that does not inspire us.** I often plan on presenting the drawing on the following day, so I make sure that we finish this part of the process with fifteen minutes of class time to spare.

We complete a quick Write & Discuss description of the OWI on the board, which the students often copy into their notebooks (but not until after we have finished writing it on the board– the W&D requires student input so they cannot be distracted by taking notes). We will also have a five minute exit quiz based on the creation of the OWI.

Post the process in English so that you can remain speaking in the target language

On the back of the exit quiz, just before class ends, I wonder aloud in English: **"Class, I wonder why oh why is this very old cucumber that likes to ski so very very sad. Why?** Look at how sad he is, he is microscopic with his microscopic tears… why is he so sad?!" Each student quietly writes their idea on a small piece of paper or note card which they then pass in to me. Students write their ideas in English… it is very difficult to be creative in a language that they are learning. **I want very creative answers to form a starting point for a story that we will create together** during the next class session.

If he is sad, then the responses will naturally lead to a problem that must be overcome in the story that follows. If he is happy, make an announcement at the beginning of the next class. **Take away whatever makes the character happy so that we must fix that problem.**

Day 2

On the following day I present the student-drawn illustration of the OWI. The moment of unveiling has a wonderful tension as we all marvel at the work of the student artists and, of course, I take the opportunity to fully review every characteristic of the OWI before explaining the problem that the character will face in the story.

Here is a pro-tip: as you present, take the time to actually write some of the description in whatever white space is left. You will be hanging these posters on the walls of your classroom and the **written language on the poster creates a text rich classroom**. For that reason, write big with a thick black sharpie so that whatever is written can be seen from far away. An OWI with text that is hard to read from far away is not useful, so don't try to copy the entire Write & Discuss onto the poster. Just add key points in full sentences (i.e. no single words either).

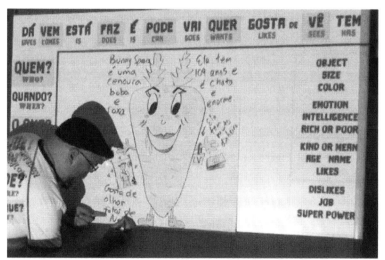

Presenting the illustration and adding captions in Portuguese

If there were no compelling problems suggested, we might not even create a story the next day. In that case I hang the picture on the wall and that character may, or may not, become the star of a future story. I may print out the text of the character description and hang it as a poster next to him so that the easy reading that we created together in the Write & Discuss can be referred to and read again in later classes.

If we do create a story, then the story created the next day is very short. There are four parts to each story and I ask a student to play the role of time keeper so that we spend no more than five minutes on each part. Occasionally I might add an extra minute to a part, but usually each story is finished in twenty minutes. The key is to express everything in comprehensible language. I use high frequency verb posters to be able to point and pause; once your students have mastered the 16 or so highest frequency verbs in the language, you will find that it is easy to express many concepts.

The first of four parts of the story simply establishes the scene by answering the following questions: Who is this story about? Where is he? Who is he with? These questions may well have been answered as we created the OWI; if not we quickly establish an answer. The last question may be useful if the OWI needs help solving his problem. Sometimes that extra character plays a role in the story, sometimes not. Often times this first part does not take the full five minutes because we have already established much of the information while creating the OWI. Be sure to ask many comprehension questions to be sure that your students are understanding you in the target language.

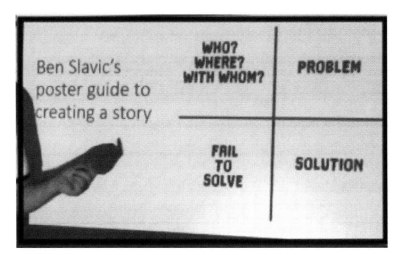

The second part simply answers the question, What is the problem? I express this in the target language. Often times there are things to explain. I make sure that students can process all of the language.

The third part is called "fail to solve"; the OWI tries to solve his problem but fails. You have to work efficiently with students because you need to be able to express this in a complex sentence indicating both what he does and why it does not work. As we do this I am working in the target language. One student might suggest (in either Spanish or English, or often a mixture) that the OWI goes to Walmart to buy new shoes, so I turn to the class and ask (in the target language), "does he go to Walmart? Does he find shoes there? Are the shoes new? Does he find shoes that he likes?". Each step along the way I am writing on the board, speaking in Spanish but writing both languages so that students are following what I am saying. When they do not understand I point at the English, but I am trying to use easy, comprehensible language. Rather than teach new vocabulary, ideally I am getting them to process common words over and over in novel situations so that they eventually process the language at the speed of a native speaker.

The final part is called "solution", where the OWI character finally finds a solution to the problem. Once the entire 20 minute cycle is finished I write the entire story on the board in the form of another Write & Discuss activity (see page 61). A completed story is typically anywhere from five to ten sentences long. Students then copy these texts into their notebooks.

Dive Deep Into Your One Word Images: techniques for advanced classes

I suspect that many of us do not truly squeeze the juice out of our OWIs because we are too intent on the beginning, the concrete descriptions. The OWI process is a great way to prime the pump of creativity, but after a few weeks even low-level classes become frustrated with the first part of the process. **Once students have acquired the language for the concrete descriptions**, spending too much time on them becomes a drag on engagement. This section suggests a few ways to expand the activity so that it remains captivating. Your intermediate / advanced students will also get a lot out of OWIs with these variations.

Ben Slavic once told me that his best images were not class-created images, but what he called "invisibles". **These are the images that students made on their own time**. He would explore them in a whole class conversation through a picture talk.

Following Ben's lead, **once or twice a year I give my students 20 minutes and a blank piece of paper to create their own characters**. At the end of the day I have a thick stack of 200 student-created illustrations that we can explore. It takes months to explore the entire pile. We have one crucial understanding: once I put an image under a doc cam, the image and the story we create no longer belongs to the imagination of any one student. It belongs to all of us.

Try starting class with one of their fantastical creatures projected against the board. Describe it; the process will take much less time than when asking the whole class for each description. **Resist the urge to describe more than one image per class period** because taking the time to imagine the story behind the image is where it gets good.

Normally making an OWI is a two day process; we create the image on the first day and I present the image and ask a story on the second day. However, once your students have already acquired the basic vocabulary frequently used in OWIs, you will probably be able to describe a new image in less than ten minutes with just a few new words to tackle. If you move quickly you'll be able to present the character and then imagine a story all within one 25 minute session. At this point, once they have mastered the concrete descriptions, try one of the following variations for a deeper OWI experience.

Troublesome character traits

The fourth question we typically ask is whether the character is happy or sad. If the character is sad, during the problem creation part of the process we simply ask why, and the story emerges easily. If the character is happy, we ask why and then take that happiness away, which sets up our character to go on a quest to regain their lost source of happiness.

In this variation we change the fourth question. Instead of happy or sad, we use one of the pairs below. **Just one pair per session; don't use all of your teaching ammunition on one day!** For example, is the character brave or cowardly? At the end of the character description, when we are establishing a problem, **we then ask how being brave or cowardly gets the character into trouble.**

Choose one pair of traits and **give your students space to explore their creativity**. How can being brave get our character into trouble? Whenever students are asked to be creative, let them start in English and perhaps **brainstorm for 60 seconds in pairs**. This will lead to richer language as long as you **reel them in before it becomes too complicated**. Here is the list of adjectives that I use in this variation:

Brave – Cowardly	Motivated – Passive, lethargic
Resilient – Fragile, low self-esteem	Leader – Follower
Enthusiastic – Downer	Amusing – Gloomy
Creative – Dull	Curious – Uninterested
Persistent – Gives up quickly	Empathetic – Indifferent, uncaring
Humble – Self-aggrandizing	Reliable – Irresponsible
Spontaneous – Cautious	Trustworthy – Untrustworthy
Hard-working – Lazy	

Incidentally, this list was inspired by a list of characteristics not typically assessed on school exams but are perhaps more important for our students to develop.

What are we really talking about?

This variation requires that the teacher be really perceptive in the moment to tease out a deeper theme emerging from the character description. This can be difficult, but is well worth it because **it leads students to start analyzing their own characters for deeper themes**.

I normally do not plan this variation ahead of time but instead start a normal OWI and then interrupt the process once I begin to perceive a deeper theme. For example, we might be creating a character who is enormous and a student suggests something that cues me to realize that our character is not just physically imposing, but obese. **Students will often use the OWI process to suggest themes that they think are taboo**, and in fact if there is a small group giggling while the rest of the class appears uncomfortable then you are right to suspect that the students' intentions are less than noble. **Don't fear the adolescents who seek to hijack the conversation**; teens explore social boundaries. But that is a blessing because they desperately need you to redirect the conversation and show them the higher ground. Their inappropriate innuendos reveal exactly what we need to address in class.

Watch a video demonstration

An online class from Spring 2020:

https://vimeo.com/416577338/d77266f9b8

Skip ahead to 26:00 in order to see the "What are we really talking about" adaptation.

Note that in this video I am both explaining the technique as well as teaching. In a normal class I would still code-switch to explore ideas, but I would not explain the process to my students. By the time we get to the W&D there is rarely need to code switch because we have made sure that everything is comprehended.

Glance around to be sure that none of your students are being mocked. This may be a moment to launch into the "Cool Generation" routine described on page 237. In fact, I would do this even if no one was explicitly being mocked. Body image is a very sensitive issue.

Now ask, "so what is this really about?" And then reframe the 'problem' that the character faces without running from the controversial theme.

"Is this about a character who is bullied because the school cannot maintain a safe, respectful environment? Because I want to be clear: no one who is bullied deserves to be bullied. No one."

You not only defuse the bomb, but **you help your students reframe problems that they face in real life**. The story that emerges then becomes a metaphor for how to problem-solve real life problems. Even if there is an element of ridiculous fantasy, solving the problem becomes cathartic.

Sometimes a small group of students will persist in trying to create a negative vibe. Take control of the narrative and tell them, in English, that **we are creating a world that we want to live in. We are solving problems to make the world a better place.** Don't make the mistake of uncomfortably laughing along in order to "have a good class".

The rest of the class is listening to you, and observing not only where you draw the line but also what you do to protect them.

"What are we really talking about?" is a powerful way to address issues faced by our students such as sibling rivalry, race and gender identity, loneliness, self-esteem and body image issues, harmful group dynamics, depression, alcohol/smoking/drug use, defiant behaviors, peer pressure and unhealthy competition. Once you have articulated the problem in English, go back to working in the target language.

Students tend to embrace these characters as masks that they wear at a masquerade ball. Let them try out several solutions; this is compelling!

A Problem Inspired by AP themes

This variation does not require the teacher to be as "in the moment", but can still lead students to grapple with real world problems within a safe classroom environment.

Complete the OWI process to create the character and, just before establishing the problem faced by the character, project a copy of the AP themes for all to see. In my own classes I have projected the entire AP themes graphic and let students choose any of them, but in workshops I found more success by **focusing on only one specific theme at a time**. Students form small groups and brainstorm in English for 3 minutes, using the graphic as inspiration for their brainstorming. Then we come back together as a large group and choose one idea to pursue in the target language.

Initial brainstorming in English is fundamental to getting great ideas, but limiting it to 3 minutes prevents the ideas from getting out of hand and allows an easy transition back to the target language.

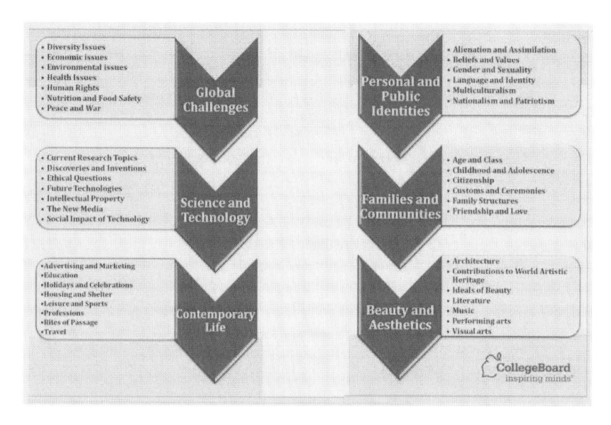

While the themes generated through this variation do not tend to be as personal as the "what are we really talking about" variation, they can still be compelling. I find that Freshman and Sophomores tend to react best to "What are we really talking about" because, developmentally, they are very much immersed in their own world. **My Juniors and Seniors, however, desperately want to have candid conversations about the real world in ways that are thought-provoking.** They want to be taken seriously, and the AP themes approach works well with that age group.

Don't be disheartened if you try this and your students do not suggest great ideas immediately. You are asking them to open their hearts in a way that is rarely done in school. **You are asking them to trust you. Earning that trust is worth the effort.** These variations may not work the first time through, but they are certainly worth trying a dozen times until your students get good at playing this game.

Once that happens, you'll be having satisfying conversations frequently with your students, in the target language. Does it get any better than that?

Matava Scripts

Matava scripts are story skeletons that make it very easy for teachers to learn to "story-ask".

I was once a younger teacher nervous about being the center of attention in the classroom. While having a seemingly relaxed conversation, any teacher is simultaneously attending to dozens of subtle classroom management decisions that looks easy when an experienced educator is running the class. I learned to become comfortable with having true conversations with my students by relying on the scaffolding of Matava scripts.

Nowadays I worry that there are so many thoroughly-scripted materials being offered to CI teachers that new CI teachers are essentially **learning to give comprehensible *presentations* to their students rather than honing the skills of story-asking and interpersonal communication**. I also give presentations in class, but being able to guide a real conversation in which neither party truly knows the outcome of the dialogue is a valuable part of any **communicative classroom**.

The original Matava scripts were written by Anne Matava and feature situations that are genuinely compelling. I encourage you to purchase her book of scripts, in **eBook form from Ben Slavic's website** or in paperback from **Teacher's Discovery**. I do not earn anything from this; these scripts are well worth the purchase.

The Matava scripts come written in English and the teacher adapts it to their target language. In my case **I translate and then copy the scripts onto large index cards and actually hold the card in front of the students so that I do not forget what is coming next**. If you translate the script before class, you won't find yourself unexpectedly confused in front of your students.

There are usually three scenes, 2-3 target structures that you want your students to acquire, and a few variables that your students fill in like a mad lib. The variables are bolded and underlined. If no student 'plays the game' with you, then you can always just tell the story written on the card. But it is a lot more engaging when students see their suggestions take life within the story, so I would strongly suggest that you ask leading questions to get students to respond in any language. You, the teacher, recast their responses into the target language.

On the next page is an example of a Matava-style script that I wrote myself to give my students plenty of exposure to three phrases: **wanted to eat**, **went**, and **there was**.

> | | wanted to eat | went | there was |
> | --- | --- | --- | --- |
> | | quería comer | fue | había |
>
> (1) <u>Juan</u> wanted to eat <u>a jar of mayonnaise</u>, but there was no <u>mayonnaise</u> at his house. He went to <u>his friend Pedro's house</u> but, unfortunately for Juan, <u>Pedro</u> had just eaten <u>mayonnaise soup</u>. There was no more <u>mayonnaise</u> at <u>Pedro</u>'s house.
>
> (2) <u>Juan</u> wanted to eat <u>a jar of mayonnaise</u> so he went to <u>his friend Julieta's house</u>. There was a lot of <u>mayonnaise</u> at <u>Julieta's house</u>, but <u>Julieta</u> used all of the <u>mayonnaise</u> to <u>sun-bathe</u>. Sorry, she needed the <u>mayonnaise</u>!
>
> (3) <u>Juan</u> went to <u>the mayonnaise</u> store. Unfortunately the <u>mayonnaise</u> store had gone out of business. All of the customers had **had heart attacks**. Now there was a new store: a <u>Kale</u> store. <u>Juan</u> bought <u>a bunch of kale</u> and cried. He did not want to eat <u>kale</u>.

Any phrase that is bolded and underlined is replaced with student suggestions.

As I start our session, I might announce that we are going to create a fictitious story but we need a real person to be the star of our story. Any volunteers? I do find it **more engaging to have a student sitting on a stool in the front of the classroom that I can gesture to, occasionally talk to and verify information as we make up our story**. However, you need to have already established a class of trust. This is not a first day of school activity because often the characters are doing bizarre things in these stories.

When you do bring someone up to be the main character, make sure to **verify the information** before accepting it as part of the story line. For instance, in this story part of the humor derives from the idea that the character wants to eat something gross. That is what I would be listening for when soliciting student suggestions. Verify to make sure your student volunteer is comfortable with the suggestion you want to accept.

So let's imagine I bring up a student named Susy. I already have the target structures written on the board, so I simply say:

"**Susy**... [walk over and touch the phrase 'quería comer – wanted to eat'] **quería comer algo**, *something*, **ella quería comer algo pero... ¿qué quería comer?**"

"**Susy**...
wanted to eat something
she wanted to eat something but...
what did she want to eat?"

The class looks at me bewildered. "IMAGINACIÓN", I say to them. "VAMOS A IMAGINAR... *let's imagine.*"

"**Ustedes** [wave with flat palm to the whole class] **pueden decir algo en inglés. DOS PALABRAS en inglés** [I hold up two fingers]. **Yo** [press my palm against my chest] **hablo español. Ustedes** [wave with flat palm to the whole class] **hablan español y inglés. Dos palabras.** *How many words in English can you use?*"	**You all can say something in English. TWO WORDS in English I speak Spanish. You all speak Spanish and English. Two words.**

Class responds, "two".

I continue: "**Susy**... [walk over and touch the phrase 'quería comer – wanted to eat'] **quería comer algo**, something, **ella quería comer algo ASQUEROSO** [write the phrase 'asqueroso=disgusting' on the board] **pero... ¿qué quería comer? ¿Ideas?**"	**Susy**... **wanted to eat , she wanted to eat something DISGUSTING** **But what did she want to eat? Ideas?**

At this point someone may suggest something too gross to contemplate. I would say in English, "oh that might be too gross even in fiction. Susy, ¿querías comer XXX? You can say no." Susy shakes her head and immediately we are looking for other ideas. I would then reinforce that this is FICTION, not the real Susy, so that hopefully when we come up with something disgusting she will agree.

However keep in mind that some adolescents will think it is funny to suggest something phallic and even Susy might not be quick enough to recognize that she should reject the eggplant idea, so keep on your toes. Don't let a few wily adolescents ruin the fun, though. This activity is very fun once your students are trained to play the game.

Eventually we get an idea like 'snails' and I'll endorse it saying, "yes, sophisticated people like myself actually eat snails for dinner! Susy, ¿querías comer [write caracoles = snails on board]... ¿querías comer caracoles?"

Susy: Sí (yes)

Then I say to the class:

"**Bueno clase, Susy quería comer caracoles.** [Walk to the target phrase on the board, point & pause and then repeat] **Quería comer caracoles. Quería comer un frasco grande de caracoles**... [write frasco = jar on the board] **pero** [hold up one finger] **había** [Walk to the target phrase on the board, point & pause and then repeat], **había un problema: no había ni un caracol en su casa. Susy quería comer un frasco grande de caracoles pero no había caracoles en casa.**"

"Good class, Susy wanted to eat snails.

She wanted to eat snails. She wanted to eat a large jar of snails
but
there was

there was a
problem: there was not a single snail in her house. Susy wanted to eat a big jar of snails but there were no snails in her house.

We continue building our story in that way, **soliciting student ideas for anything that is underlined until we have developed an original story based on the script**. Occasionally review the story in progress by asking whole class comprehension questions. After each paragraph you might even ask students to summarize what has happened thus far in pairs, in the target language. Don't let that go on too long, just long enough for them to play a little with the language.

Sometimes students develop great ideas and their creativity unites the class in a culture of goodwill. Sometimes students remain passive and the teacher relies on the script more than they might like. But in any case, the students get tons of experience with the target structures and they are developing the creative skills that make activities like One Word Images so captivating.

Ultimately it is through activities like this, **where students learn to interact and contribute in a safe, guided framework, that the creative side of a student-centered classroom blossoms.**

You can write your own scripts using language that you need to teach students—just limit it to three core phrases that are repeated in each of the three segments of the story. However, I do think that Anne Matava's scripts are brilliant. Find her book, "97 TPRS Story Scripts" on the Teacher's Discovery website.

Whole Class Community Creative Writing

I enjoy writing fiction in my own time, and I enjoy leading my students to explore creative writing in class as well. **In order to make this an effective and efficient language acquisition activity we do a form of community story creation.** One Word Images are another form of community story creation; this method creates a finished product that looks more like a traditional short story or novel. Most of the short stories in my book *"Good Stories for Language Learners"* were created through this process of community story creation, as well as my novel *"Superburguesas"*.

Students need many short, easy-to-read stories in order to make the transition from reading class-created texts (like Write & Discuss) to being able to read a full novel. Whether you are writing to fill holes in your current curriculum, to provide more windows & mirrors for your students to see themselves in your classroom library, or simply to add good stories to the language learner experience, creative writing with your students is a great second semester project.

Start with the aim of writing a short story with your classes. **One story that is developed in concert with all of your classes.** This will guide you in the process of community story creation.

Each writing session is less than 20 minutes, or you risk testing the patience of your students. **The first day is dedicated to brainstorming.**

Some teachers may allow their students to decide the genre beforehand (i.e. romantic comedy, horror, action adventure, etc.), while other teachers simply start the process by announcing, "I am writing a horror story for beginning students". That is a great way to establish that it is your story and the conversations in class are about *your* story.

Even when writing a community story, *a teacher providing input* is what students need in order to acquire a language. **Learners do not learn to write by writing; they learn to write through reading and listening**. Don't ask students to brainstorm individually, don't put them into small groups to write and don't assign writing outside of class. You will generate too many loose threads! Instead the teacher leads one group conversation through a series of questions.

So I say, "Estoy escribiendo un cuento de horror" [I am writing a horror story], and then I write the phrase on the board in both Spanish and English so that everyone understands. Pointing at the board I say, "Estoy escribiendo un cuento de horror para estudiantes de español, como ustedes." [...for students of Spanish, like all of you]. "Vamos a imaginar" [Let's imagine]. Then I draw a circle in the middle of the white board and write "un cuento de horror" in the middle. This is our brainstorming graphic organizer. "¿Qué pasa en el cuento de horror? Tienen ideas?" [What happens in the horror story? Do you have ideas?]

And the crucial additional instruction: "Denme DOS PALABRAS" [Give me TWO WORDS].

Limiting each students' contributions to only two words at a time is the difference between one student dominating the conversation and a true community collaboration. As ideas are generated in English or the target language **the teacher adds to the brainstorming web in the target language**. Don't slow down to repeat everything for acquisition—this is just to get a bunch of ideas floating about.

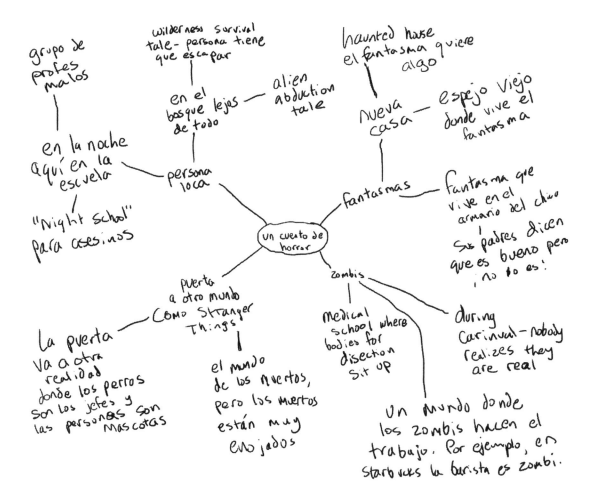

As you brainstorm, use the Artful Questioning technique (see page 56) to add additional stems to the web of ideas. "There is a crazy person? Where?" **Remember that with brainstorming, there are no bad ideas.** Write everything (that is school appropriate, of course) knowing that you are the person who will ultimately decide whether or not to follow an idea. Follow up: when a student says "ghosts", write that on the board and try to develop several different ideas related to ghosts. **Brainstorming is not the time to establish one storyline; it is a process to develop as many ideas as possible.**

The brainstorming session is enough for the first day. Take a photo to keep the ideas and thank your students for their contributions. **Right now they don't even know that they will help you write the story**—you've only told them that you are writing a story and they helped brainstorm ideas. If nothing inspires you, you can drop the story and never return to it! However, after brainstorming with all of your classes, I hope that you have generated at least something intriguing.

One crucial guideline that we developed in my writers group dedicated to teachers who write creatively with their students is that **we write ONE story with the help of all of our classes**. The evolving story does not belong to any one class; instead we work on pieces throughout the day so that no single class will recognize the final product. The teacher has a manageable process that takes the best ideas generated throughout the day.

This activity, like everything we do, is a pretext for class conversation in the target language.

Once we have finished our day of brainstorming I will look at all of the ideas and develop a story idea that can be expressed in one sentence. The classic way to do this is to **write a one sentence story premise that includes the character, their goal and the problem they have to overcome**. I write this outside of class. I often find that beginning writers—whether they be teachers or students—don't appreciate how important it is to include both the goal and the problem faced by a protagonist. You want a character's goal to be closely tied to solving the problem.

In the brainstorming graphic from the last page, I think that the idea of a Starbucks that relies on zombie workers is something I might pursue. **But that is just a setting. Who is our protagonist and why are these zombie workers a problem?** This is the hard work of creative writing that I enjoy doing outside of the classroom. When my classes return to this project I already have a story premise created, but very little else. We are still in the brainstorming phase, but now we have a story premise to guide the conversation.

Maybe a week after our first brainstorming session, students enter the classroom and I'll have my story premise written on the board in both English and the target language. "Hay un mago joven que quiere salir con una chica, pero descubre que ella ahora es zombi que trabaja en Starbucks [There is a young wizard who wants to go out with a girl, but he discovers that she is now a zombie that works at Starbucks]". **I can brainstorm various pieces of the story premise with different classes.** Who is this young wizard? Who is the girl and why does he want to go out with her? Is there a path back to being a normal girl once you've been turned into a zombie? Is it taboo for a wizard to date a zombie? Why must he date this specific girl?

In the brainstorming sessions my classes might provide an alternate to the hetero-normative love story that I first imagined. Or they might think that Starbucks is lame, but In-N-Out Burger is funny. They might develop a backstory that is completely unexpected. Actually, I hope they do. But remember, their suggestions are always just suggestions. Ultimately it is your story.

After the second day of brainstorming **I take the information generated and write a longer story premise paragraph.** Again, this is done outside of class. I am taking ideas I like and rejecting the ones that don't work for my story. Don't create a Frankenstein of a story, stitching together all of the ideas with the hope of pleasing all of your students. That's crazy.

Once the story premise paragraph is complete I will write five to ten sentences that describes each scene we need in order to tell this story. For example, in my story let's imagine that at the end of the second day of brainstorming we have established that the young wizard is not a young wizard after all but rather a teen who discovers that his best friend has been turned into a zombie by his parents. The teen zombie does chores all day. **I didn't see that coming either—and that is the power of brainstorming all day with all of your classes.** We also brainstormed the goal of the protagonist. It isn't a romance, but rather the two best friends compete on Saturdays in mountain biking races. Competing alone just isn't as fun, so the protagonist is eager to break the spell that the parents have cast so that his friend can join him on Saturdays again.

When I write those 5-10 sentences, they are called "scene goal statements". **What must happen in this scene to move the story forward?** Each scene goal statement is a new brainstorming session with a class. I don't need to tell students the whole story. I'll just tell them what they need to know to complete the scene goal: "okay, so I have this kid whose friend is under a zombie spell. How does he break the spell?", and off we go imagining how to write this scene. We write one or two paragraphs for each scene goal using the Write & Discuss process to make sure that it remains comprehensible. Students will want to push forward quickly to create a complex plot—resist them as you write slowly and make sure that the writing remains understandable for all. **The key to making this good language acquisition material is to constantly be writing on the board. Allow students only two words at a time so that students piggy-back off of each others' ideas. No single student should control the conversation. The teacher helps them express it all comprehensibly in the target language.**

Work with one scene per day; let period 1 develop it, let period 2 hear their ideas and tear them apart, start fresh with period 3 and perhaps build on all of that with period 4. Create a Write & Discuss text after every period to record the ideas that you may or may not incorporate into your story. **By the end of the day you might have a single rough draft paragraph that you can place within your plot outline**. As a product of Write & Discuss, that paragraph will be co-written between students and teacher so it will already be simplified.

Your students will be crucial as you orally retell parts of the story. Take note of how to simplify the language for your audience. You never have to explain the entire context of the scene; simply say, "I am writing a story and there is a scene where a zombie finds the protagonist. So... (in target language), *'there is a zombie. Where? Let's use our imaginations...'*"

As ideas evolve you will be changing your plot outline by adding scenes, building and eliminating characters, adapting ideas as a strong theme emerges and modifying plot so that the story flows well. This is done outside of class without students.

The teacher's role outside of class is significant. After accepting some general ideas of what the story is about, take the time to write the plot outline with a scene goal statement for each scene. **Speak about particular scenes with classes, but never the entire story until the whole story is complete.** The plot outline describes what needs to happen in each scene; the discussion in classes shapes how that happens. One class may have a brilliant idea about how the protagonist gets from A to B, but another class tweaks that idea and a third class has a different idea that I decide to incorporate so that the final chapter is unrecognizable to any of the students.

Sometimes the students take on a big role in imagining plot; sometimes the teacher merely presents a range of choices that students tinker with, but students do not create the plot of the novel. The teacher is the author who determines which choices to accept. **Remember that it is the teacher providing input that leads to acquisition, so make sure that your voice as you incorporate student ideas into the paragraphs is front and center.**

In my writing group we found that teachers who announced to the class that 'we are writing a story together' faced insurmountable problems that led them to abandon the project. Instead, **maintain ownership of your story and entertain students' ideas about *your* story**. For students, this process is more like painting a piece of pottery at a pottery studio than actually creating their own pottery.

Once you've completed the story (it may take a month or more) it is rewarding to share the finished story with all of your classes. Often students will recognize bits and pieces that they helped develop, but the story should feel new to them since no class witnessed the creation of the whole story. Better yet, **if you truly did create the story through the Write & Discuss process, the text should be fairly comprehensible** with only a bit of footnotes provided. If you have a text that is still too complex, you'll need to wordsmith focusing on the low-frequency words before sharing with students.

Truthfully, **you now probably have a first draft**. It's fine to share a first draft with students, but before you consider publishing the story you'll want to go through a process of rewrites. Examine the themes and how to make the big ideas emerge. **Even silly class stories often have big themes hidden within.** In our zombie story, I might work to bring out the theme of adolescent autonomy. If I look closely I might find that our zombie story may truly be a coming-of-age tale! Listen to your students as they react to the first draft and consider altering the plot and the characters. Allow them to show you where they get bored with the text so that you can cut portions that don't work, and build upon parts that bring delight.

If there is one piece of writing advice that I constantly give, it is "**start with the action**". Many teacher-authors plan a novel with the first five chapters consisting of background description, when they really need to start with chapter 5. A student reader judges a book by the first paragraph, so **make sure that a compelling character, their goal and the problem they must overcome is introduced in that first paragraph**. For a short story I urge you to communicate that information in the first sentence.

Ultimately before publishing you'll want to consult with several layers of professionals: native speaker reviewers, proofreaders, cultural sensitivity reviewers, illustrators. But don't let the process rob you of the delight of writing, and reading, with your students. If you have publication as a long term goal, I recommend that you consult the website created by Anny Ewing and Kirsten Plante:

https://www.whats-your-next-step.org/

– 'Voices of Others' Activities –

This is the second module that presents the main activities done each day in our classes.

The activities in the 'Voices of Others' module seek to expand the students' worldview and present the target language culture.

Picture Talk

On page 148 I described Picture Talk with student photos and student drawings to generate student-centered conversations. We also can use the same skills to describe the world outside of students' life experiences. There are two types of images that I like to use for this activity; either an illustration taken from a story (like the ones here) or a photo from the target language culture. In either case, the *Picture Talk* will not always develop into a story... and that is okay.

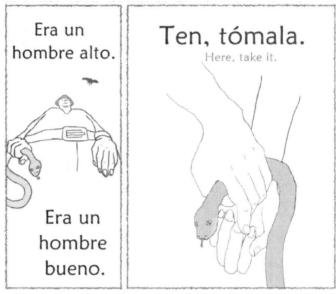

A scene from *Un mundo raro 2: Comic Strips for Spanish Students*

- **Start by describing the image** using your skills to remain comprehensible.

- Point and pause, write on the board, and use all of the interrogative words as you ask artful questions. Verify comprehension. **Look at your Sweet 16 verbs and ask a question without an obvious answer**. Sometimes I accompany this question by pointing at my head and saying, "¡imaginación!" (Imagination!)

- **Continue asking questions with different Sweet 16 verbs**, matching them with various interrogative words as well (see page 56).

- **Students may respond with a word or two in English**. Simply translate them on the board, and repeat in L2 so that students hear the new words used several times.

- This activity is an excellent way for the teacher to develop their own story-asking skills. **Sometimes this**

Scene from *Superhamburguesas*

activity develops a full story, more often we develop a snapshot of a moment within a story. I think that is fine. We do not want students to feel like creating a story is a heavy, troublesome process. Enjoy the moment. As the energy begins to fizzle, wrap it up.

- **Always end with a Write & Discuss** so that students can see the full story (or simply the scene) created through the questioning process.

Note: using an image from a book in the classroom library can be an effective browsing activity. Even if the story you create does not relate to the actual book, be sure to hold up the book that the illustration came from.

While any picture will do, **I prefer pictures that come from stories**. These often naturally lead students to imagine a bigger scene than that depicted in the picture. I call them "pictures loaded with story-telling potential". For example, the pictures included here all come from my books. Also **choose photos from the target language culture and build small, observational sketches together as you imagine what life is like for the people in the photos**. I try not to be heavy-handed with photos from target-language cultures. Instead this is a moment of discovery when many of my students are first exposed to the diversity of human cultures. These are great moments to quietly let students process the myriad conditions of humanity and gently nudge them to grow.

When looking for photos, **I actually favor gentle photos over startling pictures**. A startling photo may appear at first to be loaded with story-telling potential. For example, I used to use a photo of a "vomiting pumpkin" each Autumn. The pumpkin was carved to look like a head vomiting out his own pumpkin seeds. It always generated a strong student response, but found that beyond the initial shock and amusement, I could never get much out of the students afterwards. There simply was not much to say about the photo.

Shocking images do not always lead to good conversation.

On the other hand, a photo of Amazonian children on a canoe in the early morning on their way to school seems pretty bland but leads to many interesting stories when we slowing go through the process of artful questioning.

Do not feel compelled to tell the story that the picture came from. I like to use pictures from novels in my classroom library, but I do not even try to contextualize the picture within the real story. Same with fables; the conversation may lead towards the story, but **listen closely to students' responses** to your questions and follow their ideas first.

If an answer seems obvious, try the opposite. When I ask workshops if the mother holding the child's hand knows that he is stealing a toy, most crowds respond "no". It is always interesting to turn the tables and say, "yes she does!" Or "is that a mother? Maybe she's a teacher…"

If unplanned conversation seems scary to you, Picture Talk is the perfect activity to start your journey into this conversational approach. **The picture scaffolds the discussion so that you never feel lost.** It is also an activity that packs a powerful punch. I think of Picture Talk as the foundation of so many other powerful techniques such as Card Talk, One Word Images, Movie Talks and Cultural Presentations.

While you do a Picture Talk in class, focus on the techniques to remain comprehensible to your students. **Pause** whenever you say a word that has not been fully acquired by your students, casually stroll over to the poster or white board where you **wrote the word**, lift your arm up and physically **touch the word**. Repeat it. Some students will roll their eyes. Some students will react with impatience as if this were the worst thing they have experienced today. Keep doing it.

You are teaching for the slowest processor, the student who is just putting the language together and who will not speak up. Learn to **ask artful questions** and **require choral responses**. Even the fast students are benefiting from your deliberate pace because they are learning to process the language at the pace of a native speaker.

Watch a video of me Picture Talking using an illustration from a story:

https://vimeo.com/731939441/6bfcc40426

While all of the examples provided here come from illustrations from stories, a large part of the photos that I like to Picture Talk in my classes come from photographers that have posted photographs of target language cultures.

Movie Talk

Movie Talk is a technique that I recommend for beginners, both students and teachers who are new to a conversational classroom. **It is fairly easy to keep students engaged** while the teacher is perfecting their basic skills to remain comprehensible. If this sounds like you, feel good about doing lots of Movie Talks!

Movie Talk was **originally designed as a technique for true beginners who did not share a common language**, and it is a very powerful way to develop listening comprehension. I also appreciate that Movie Talk leads teachers to speak naturally, describing the plot of the video while leaning on high-frequency verbs such as the Sweet 16 in order to remain comprehensible. If you plan on using a TV series or movie as an ongoing anchor text, I recommend that you first spend several weeks practicing with short videos in a Movie Talk format. As you improve your own skills you also **train your students what to expect when watching videos in language class.** It is okay to burn a few sessions as students are learning to follow your explanations and not whine that "they just want to watch the video", but if you try to teach a tv series before students have learned to prioritize the teacher talk then they may easily lose the thread of the plot while focusing on the visuals. **The teacher leads students to process the target language with the aid of the visuals.**

There are three parts to this essay introducing Movie Talk.
1. First I present **a no-prep, 55 minute lesson** based on a 45 second wordless video.
2. Second, I present **a Movie Talk lesson with a prepared reading**.
3. Third, I provide a list of about 50 videos that I approve for Movie Talks. You can explore this technique without having to spend hours scouring YouTube for videos.

I like both ways of doing Movie Talk, with prepared readings or without**. Prepared readings help the teacher retain a tighter control over the class and gives the illusion of rigor** for students who need a worksheet to value the work done in class. If you have trouble with classroom management *(every teacher will face difficult classes at some point in their career)*, a prepared reading to go along with the Movie Talk is an excellent solution. My prepared lessons are in Spanish, but for other languages **you can do any movie talk in any language and then save the Write & Discuss generated in class for the following year**.

I do these lessons as described in any level class, assuming that the complexity of language will differ according to the students that are in the class. I can bring up AP themes as they occur to me in a level 1 class, as long as I can keep it comprehensible, but I am more likely to stick to concrete description. Likewise, in my AP class I will lead students to delve deeper and make observations that move beyond surface level comments, but we will also include concrete descriptions.

LESSON 1: NO-PREP MOVIE TALK LESSON TEMPLATE

The basic skills used in a Picture Talk will prepare you to do Movie Talk. I recommend that you start the school year with Picture Talks using student photos from their childhood (see the "Student Voices" module), your own photos (no beach photos!), and some photos that elicit a story such as the illustration of the child thief that I discuss in the Picture Talk essay from this module.

The following lesson template can be used in its entirety to fill a 55 minute class, or you can cut corners and squeeze this into one of the 15-20 minute blocks that I use to plan my lessons. I tape **this small lesson template** to the wall at the front of the room so that you can remember the sequence without having to consult notes in the middle of class.

> **Copy and tape near front board**
>
> Movie talk lesson template
>
> 1. Picture Talk a frame of the video
> 2. Talk through video
> 3. Paired retells while viewing
> 4. Personalized questions
> 5. Students write questions
>   Choose other students to answer
> 6. Whole Class Write & Discuss
> 7. Fluency Write (optional) or an exit quiz

(1) Picture Talk one frame of video

First I show them just one frame of the video, as if we were going to do a Picture Talk. Looking at the frame to the left, I ask them ¿Qué ven ustedes en la foto? (What do you all see in the photo?) and we spend a few minutes commenting on everything we can think of, including asking if the man is happy or sad and guessing what might be in the photo. My all-time favorite student response was: *es una foto de una hamburguesa y el hombre está muy triste porque comió la hamburguesa.* [it is a photo of a hamburger and the man is sad because he ate the hamburger].

(2) Talk Through Video

Then we watch the video, pausing every few seconds while the teacher talks about what the students see. This example lesson uses a wordless video called "Rain". You can find a link to the entire video in the Movie Talk database provided at the end of this essay on page 197.

The first time through I stop it as often as possible, simply describing what we see. I stand in front of the classroom at the screen and tap on the screen whenever I want my student, sitting at my computer, to press pause or play. **Simply standing up front is very important to keep my students focused and engaged**; when I am in back behind my computer they tend to be less engaged.

I rarely write anything on the board the first time through (unless a student explicitly asks); I want them to hear the language first. **While teaching I am looking at the list of sweet sixteen verbs posted on the wall**, so it is easy for me to improvise, drawing from previous learned verbs. When the man in the video puts the photo on his nightstand, of course I say *Pone la foto sobre la mesita de noche* [he puts the photo on the night table] and then I ask artful questions around that phrase. I can also say ¿**Oye** un ruido? [Does he **hear** a noise?] ¿**Quiere** otra foto? [Does he **want** another photo?] ¿**Sabe** que **hay** algo debajo de su cama? [Does he **know** that **there is** something underneath the bed?] because **all of these verbs are part of the Sweet 16**. In all we spend about five minutes with me mostly narrating and asking pointed questions to verify student comprehension.

(3) Paired retells

Do you have students whose language is bubbling over, demanding the opportunity to talk in class? Or do they *all* remain silent? **If some enjoy speaking then we have the luxury to watch the video again, this time in pairs**. I stop it at three places and ask them to describe, in pairs, everything they can for about 30 seconds. **I spend much less time on**

this step than on the first step. You can skip this step, but I actually like to give students the opportunity to observe that, even though they can understand me fine, they need a little more input before they are ready to speak. Make sure it is a low-stress environment among peers; don't correct anything you hear and quickly move on. **Preserve the feeling of enchantment and laughter characteristic of the early stages of learning a language**, but if there is no enchantment just move on.

(4) Personalization

This is the most enjoyable part of the lesson. Even though this is a "Voice of Others" activity I still like to pull in students own lives as we discuss a part of the Movie Talk. For each movie talk I have a prepared question related to something on screen that I ask.

For this particular movie talk, I stop at the beginning scene of the man gazing at a photo on his night table and I ask a student: *¿Tienes una foto en la mesita de noche al lado de tu cama? [Do you have a photo on the night table next to your bed?] ¿Es una foto de la clase de español? [Is it a photo of Spanish class?] ¿Es una foto de tu perro? [Is it a photo of your dog?]* We build a word image for several students, comparing their bedrooms and using the vocabulary from the video. *¿Hay una ventana en tu dormitorio? [Is there a window in your bedroom?] ¿Te gusta abrir la ventana cuando llueve? [Do you like to open the window when it rains?]* When we find something interesting we could follow it, asking artful questions until interest gradually dissipates, but normally I cut this off after about 15 minutes. If you are working this movie talk into a 20 minute block in your lesson plan, I would spend just a few minutes on the personalization part.

(5) Questions

I ask students to write nine questions about the video using different question words. After about five minutes I start to ask for student volunteers: they read their questions aloud and I write them on the board, corrected. Although they hear many questions everyday in my class, once they try to write their own questions they tend to make mistakes with word order. It is interesting to watch the recognition on their faces as I rewrite their questions and they recognize proper word order. It is common to hear kids mutter, "oh yeah, that sounds better", which is appropriate for their level of acquisition.

Once we have nine questions on the board I ask those same questions to nine other students who did not volunteer a question, allowing us to reread the questions again. **Here is a secret to training students to eagerly participate when an outside observer comes in**: students learn to always volunteer the questions if you make it clear that those who do not ask are required to answer. Altogether we spend around 12 minutes on this section.

(6) Whole class retell

I write on the board: *Hay un hombre que...* (there is a man that...) and then students add suggestions. It goes without saying that this and all other activities are conducted entirely in Spanish, with the exception of when I write words in Spanish with their English definitions on the board. With the class retell we are trying to fill all three whiteboards (my handwriting is fairly large) with long, complex sentences. *Hay un hombre que / mira la foto / de su perro / y el hombre está triste / porque su perro está de vacaciones en México.* What I like about this activity is that students add what they can but learn how easy it is to construct a more complex sentence. After 8-10 minutes we have a student-generated (but teacher corrected) summary on the board.

Make the text a bit more complex by going back and adding transition words (have a list already posted), or add entire new phrases so that the original text slowly gets larger and more descriptive. Essentially you are creating more and more complex embedded readings. Save them for next year as readings to accompany the Movie Talk!

Yes, this is a Write & Discuss. With Movie Talk I always do the W&D immediately to help train students to recognize that simply watching the video and tuning out the teacher's voice is not enough. They must be able to read a text related to the video. When you later watch a film or a tv series with an ongoing plotline, it is important that students save the texts generated to be able to review and understand complex plots.

(6) Fluency Write or Exit Quiz

We just barely have enough time for a quick write, although we can just as easily extend the personalization part of the lesson. As a prompt I write on the board: *Yo tengo una foto en la mesita de noche al lado de mi cama...* ["I have a photo on the night table beside my bed..."]

In my classes the responses have varied from goofy stories about a girl who has a family of cows, to a touching story about the photo of one of my student's recently deceased grandmother. Reading these quick writes sometimes helps me build a relationship with my students, and students feel great about their language abilities because they can see the great progress they made in one class period. Scheduling a fluency write immediately after a long Movie Talk is great if your students have not done too many fluency writes and they feel somewhat intimidated by all that writing. The massive amount of listening and reading beforehand will boost their confidence.

LESSON 2: MOVIE TALK WITH A PREPARED READING

I use prepared readings along with a movie talk whenever (1) I want to expose students to specific themes or vocabulary and (2) **whenever classes are quieter, less cooperative or simply harder to manage**.

'Less creative classes' are not bad. There are good reasons that students may choose to hold back, including class culture and the unique mix of personalities that make up any class. Some teachers react by trying to find crazy activities that they hope will create a lively class community, as if that were the key ingredient to getting kids communicating in the target language. I call that "*the birthday party*" approach to lesson planning. **If you have a birthday party every day, kids will get bored with the same old birthday activities and the teacher engages in a constant search for new, more exciting ways** to capture the attention of adolescents.

I suspect that the true problem is often not the class community but rather that your students are in a natural phase of language acquisition where students feel shy, awkward and unsure about speaking the target language. These feelings are augmented by emotions of isolation, awkwardness and insecurity that all adolescents naturally feel, just going through adolescence. The "*birthday party approach*" addresses students' feelings by providing a warm community of laughter... not a bad thing!

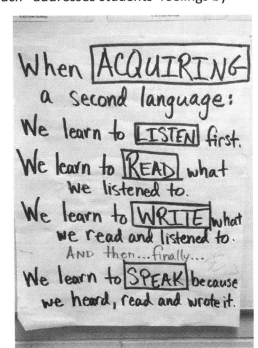

However, **if the root cause of a lackluster student response in class is that students do not feel confident speaking the language, the only thing that will get them out of this phase into a place with more confidence is through more language acquisition.** I reproduce Grant Boulanger's great poster (right) to remind us of the natural path we can expect our students to follow. They need A LOT of targeted listening & reading before graduating to a little writing & speaking.

Unfortunately many "birthday party" activities are not the strongest, most efficient sources of language. If you react to students pulling back by watering down your class activities with group games (which provide weaker exposure to the target language), you only prolong the non-communicative phase in which students feel awkward.

For that reason, I make movie talks paired with readings a significant part of my curriculum around late October through to the end of first semester of level 1 (or other levels, if needed).

My key insight here is that adolescent moodiness is not always an indication that you need to do something fun in class. Don't let students complain and bully you into being silent as you watch the video or watching videos longer than 2-3 minutes. *This is a language acquisition activity; they can watch YouTube on their own time.*

When I have a prepared reading (which I write before class) I will:
  (1) watch the video like normal, with **me narrating and asking choral response questions.** Upon finishing I
  (2) pass out the reading but **ask that all pencils & pens remain under their chairs**. The first time through the entire text
  (3) I read slowly but without answering questions. Then
  (4) students can take out their pencils and ask questions, one paragraph at a time. They can take notes on specific words, **but are not allowed to translate yet**. Once we have gone through the entire text students then they
  (5) translate everything in silence, no group work and **no more questions for the time being**. The paragraphs are written to be just slightly above their reading level so students generally can race through these translations in 10 minutes. **At the end of the quiet translation period I allow**
  (6) **more questions so that everyone has a full, correct translation**. I collect these for a grade, quickly scanning to make sure that the translations written above the Spanish match. Everybody should get a 100%.

This is the quietest Movie Talk that you'll ever do!

Although translation feels like an old school activity, it is surprisingly effective. This feels like rigorous work for students who need that to respect our class, but since the translation only lasts about 10-15 minutes with texts that are nearly transparent to the reader (with help), it is a good experience that ends with all students feeling success. **I think that these texts are good whole class readings that teach students the stamina & reading skills they need in order to be successful with their own independent reading.**

Therefore I would argue that movie talks with prepared readings are an essential piece of a second language classroom. Your independent reading program will not blossom as quickly if you chose to leave them out of your routine.

By the way, **the easiest way to develop a set of readings to accompany your Movie Talk videos is to simply save the Write & Discuss texts made in class**. One year I had a strong period 3 class, followed by a weak period 5. I routinely took a photo of the period 3 Write & Discuss text of the Movie Talk and then inserted it as a quick reading for period 5. After viewing the video in period 5 we would read, and then write our own period 5 W&D. The extra reading made the period 5 class 'the strong class' by the end of the year!

Sometimes when I have a few extra minutes in class we will play a game in pairs that gets students listening closely & actively. **Students pair up and** place something between them (a cup, a notebook, a bag). The teacher says one true or false statement about the movie talk. If the statement is true, the first student to grab the item wins a point. If a student grabs during a false statement, they have lost a point. Try to say at least two false statements for every true statement to give them plenty of listening opportunities. When you review the Movie Talk, it is now perfectly natural to use past tenses.

List of Movie Talk Videos

tinyurl.com/fesxjbk9

Don't worry about the language of the video. Students are not acquiring the target language from the video; they acquire it from the teacher. I regularly show videos in Japanese, French and other languages to my Spanish students.

Cultural Presentations

The origin of my approach to cultural presentations comes from an evening flight between New York and Los Angeles when I was stuck in the middle row, unable to wedge my computer between my seat and the seat back and unable to move my arms to write without constantly bumping my elbows into the space of the people sitting on each side. I was stuck watching the tv screen of the passenger in the row ahead of me. Although I could not hear the audio, I easily followed the plot of the film he was watching. That night I recognized how easy it is to scaffold a short videoclip so that language learners can be prepared to read a text that would have been otherwise too difficult.

There are four steps that I always follow. The key is to remember that **the language spoken during the video is not meant to be acquired**; instead, in the first two steps, the reader is building a visual memory that will help him or her make inferences while reading in step three. In fact, I suspect that many of our students are poor readers because they do not visualize what they are reading. **This process leads them to visualize before reading the text**.

In order to create a cultural presentation I start by searching for the right video clip. The best are no longer than three minutes… even better if they are shorter. Finding a discrete video clip is probably the hardest part.

During class I start with a Picture Talk. I usually preplan this picture talk, taking a screen shot of the video and supplying a vocabulary word or two that we will use later during the reading and community writing portions. I might take two or three screenshots to present different elements of the video, but I don't attempt to explain the entire video. Instead I am merely introducing the topic.

> **The Four Step Process to a Short Cultural Presentation**
>
> **First**: Picture Talk with a few key words presented *in context*.
>
> **Second**: Play the captioned video and instruct students to watch the visuals, don't worry about what they don't understand.
>
> **Third**: Read the prepared text which is written to be slightly above their reading level. Code switch while reading to clarify, ask questions in the TL, chorally translate.
>
> **Fourth**: Group Write & Discuss to verify comprehension. **Any assessment should be based on the W&D**, not the video or prepared reading from step 3.

During the second part of the presentation I play the video, captioned in the target language. I use a free video editor called Shotcut to include the captions on the video. There is a bit of a learning curve to using this program, but there are other programs that will allow you to add captions to a video. Shotcut is free, and there are tutorials on YouTube. Personally I rarely show videos without captions in class; even advanced students get much more out of the video with captions.

However, keep in mind that the purpose of the first two sections (Picture Talk & View Video) is to build a bank of visuals in your students' minds. They don't have to understand the video. In fact, I tell them not to worry about following the target language but to just focus on the visuals. We'll explain it thoroughly after viewing the clip.

The third step is to read a prepared text about the video. After having watched the video my students can make better inferences and this step often moves along easily. Nonetheless I usually have students do a choral translation to make sure that every word is crystal clear. The fourth step, the Write & Discuss, verifies reading comprehension. If students fail to include a major detail, it is a sign that maybe they were not following the reading as well as you thought.

The second conversation in the Two Conversations Classroom exposes students to 'the other' and seeks to expand their worldviews. For this reason my approach to our cultural presentations centers around authentic videoclips in all levels. The fundamental element of the presentation is that it is made comprehensible, regardless of the complexity of the language used in the video, by the reading that is scaffolded by the Picture Talk and the visuals in the video. The Write & Discuss verifies what students have understood.

Examples of cultural presentations

The *Maravillas* are an example of cultural presentations that bring Latin America into the Spanish classroom. **I want students to *marvel* at the creativity, the ingenuity and compassion of people across the world.** I have also worked with French teacher Cécile Lainé to develop a set of French maravillas, *Les merveilles,* both of which you can find in the online Master Class if you received this book as part of a full workshop. If you purchased this book separately, you still have access to the following two presentations that will show you how to make your own. These presentations focus mostly on the lives of ordinary people who do extraordinary things.

The last quarter of the school year is the perfect time to bring the *Maravillas* into your Spanish class. After a year of crazy class created stories, I like to get serious with some authentic target culture scaffolded so that students of all levels can embrace it. I originally developed the *Maravillas* to introduce inspiring Latin Americans to my students, who had only known the cardboard stereotypes of Latin America portrayed in US media. I have since expanded the project to include places and cultural customs that beguile, intrigue and lead my students to marvel.

The first *maravilla* is about a woman who was sad about the many stray dogs in Costa Rica, so she decided to create a home for them in the mountains. That quickly spiraled out of control!
Each *maravilla* has four parts: (1) a picture talk, (2) a captioned video, (3) an embedded reading, (4) a Write & Discuss activity. I present these to every level I teach, from level one beginners to my level 4 AP students… simply modifying the language and remaining comprehensible to the class in front of me. I write on the board when necessary to clarify, and watch their eyes for signs of confusion.

Download the PowerPoint:
https://wp.me/a32vth-1R1

If you choose to add an assessment, I recommend that you have your students copy the Write & Discuss created in class and base the assessment on that text so that the assessment closely mirrors their actual comprehension.

If you download the presentation but cannot play the video, or the embedded video has been stripped from the presentation, in many cases this can be fixed. First, make sure that your edition of PowerPoint is from 2013 or more recent (prior to 2013 PPT did not embed videos). Second, download to a PC (sometimes Apple products do weird things when translating a product made for PCs to the Apple environment). Third, do not host the presentation on a cloud platform like Google docs, which often strip videos to save space. Instead load it to a removeable hard drive or a zip drive, which is better anyways because the file will still be available if your school internet is down. Finally, try right-clicking on the PowerPoint frame with the embedded video; you might be able to "download media" to your own computer so that, if your computer does not allow you to play the video when embedded in the presentation, you'll still be able to play the video.

The second *Maravilla* presentation is about a group of young people in rural Mexico who create machines out of bicycle parts to make rural living easier and healthier. This is captioned in Spanish, but do not worry if your students do not catch every word. The purpose of the picture talk and captioned video is simply to prepare students for the embedded reading that follows. We know that struggling readers often do not visualize the reading, so the first two activities serve to create images in the minds of students... any language they pick up in these first two activities is bonus! During the last two activities, the embedded reading and the Write & Discuss activity, students process the language while relying on the "pictures in their minds".

I particularly love this cultural presentation because it highlights the ingenuity and compassion of the young people involved. These are key characteristics that I look for when searching for subjects of a cultural presentation: I want to present people that my students will admire. For that reason, I avoid creating presentations solely about problems faced in the target culture. As a Spanish teacher, I am aware that my students already harbor a worldview about Latin America that is full of images of poverty and violence. I want to

Download PowerPoint:
https://wp.me/a32vth-1R2

spend our precious time together expanding their worldview to include why I fell in love with the cultures I study. If poverty comes up in the presentation, it is in the context of a group of people who are doing incredible things despite the poverty or are developing awe-inspiring projects to change their world.

I am also less likely to create a presentation solely about places, customs or abstract cultural concepts that are not connected to precise people. If, for example, I want to create a presentation about regional Mexican dances, I will search far and wide for a video that highlights a particular dancer by name so that I can talk about that person's life. This is how I avoid making overarching, generalized statements about a culture. Rather than stating, "Mexicans value family", I will describe the love readily apparent in these young people's hard work that has made life easier for their grandparents.

Watch the full 15 minute presentation:
https://vimeo.com/426186705/ae8396f619

Oral Storytelling

When I transitioned to a student-centered conversational approach, I temporarily lost a lot of the cultural foundation that had been a hallmark of my classes. In the first half of my career I collected many great short stories that I loved to teach. I had portraits of inspiring Latin Americans lining my walls that I would refer to as *our family*. Latin America was vividly present, even though I wasted far too much time teaching grammar and vocabulary that kids quickly forgot from one day to the next. Oral storytelling in class brought me back to incorporating a lot of target language culture.

At the time my Heritage Learners class was reading the classic short story *Un señor muy viejo con unas alas enormes* by García Márquez. I had been feeling guilty that I had not planned anything lately for the higher ability learners in class (about 30% of the students in a very differentiated class) so I pulled out some challenging but truly rewarding reading. Higher ability kids in the past had really warmed to this tale, so I thought that I would collect all of my best reading activities together and fly through this beautiful story the best I could.

The funny thing is... wow, those first two days felt horrible. I could feel the joy withering in my artless hands as together we started doing the first vocabulary activities. My intention was to micro-develop skills so that the students who couldn't yet read the original text would quickly develop reading skills to be able to read this specific story. Instead we were slowly trudging through a series of humorless vocabulary activities that was killing the joy before they ever met the original story.

At night I had been reading about the story listening technique developed by Beniko Mason, who questions whether "reading activities" are more efficient or more effective at developing language than simply providing more interesting and comprehensible reading and listening. That is when it occurred to me that my reading activities, meant to scaffold the reading of a story, are putting the brakes on enjoying the *soul of the text*. My ah-ha moment: **the oral tradition is strong even in illiterate communities. Why not present an oral version of the text first so that the storyteller can closely tune the telling of the tale to the audience?**

It is worth asking: why was I pushing an incomprehensible text towards my students in the first place?

Because the reading is beautiful, because it occupies a central place in the target language culture, because I want my students to gasp at the mind-blowing creativity of a writer like GGM.

All of these objectives can be reached through an oral retelling of the tale, so I dropped my canned reading activities mid-week and decided to *meet my students where they were* through oral storytelling.

> The more we try to make our classes look like the rest of school, the more disengagement we'll see. Our classes need to be refuges from the monotony of the ever more homogenous classroom. Accepting acquisition is subconscious frees us to make class ever more compelling.
>
> 7:15 AM · Apr 12, 2019 · Twitter Web Client

Once I looked at the story with new eyes... **not to prepare students to read the original text but rather to enjoy the most marvelous moments of the tale**, it changed everything. I realized that I can tell this tale to my non-heritage learners. And I did, in one period. As I was reviewing the video of my teaching I heard for the first time the voice of one of my students who sits next to the camera. He was muttering, midway through the story listening session, "*This is getting serious... I am

Watch the lesson *(in Spanish)* https://vimeo.com/195024952

so invested in this story!"

Although it sounds planted, it was not! There were 37 juniors crammed into that room but, by their silent attention, one could easily make the mistake & believe it was just me and that one kid. The first few minutes of the video are a bit dull as I set up the class, but the story picks up after a few minutes.

I did stray in one important way from the ethos of story listening: I had my students illustrate the story as I told it, and when I was finished I had them go back and write in text to their cartoon versions. I just could not trust that they would listen to me for 36 minutes straight without daydreaming or outright snoozing. Perhaps this lack of faith reflects my own uncertainty in my skills as a storyteller, recognition that school has taught them to play the accountability game, or maybe my belief that the illustrating helps them maintain the thread of a complicated story in their own minds. Maybe a bit of all three.

Try this in class with any story that you love. Tell the story of Star Wars in twenty minutes, or your favorite episode of a TV sitcom. Or try a classic fable: look online for "Aesop's fables" or "the fables de la Fontaine". Learn to simplify a story first, and then turn to the target language culture for the stories that you learned when you were getting to know the language.

In order to do this **I recommend that you break down the story into no more than eight sentences. Simplify!!** In the story I tell in the video I eventually rewrote the characters so that five characters turned into three for the sake of simplicity.

Students fold a normal-sized piece of paper twice, making four squares on each side. They illustrate each sentence in one of the squares, so they will have a maximum of eight squares to complete. Do not dictate the sentences for them to copy; instead describe the scene in a repetitive manner so that students can continue to add details as they draw.

After they have finished illustrating, then tell them to go back and caption each drawing.

Oral Storytelling Process:

(1) Choose a favorite tale to tell. Familiar stories are fine; student pre-knowledge will help them understand.

(2) Simplify your story into no more than eight sentences. Four or five is best.

(3) Have students fold a blank piece of paper into four parts.

(4) They illustrate each part as you tell it.

(5) Students add captions afterwards.

The next few pages contain some of the cartoon panels that my students passed in (all non-heritage speakers).

Using Target Language TV and Movies

Authentic television and movies can be used in even the lowest level classes as long as the teacher plans for one important thing: **the videos themselves rarely provide good, comprehensible language for students to acquire**. Yes, that's right: even in an advanced class there will be a small group of students who acquire language from the video while, for the vast majority of students, the language speeds by too quickly. So, if students aren't acquiring from the video, why use authentic media at all?

There are two reasons that come immediately to mind: first, find a video that is compelling. **The compelling nature of the video will draw students to engage closely with the class conversation about the video.** You should remind yourself, when you are tempted to just let the video play because everyone is enjoying the video, that it is the conversation after the video that leads to acquisition. We have already seen this with the Movie Talk technique in which we use short video clips to engage students in a class conversation.

The second reason to use authentic tv shows or movies is to provide an ongoing plot for class conversation. Once you have established the nature of the characters and the drama involved, it is easy to rely on students' pre-knowledge of the series to discuss new scenes. Of course, this is exactly what you would do while discussing a class novel as well, but the video has an advantage. In the video there are **compelling visuals that you can refer to, making this the perfect medium for beginners**.

The irony is that so many teachers save their most intriguing cultural products, movies and tv shows, for upper level students when they could be establishing their students' long-term interest in the language **in the first years of study**.

How do you show an authentic TV show to first year students?

Most importantly: **don't just press play and sit back!** We use authentic media because it is compelling, but we have to do the work of providing language that our students can understand. Over the years I have developed an approach to watching TV shows in the lowest levels that requires the teacher to do the exact opposite of what is normally done when a film is played in class. These are my best insights:

- The normal expectation is to watch a sizeable chunk of video before stopping to discuss. Instead, you want to watch the minimum amount that will allow you to stop and discuss. **Plan on watching 1-2 scenes, no more than 5 minutes.** In fact, watch those scenes the night before and do not show more in class. If you watch a scene or two the night before, you will never accidentally show school-inappropriate material in class. 5 minutes of prep work each night will save you from the embarrassment (and possibly being fired!) for showing something that should not be seen in school. If you do find something objectionable, just skip the scene without explanation. Trust me, no one will notice.

- Normally teachers like to have one day dedicated to the show, like a Friday watch & relax party. *Fight that urge*. Instead, **watch a little every day**, not a lot occasionally. Reserve 20 minutes at the end of class every day in January & February. And don't relax; you'll spend most of those 20 minutes up front talking, discussing, asking questions about the show and leading W&D. You want to develop a continuous class conversation about the drama and characters; once a week is infrequent enough that students will lose the thread of the plot. Even worse if a student misses a Friday (which will happen). For the month or two that you all watch the show, you want this to be the beating heart of your classroom. **Every student needs to be eating, breathing and swimming in the plot**. You cannot allow even one student who had a doctor's appointment to get lost. Do this every day and you'll easily be able to catch up an absent student.

- Remember: the video does not provide the comprehensible language for acquisition. The teacher provides that language. **The class discussion and Write + Discuss are essential for deep language acquisition**. Once we get in the habit of concluding each class period with the creation of a Write & Discuss text, we have the tools to make impressive leaps in literacy. It is valuable to have students reread the texts describing student interviews and the other activities we do daily in class. However the collection of the W&D texts reach a whole new level when we use them to track an ongoing plot line, such as when we take notes on the development of a target language television show. This collection of W&D texts truly becomes a class anchor text if we frequently refer back to the texts as we recognize character and plot developments. An anchor text is a text that is read and referred to often in class because we use it to build a variety of skills.

- When you preview a scene at night, break it down into one sentence that summarizes the scene. **Focus on what the main character wants in the scene and don't worry about anything else**. For instance, if Carolina wants to kiss Marcos, don't bother describing the homework assignment that they are both talking about in the scene. SHE WANTS TO KISS MARCOS!! Before watching the scene, tell your students what Caroline wants. During the scene, point out the visual cues and hammer that key point. After the scene is finished, keep hammering variations of that point because this scene is not about homework. If you identify what a character wants, students will follow the plot of the show easily. If you insist on talking about every little thing brought up in the show, students will get confused and bored, thinking that the show is about two kids doing homework.

- **Do not translate dialogue!** Translating each line will just distract. The conversation about Latin homework is irrelevant, because the scene is really about Carolina who wants to kiss Marcos and MARCOS DOES NOT KNOW!!! He is so clueless!

- Have students maintain a notebook of the Write + Discuss texts related to the series so that they can go back and reread to trace how the plot has developed.

- Maintaining a notebook is crucial for absent students.

- This notebook is also helpful if the plot line is complex.

As a Spanish teacher I enjoy watching *El Internado* with my level 1 students from January until Spring break. With my level 3 students I watch *Gran Hotel* from early October until Winter Break and then movie-talk authentic movies until Spring break.

Over the years I have saved the best Write & Discuss texts from the various TV shows and films that we have watched in class so that we now have a great selection of pre- and post-readings. Definitely save the Write & Discuss texts! On the next page I have examples of how I have transformed the Write & Discuss texts created in class into interactive reading guides. Don't try to do it all in one year, simply save the Write & Discuss texts and, when you have time, make a reading guide to review past episodes. Over the span of a year or two you'll develop reading guides aimed precisely at the reading levels of your students that you'll use for the rest of your career.

Whenever I decide to include a show into my class, I first watch the series (with teacher eyes) to make sure there are only a few scenes that I have to skip. *El Internado* may not be appropriate for your school due to frequent coarse language (my students don't notice it), but the truly objectionable material (a teacher-student relationship) does not emerge until the third season. If you follow my guidelines, you'll be struggling to finish the first season even if you make *El Internado* the centerpiece of your class. Gran Hotel has only a small handful of inconsequential scenes to skip, making it a good choice. The language is clean. I've never made it past episode 7 (season one) with a class. There are 50 or so episodes... it is okay not to finish a show. In class we are just finding conversation topics.

If you do find a show that you can use for many years of classes, try to **buy the series on DVD**. Netflix shows come and go, videos are removed from YouTube and other websites frequently. Don't put all the effort into making reading guides for a show that you won't be able to find online; it is a good investment to buy the DVDs.

El Internado -- Primer episodio – Guía para estudiantes (1)

Una mujer se escapa de un _____. Ella se llama María. En el autobús vemos que ella tiene una carta del colegio *Laguna Negra*, y podemos ver la palabra "_____". ¿Es estudiante? _____. Un hombre en el autobús la (besa grita reconoce) y ella se escapa de nuevo.

Corriendo por el bosque ella decide cambiar de (dirección idea ropa). Así nadie va a reconocerla por la ropa. Mientras que se desnuda se acerca un (estudiante hombre lobo). Ella sube un árbol y el lobo se va. Antes de que pueda bajar del árbol un hombre llega (corriendo hablando llorando). Ella se cae en sus brazos, más o menos. Este hombre se llama Héctor.

Los estudiantes llegan al colegio para el nuevo año escolar. La primera chica es hija de una actriz famosa, ella se llama _____. La segunda chica, Victoria, habla con su madre. Su mamá es (más guapa que   menos guapa que   tan guapa como) la madre de Carolina. La madre de Victoria le da una (bufanda manzana toalla). Victoria es de una familia (pobre rica).

El primer chico es Iván. Su padre no le (da la mano habla dice adiós) a su hijo. ¡Qué antipático! Además de las dos chicas Iván tiene dos amigos, Cayetano y Roque. Roque tiene el pelo corto. También hay un chico que llega en un coche negro. Es nuevo y Carolina dice que es muy _____. Se llama Marcos y su hermana se llama _____. No llegan con sus padres, él que maneja el coche es el (abogado médico profesor). Son huérfanos; es decir que sus padres están _____. O mejor dicho, sus padres se han (aparecido desaparecido reconocido). Marcos cree que todavía están vivos.

Gran Hotel – guía estudiantil – primer episodio

escena 1
0:00 – 3:07

clase social
PQA: ¿De qué clase social son los Kardashian? ¿Tienes amigos de otras clases sociales?

Un joven prende (un cigarrillo un fuego una luz) en una estación de tren. Se ve por la ropa que es de una familia (árabe humilde rico). Él se llama Julio Olmedo, y va desde Madrid a un pueblo en el norte de país que se llama (Bilbao Cantaloa Santander). Una mujer joven, vestida lujosamente, camina hacia el (edificio lago vagón) de primera clase. Ella se llama (Alicia Susana Julieta) y viene de una familia (adinerada francesa pobre). Ella también va a Cantaloa. El joven la mira; ella (lo besa le grita ni lo ve). El joven sube al vagón de segunda clase y habla con (un perro una mujer vieja un payaso del circo), revelando que va a visitar a su (hermana hija sobrina). En el tren él lee (una carta un libro un poema) que le escribió su hermana, Cristina.

---

escena 2
3:08 – 5:39

se extraña
La vieja en el tren se extrañó cuando Julio le dijo que iba a Cantaloa. ¿Por qué?

Cristina era la jefa de la planta; quiere decir que era una de las jefas de (los osos las mujeres los niños) que trabajaban en el Gran Hotel. Sin embargo ella tenía (dos amigos mucho dinero un secreto). Vimos en flashback lo que pasó la noche (del desfile de la fiesta del partido) de la luz, una fiesta para celebrar la llegada (de la luz eléctrica del sol). Doña Teresa, la dueña del (hotel tren elefante), quería que Cristina subiera a su habitación con (el té las drogas el nuevo camarero). Cristina se extrañó (quiere decir que creyó que era muy raro) porque llevar la comida y la bebida a los cuartos solía ser el trabajo de los (camareros elefantes clientes). Al subir Cristina descubrió que Doña Teresa quería hablar con ella (a solas como si fuera su mamá para darle las gracias).

- Essays about teaching -

Letter to parents about advantages of a deskless classroom

Teachers who are going deskless frequently ask me for a version of a letter I wrote to parents when I first went deskless. I think that this letter is gold; it places the deskless classroom within the context of solid teaching practices and describes why this change is an improvement. My administrators and parents were happy once the change was explained, and even students recognized that desks often are used to hide phones or homework for other classes.

I have edited this letter so that you can simply print and sign it if you want.

The first year that I went deskless I left one desk in the back for students whose parents insisted that their child "needs a desk in order to learn". Within a day or two I always found the student using the desk to hide non-class activities. *EVERY SINGLE TIME.*

However, leaving a desk or two in the classroom may be helpful for a student feeling anxiety about the change. I still would not let them take notes during the class, but that is a paradigm shift that many parents (and teachers) may not understand. This letter is a good way to open that conversation.

Dear Parents & Guardians,

Our World Language class has replaced standard student desks with free standing chairs. This one change has had a tremendous impact on the classroom; instead of having several rows across and deep, we now have the possibility of arranging a classroom with no far back corners inaccessible to the teacher.

A simple circle, or two half circles arranged like an amphitheater, allows every student a privileged position to observe and interact with the lesson. Teachers can monitor engagement by teaching to the eyes of students, something nearly impossible when a sea of heads extended back thirty feet.

Student desks can serve to inhibit student learning in language classes. With a sea of desks obstructing the teacher´s vision, it is easy for students to surreptitiously spend the class period monitoring social media on their cellphones. By placing work for other classes on top of their notebooks, it is easy to spend the class period completing math assignments while it appears that they are taking copious notes.

Now there are no longer desks for students to rest their heads and disengage. In fact, the student desks get in the way of what your child needs most to acquire a language: their full attention during class.

Student desks are still useful for lecture courses that require a lot of note-taking. World language classes, on the other hand, no longer require extensive note-taking. In a typical class period students dedicate the first few moments to copying the phrases of the day into their notebooks. Notebooks are then placed under the chairs and the rest of the class period is dedicated to activities that help students develop the ability to use the target phrases naturally. Students hear and react to the phrases in a variety of contexts so that they develop an ear for the language. If you were to visit one of our classes you would see students actively responding to the spoken language throughout the period. In order for this to work, teachers must verify that students comprehend everything said in class. Thus it is important that teachers are able to carefully observe the eyes of all students for signs of wavering or lack of comprehension.

Listening, reading, speaking and writing all still have a place in our classrooms. Often the last five to ten minutes of class are dedicated to a writing activity. Positioning their notebooks in their laps has proven to be sufficient for such a short duration of time. Overall the use of chairs helps students engage in class to become more active learners while using the language, rather than passive note-takers. It is an exciting pedagogical shift, and I hope you share our excitement.

Aligning with a textbook

I once led a workshop where teachers brought their worst examples of textbook vocabulary lists that they had to cover in the school year. Textbooks tend to present thematic units which, in the best cases, theoretically lead to interesting conversations in class. Unfortunately in the real world many busy teachers see these lists and feel pressured to turn their classes into vocabulary drills for fear that their students are not going to 'learn the vocabulary'. **Drilling isolated words does not lead students to acquire language. They need to hear complete messages.**

Observation #1:
Regardless of however long the list of words we have been tasked to teach, **we must always embed each new vocabulary item** *that we choose to present* **within communicative language that the learner is already processing with ease**. Researchers tell us that native-like language acquired via the implicit language acquisition system only happens when the learner understands a message. "*You should fall asleep before midnight*" is a message, whereas "*dormirse (ue): to fall asleep*" is not a message.

Lengthy vocabulary lists are not the only problem with thematic units. If you are currently stuck in a "daily routines" unit you might be having a hard time getting student buy-in with preachy little phrases about the evils of staying up late watching Netflix. **Students acquire best when they think that the class conversation is** *comprehensible and interesting,* not comprehensible and nagging.

Observation #2:
Use the "Student Voice" activities to embed new vocabulary into activities with compelling language.

For instance, ask a student in a student interview at what time does he/she fall asleep. Don't mention that it's a stem-changing verb in Spanish, don't interrupt to clarify that *acostarse (ue)* means to go to bed while *dormirse (ue)* means to fall asleep. Just simply ask in the target language, *¿A qué hora te duermes?* (At what time do you fall asleep?). The student will understand because the translation is on the slide projected behind her. **Act surprised and interested in her response and-- this is crucial-- ask follow up questions.** "*¿Te duermes* (point and pause at the phrase *te duermes* on the slide, which also has the translation *you fall asleep* written directly below) *a las dos* (hold up two fingers to indicate "at two") *de la mañana?*" When she affirms that this is correct turn to the class and ask, *¿A qué hora se duerme Sarah?* (palm of your hand facing up and outstretched toward Sarah so that the class understands you are talking about Sarah, not to Sarah). REQUIRE A CHORAL RESPONSE from all students in class. Repeat the question if necessary. Ask more questions, going up and down your interrogative words poster.

It is always tempting to follow up with *¡¿Por qué?!* (WHY!?), but put yourself in the shoes of your students: **"why" questions are always the hardest to answer and thus often kill the conversation.** I try to avoid asking questions beginning with *why* and instead either offer a choice or ask a yes or no question. *¿No te gusta dormir?* (Don't you like sleeping?) *¿Es difícil* (write the word *difícil* on the board and then write *difficult*) *dormir?* (Point and pause at *te duermes* even though you said *dormir*). (Hold out two hands, palms open and facing up to indicate a choice between two things): *¿Tienes miedo de dormirte o prefieres mirar el Netflix?* [Are you afraid of falling asleep, or do you prefer to watch Netflix?]

I rarely spend more than 10 minutes on a student interview. Even a student who does not find Sarah to be compelling can be reasonably asked to follow the conversation for 10 minutes, whereas spending 40 minutes will wear students' patience thin and make them less open to more student interviews in the future. Short and sweet is always better. However, I will follow-up with a five minute **Write & Discuss** so that students get to see the words written in full sentences and process the language again.

Calendar Talk is not about dates and weather!

Other activities that lend themselves well to introducing new vocabulary include **calendar talk,** which is a natural choice for talking about routines. However, you can fit anything that students do into a calendar talk. Stuck in a sports unit? "Who is playing rugby this week?" (I ask in the target language). "Nobody!?" Then I write on the side of the calendar "Nobody in our class plays rugby".

Or do a **picture talk**: find a picture of an exhausted person (or, **even better, have your students send you photos of themselves looking exhausted and choose JUST ONE to discuss**). Hold out your hands, palms facing up to indicate a choice: "*Sí o no: ¿Él se duerme a las nueve?*" [Yes or No: Does he go to sleep at 9?] Follow up by glancing at your question words poster and asking several more questions. *¿Dónde se duerme? Imaginación, chicos... él no se duerme en la cama. ¿Dónde se duerme? Quiere dormirse, pero no puede. ¿Por qué no puede dormirse? Cuántos... hmm... ¿Cuántas horas por noche duerme?* [Where does he fall asleep?

Imagination! He does not sleep in a bed. Where does he fall asleep? He wants to fall asleep but cannot. Why can't he fall asleep? How many... hmm... How many hours per night does he sleep?]

Then try a **card talk** in which students draw something that represents what they like to do immediately before going to sleep. "*Antes de dormirse... clase, ¿qué quiere decir 'antes de dormirse'? [Before falling asleep... class, what does 'before falling asleep mean?]* (write on board 'before falling asleep')... *bueno, antes de dormirse [okay, before falling asleep]* (point and pause at the board again) *a Andrea le gusta* [Andrea likes to] (pick up her card and show everyone the illustration of a toothbrush) *cepillarse los dientes. [brush her teeth]* Andrea, *¿dónde te cepillas los dientes? ¿Dónde te duermes?* [Where do you brush your teeth? Where do you fall asleep?] *¡Clase!* (I say this to alert everyone that I am asking the entire class a question) *¿Se cepilla los dientes en la cama?* [Does she brush her teeth in her bed?] REQUIRE A CHORAL RESPONSE TO QUESTIONS POSED TO THE ENTIRE CLASS. *¿Se duerme en el baño?* [Does she fall asleep in the bathroom?]

However, **we still have a problem with creating compelling class conversations because textbook thematic units are generally not compelling**. When was the last time you had a fifty-five minute conversation in your first language about daily routines? If, by some odd chance, you really did recently chat about brushing your teeth without boring your conversation partner... did you continue having such conversations for 55 minutes a day for two weeks, after which you stopped talking about daily routines and instead dedicated the next two weeks to discussing modes of transport?

I love **One Word Images** because they are compelling and provide a lot of natural language. **If I were stuck in a daily routines unit, I would do some of the activities listed above but also modify a one word image.** After the first four characteristics, just after the class decides whether he is happy or sad, I would add one thing. I would tell my students in the target language, "class, I have to add one important detail: he is very, very tired". Then we would continue the one word image process like normal. The following day instead of asking the class for a problem I would have prepared a prompt to start our story. I present the illustration like normal, then I would say in the target language, *"Class, our very tired and sad* **box of cereal** *(or whatever the object is) has a big problem. He falls asleep very late, very very late, and he always wakes up late. Class, he wakes up so late that he does not* **brush his teeth**. *He comes to school and he says 'hi' to the cute* **box of cereal** *that he likes, but that cute* **box of cereal** *leaves quickly and does not talk to him. He does not know why. Class, I have a secret: it is because he does not* **brush his teeth**. *It is because* **he falls asleep** *very, very late and then does not* **brush his teeth**.*"*

Once the problem has been presented, your class can resolve the story using the normal OWI story template presented in the OWI section. **When we embed key vocabulary into a story, our students are more likely to acquire the language than from a list.**

Observation #3:
Not all vocabulary words are equally important.

You might be thinking that you cannot spend so much time on one word when you have a gigantic list of words to cover. Perhaps you are looking for an activity to quickly cover all of these words, so that you can do what linguists tell us should not be done. From a research perspective, it is essential that you focus on a few specific words.

"Well designed programs need to draw on [vocabulary] frequency information and also need to have the flexibility for teachers and learners to play a part in choosing the vocabulary to focus on."
- **Paul Nation**, linguist and expert on vocabulary acquisition

---

I was shocked when I first started paying attention to a **high-frequency word list** to guide my curriculum. While I was eager to rid my students of such low-frequency words such as *fregadero* and *algodón* in favor of words that they would use spontaneously on their own, I was unaware that even words like *azul* and *octubre* are much less frequent than many words that I saved until their third or fourth year of language study. I am not arguing that colors and months be altogether dropped from level 1 courses, but **if you want your students to quickly become communicatively proficient then you should emphasize the highest frequency vocabulary**. I have seen estimates that the most frequent 100 words make up half of the spoken language and the top 1000 words make up 70-80%!

Most textbook vocabulary does not even appear in the top 1000... some not even in the top 10,000. "*Encestar*", a Spanish 1 word from the *Así se dice* textbook, shows up among the top 36,000. Stop the madness!

You are wasting your students' time if you force feed them mountains of vocabulary. Instead, **focus on high frequency words and allow students to suggest the low-frequency words that *they want to learn***. They don't need to learn "cereal box", but will embrace that word if they themselves choose it. If necessary, ask them to choose from your word walls of thematic vocabulary rather than treating every vocabulary word as equally important.

Here is my final advice if you are trapped in a textbook department:

Post the Sweet 16 verbs and the interrogative words at the beginning of the year and prioritize their acquisition. Even if your school district insists that you follow a certain textbook closely, posting and actively using the sweet 16 verb posters in class will lead your students to develop an amazing native-like fluency with some of the most commonly used words in the target language.

If someone if forcing you to "cover" a large list of words, place weekly thematic vocabulary that you must cover on a **rotating word wall with the English translations visible**. Use that wall as inspiration, not as a list that students are required to memorize.

Limit vocabulary. *Don't kill yourself* trying to get all of the vocabulary from the textbook into your lessons. If required, assign Quizlet lists for out of class study.

Use your question word posters to help you park on one word or two from the thematic unit that you are focusing on.

Do not strictly follow the textbook order. Textbooks tend to drip out the Sweet 16 verbs over the course of the entire first year, if they even present them all. You can introduce the third person form of those verbs within the first few hours of classes, setting up a much more communicative class far earlier than the textbook anticipates.

Regardless of what you do in class, be sure to end with a Write & Discuss and an exit quiz. It will be effective even if you have to write (in the target language), "today we read the textbook and half the class fell asleep. We talked about rooms of the house and Bobby dreamed about his bed while Tricia wanted to watch TV in her living room..."

"**If learners spend time learning low-frequency words... this learning would be largely wasted because it will be a long time before they meet or use these words again.**"
- **Paul Nation**, linguist and expert on vocabulary acquisition

Common sense activities that simply waste time

When I started my career almost 20 years ago I was taught to immerse my students in an eclectic grab bag of language games and activities, ready to use so that my classes never lost their novelty. Over time I have shed many of these activities from my repertoire.

The issue is not whether they work; most often there is something valuable. The issue frequently comes down to **whether the activity is an efficient as well as effective use of class time**. Language acquisition takes place on the scale of thousands of hours; the average high school language program offers students a total of between 400 and 650 contact hours spread over four years.

We have to optimize our class time, choosing the most efficient activities so that students leave our programs prepared to continue the process of acquisition without us.

This essay lists nine activities that I once understood as part of a common sense approach to language acquisition, which I later re-evaluated with a critical eye. If you are transitioning towards a more conversational approach to teaching but have a hard time adding more to your already packed classes, this list might help you simplify your teaching life.

(1) Conjugation games: Conjugation races, games with verb ending manipulatives, and all sorts of other activities in which kids had to conjugate verbs were a staple of my classes when I first started my career. **They were dropped when I discovered that my students learn to conjugate just fine by being exposed repeatedly to rich, comprehensible language in class.** The key is to write full sentences on the board, such as in a W&D activity, and to occasionally draw their attention to the verb endings so that they associate the endings with changes in meaning. If you let students always infer the meaning, they will get the gist of the reading but not pick up on the subtle differences between "he runs" and "they ran". It is incredibly powerful to insert an occasional pop-up comment, such as, "Why does '*corro*' end in an *o*? What does the *o* mean?" A pop-up grammar comment should not last more than 10-15 seconds. It is sufficient to do it 5 times per class period (a total of 50-75 seconds per class spent on grammar). Point out the same grammar point each time so that students are screaming the answer back in exasperation.

However, **the huge game-changing advantage of teaching conjugation in context is that students unconsciously observe all of the minor grammar points** that would otherwise eat up your entire curriculum if you were to explain it all explicitly. I have not even mentioned "the personal a" in years, *in any class*, yet my level 3 students naturally use it fairly consistently. Never mind all of the prepositional constructions that accompany specific verbs, or the myriad rules governing the usage of *por* and *para*. Linguists Stephen Krashen and Bill Van Patten both argue that even a grammar pop-up is not needed, so don't feel bad if you forget to interrupt your class conversation with grammar pop-ups. *In fact, feel great about it.*

(2) Correcting writing samples: On a practical level, can we take a moment to mourn all of that precious time spent marking up papers that students do not even glance at?! Surely the "efficient use of time" argument can eliminate this practice. **But if you need research, take a look at John Truscott's review article, "The Case Against Grammar Correction in L2 Writing Classes".** He indicates that correction is not only a waste of time, but possibly harmful in many cases. "Waste of time" is good enough for me to throw this practice in the trash bin.

> **A link to Truscott's article online:**
> https://lecture.ecc.u-tokyo.ac.jp/~cwpgally/references/2009S_TEW_Truscott_original_article.pdf

If you must, try gently rephrasing learner language orally. While completing a W&D, listen to the learner language and then write it on the board in the correct form. Sometimes after a movie talk I ask students to pose follow-up questions so that we can delve into the story. As they ask questions, but before we start answering them, I write the corrected question on the board. These are productive ways to provide feedback.

Or better yet, simply do not correct your students' written or spoken output but rather continue to model lots of correct language. Research has found that language learners will go through predictable stages, including some stages (when their output is getting more complex) that may look like students are making even more errors, not less. These stages cannot be avoided.

"Direct error correction by the instructor does not promote linguistic accuracy and the absence of error correction in the early stages of acquisition does not impede the development of linguistic accuracy."
- **Bill Van Patten,** linguist and expert in Second Language Acquisition

---

(3) Pair work (for the most part): Krashen's research indicates that people do not learn to speak by speaking; they speak after much listening and reading (input). For that reason alone it is more efficient to expose students to more input than burn class time on non-input activities.

Listening to partner speech *is* input but, as Terry Waltz says, "it is the McDonald's of language acquisition". It is better to expose students to the correct, rich and comprehensible input provided by the teacher than the error-riddled, simple and at times incomprehensible speech of a learner.

However, there are times that I do encourage students to briefly engage in pair work: occasionally as a short 1 minute bail-out move I tell students to summarize our class conversation in pairs so that I have a moment to consider what to do next. I also believe that it is empowering for students to occasionally speak in small groups without being assessed. They are often amazed at how the language just flows. I might even give students the opportunity to voluntarily choose a speaking activity among a variety of options designed to review a reading or class discussion (it would probably be recorded on their phones and sent to me via email). Occasionally I break for very short paired conversations when students are bubbling with language and want an outlet to enjoy speaking.

Voluntary speaking can lead to positive language experiences, but that is a far cry from routine pair work in class to *practice* the language.

(4) Readings designed to practice X language (vocabulary, grammar): Students acquire best when they are interested in the message being communicated. Or better yet, the message should be not just interesting, but compelling. While students may judge our class conversations as less interesting than their lunchtime conversations with friends, a text designed to practice "parts of the house" or "usage of the subjunctive" is sure to be a loser. My rule is if we would not be interested in the conversation (or reading the text) in our first language, don't bother forcing it in the second language. ***Life is short, let's be interesting.***

(5) Speaking assessments: Instead of regularly burning a significant amount of class time on scheduled, forced speaking activities, **simply give ample opportunities and encouragement for students to speak when they are ready**. My class rule that "one person speaks, everyone else listens" motivates students who are capable and eager to actually talk in class, but forcing speech does nothing for language acquisition. Nor is it necessary to run an effective class.

Speaking assessments are also a tremendous time suck for teachers both in and outside of class. That time could have been spent developing more compelling readings and conversation topics.

Please note that *I am not against student speaking in class*; just squandering time assessing it. From the perspective of efficient use of class time, whatever advantages that students gain from a forced march through a speaking assessment pales compared to the time that could have been spent on an interesting reading.

I do start giving speaking assessments in level 3 because we are preparing for an exam in level 4 (AP/IB), but even then the speaking assessments are recorded in private (much like the exams). That is for the purpose of test prep, not language acquisition.

(6) Studying grammar: Linguist Bill Van Patten has said that our attempts to describe the grammar we have in our minds is like seeing a constellation of stars in the sky; the constellation that looks like a bear is just an illusion of our perspective in space. In the same way, grammar is actually a lot more complicated than our minds consciously grasp, yet when exposed to natural language our unconscious minds soak it all up. Even something like usage of the subjunctive can be taught simply by exposing students to rich, correct input.

In my practical experience, as long as my input is grammatically rich from day one, it is a more efficient path than grammar study. The key is to **make sure that your own language as a teacher is both comprehensible and not unnaturally simplified**. For a non-native speaker of Spanish I would recommend that you consciously try to use the phrase "para que" in your W&D texts. As long as students thoroughly understand the message, they will eventually acquire the correct form.

However, there is a *limited place* for explicit discussion of grammar outside of brief grammar pop-ups: during the editing phase of the writing process for advanced students. In my teaching that only shows up in upper level courses for heritage language learners. For my non-native speakers I am more likely to spend class time in our level 4 course discussing, as a whole class, how to use transition words to build a logical argument (once again, part of the editing process as we write AP essays).

Four years of exposure to real language in my school's program leads the majority of students to develop an intermediate mastery. Explicitly reviewing the imperfect and preterit will help students pass an explicit grammar test, but it will not impact their implicit, instinctive language use. The best way to develop their instinctive language use in upper levels is even more reading, including models of the kinds of essays that you want them to write.

(7) Unit Exams: I don't even teach units anymore-- almost all of our class activities are self-contained within one class period. This is a strategy that I adopted to help my kids with high absenteeism due to the chaos of living in poverty. Placing my teaching situation to the side, however, the idea of burning a whole day on assessments, and then losing sleep and valuable prep time to correct them all... **that is an inefficient use of time**. Instead **pinpoint exactly what you want to learn about your students, give them a five minute assessment in class to gather that information and then REACT to the assessment**.

Many teachers give assessments to get some grades in the grade book. We should be using those assessments to modify instruction. If you are not reacting to the information gathered, why burn the time doing the assessment in the first place? This leads to a more reflective practice on part of the teacher who interrupts the flow of input only when necessary. You will find that you need to interrupt that flow less and less. As the old farmers saying goes: "*weighing the pig frequently does not make it grow any faster*".

(8) Vocabulary games (for the most part): I still occasionally play a word game like Boggle in class because it is a fun bailout move, but that is different from routinely playing vocabulary games as a way to learn vocabulary. **Most vocab games focus on one word, whereas what really drives language acquisition is communicating whole messages.**

It might feel satisfying to cover 30 words in a 10 minute game of Flyswatter, but that game has a frustratingly feeble impact on students' ability to later use those words. I used to consistently use these kinds of activities to front-load vocabulary in my Spanish heritage language learners classes before reading stories. As much as my students mastered the vocabulary out of context, it seemed to have little impact when they later read the story. It comes down to efficiency; students need to experience words in many contexts before actually acquiring the word.

The superficial, short-term learning of a list of vocabulary words fools us into believing that those words are well on the way to being acquired, when in fact it would be much more efficient to embed a single new word in a compelling context for 10 minutes. Beniko

Mason's research on vocabulary acquisition related to reading finds that **vocabulary games and activities before and after reading actually lead to less long-term acquisition than simply using that time for more reading**.

(9) Reading whole class novels: This might get under some teachers' skin, but I truly believe that a forced march through a whole class novel is an inefficient reading practice. Reading a whole class novel together is a lot better than a textbook, but why struggle to push your classes through four novels per year (and that is a lot for enthusiasts of whole class reading) when your students could enjoy reading between 15 to 25 novels on their own with a pleasure reading program?

It is better to stretch their reading skills with short, whole class Write & Discuss texts based on the daily conversations in class. Save your library of comprehensible novels for pleasure reading.

The irony is that if level 1 students read 20 easy novels on their own, by level three they will be reading the level 3 novels... without the teacher's interference. **Pleasure reading empowers students.**

Keeping it fresh all year long

There are times in the course of a school year when students just seem "done with school" and there is nothing we can do to revive the flash of goodwill that we enjoyed in our first weeks together. Personally I have always found November and February to be the hardest months to slog through, but of course I don't let my students see that.

There are a few tricks that we can employ to keep our classes fresh and not become demoralized by students that simply stare at us. **When students refuse to contribute, their apparent passive aggressive non-compliance is often masking a deeper discomfort with speaking and feeling foolish.** Even if you know that they 'can speak', respect this awkward moment and instead invest in activities that provide rivers of comprehensible input. That is what your students truly need to eventually emerge with a desire to speak.

Plan the flow of your year

Take a look at the **lesson planning essays**. The thrust of the **Two Conversations Approach** is to teach you a set of skills that you can use to interact with your students in the moment. Each activity and skill leads educators to have real conversations with their classes, rather than canned, 'fake dialogues'. Stop spending prep time developing beautiful content lessons that students seem intent on ignoring!

I plan my year so that the featured activities develop the skills required later in the year. For example, we start the year with frequent book talks so that, by second semester, students can read from my class library independently. **My book talks in first semester also prepare them for their own gallery talks in second semester**, modeled after what they have seen me do. Planning the flow of your year may build just enough novelty in class, but it also will help you see the big picture of the skills students are developing even if they stop contributing orally to class.

Movie Talks and authentic media
Looking at the graphic showing the flow of my year on page 16 you may notice that around mid-October I start leading many movie-talks and "telling a tale" activities. In part this is because students are gratified to find a few more "passive" activities such as movie-talk in this part of the year.

With the movie talks I am training them to participate appropriately before we begin a TV show in January. In October students will whine because they want to chat with friends during the movie-talk. They do not want the teacher to pause the video and discuss. In

October you should teach students to expect the video to be interrupted, to expect to listen to you talking about what is on the screen, and to maintain a silent room while doing so. Do this in October so that the activity will work in January when you start **movie-talking an entire TV show**.

It is not the worst thing if you burn a movie talk or two in October because your students are not listening to you talk through the video in class because there is no ongoing plot line. **However, in January if students are not paying proper attention to the movie talk each day, they will become hopelessly lost in the complexity of a plot that lasts until Spring break.**

Simply telling tales through oral storytelling
By October students' listening abilities have developed considerably, but they may be self-conscious of their speaking which is weaker. They can now 'hear' more of their mistakes. **Some teachers mistakenly believe that students at this point need more practice speaking; what students really need is a heavy dose of listening and reading until the language falls naturally out of their mouths, unforced.** This is the perfect time to give them an extra dose of rich language through **oral storytelling activities**.

Fables, fairy tales, and folk tales all work as great sources of inspiration and many students are not acquainted with these timeless tales. Aesop's fables are just the tip of a bountiful genre; certainly delve into the many fables attributed to Aesop but also do a google search for "Jean de la Fontaine fable", "Hans Christian Andersen fable" or "Félix María de Samaniego fable". But why stop there?! I have heard of teachers telling the Star Wars saga in short installments in class! **The key is simply to avoid telling the story word for word, or translating it into the target language. Instead glance often at the Sweet 16 verbs posted on the wall of your classroom and use those to help you tell the story in language that your students can understand.**

Subtle changes

An occasional subtle change can have a great impact on the energy in class. Do you always stand in front? **Try sitting among your students, facing the board like they do.** Nothing sends the message that you are not the performer on stage quite like simply joining the audience and commenting on a movie talk from '*the peanut gallery*'. This is easy if you have a student at your computer.

I am always impressed at how the lighting in a room profoundly impacts the mood of the class. Switching from industrial overhead bright white lights to several soft lamps, specifically during the storytelling portion of class, may impact student's willingness to participate.

Have a bailout move ready
Bailout moves are essential, like the net below a circus acrobat. I always have a bailout move ready so that as an activity loses steam I can quickly transition without losing the attention of my students. **There is a list of bailout moves** on page 70. They are student-directed, allowing me to pour myself a cup of tea, and they can be dropped into any class for a quick transition. I also love the subscription website Textivate to keep track of my Write & Discuss texts, which can supply a text game at a moment's notice.

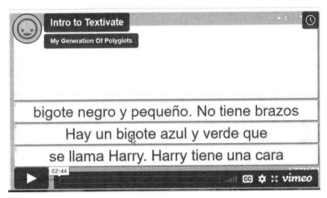

https://vimeo.com/715795159/5d8c5f1849

What not to do

The one trap I avoid is continually searching for the next big thing that will delight students *so they hopefully love my class again*.

I could, of course, plan out a non-stop string of surprises that flow throughout the year, and on paper that does not sound too bad. However, there is a problem with what I call "the birthday party" approach to lesson planning: **students become more and more passive as they expect you to entertain them**. *I don't want to be an entertainer.* I don't want students to passively expect me to perform tricks for their amusement. **What happens after the performance is over?** Honestly, I suspect the 'entertainer-teachers' may be robbing their students of the internal motivation they need for a lifetime of language acquisition.

When the school year is over, I want my students to be aching for more Spanish, not for more *crazy Spanish class antics*.

Fear & Creativity

Today I want to talk about creativity. And fear.

Some of us shy away from free-form activities that require improvisation in class, while others thrive in an 'anything goes' environment. Fear of losing control (or simply having nothing to say in front of a snarky group of students) holds teachers back. Others worry that the time sunk into nurturing students' creativity is simply not an efficient or effective use of our limited class time. Our own 'comprehensible input rallying cry' undermines the case for significant student creative writing: "Input input & more input is the path to language acquisition".

If you agree with the basic tenets of comprehensible input instruction, you understand that **writing and speaking abilities do not emerge from practicing writing and speaking**, but rather from listening and reading.

It would seem logical that what language teachers really need are abundant sources of comprehensible texts with which to smother our darlings. And so enterprising educators have set up shop on Teachers Pay Teachers and churn out unit after unit of interesting lessons, chock full of readings and guided talks that a CI teacher can use to *smother their students with the target language*.

And this works. Students acquire language, teachers have recognizable units that 'look' like school while accomplishing what the old textbook units never accomplished. We can even give the same kinds of assessments that kids see in their other classes. No parents object when there is an exam that students can study for, covering discrete facts, all in the target language.

> **It's a win for snugly fitting CI into an antiquated educational system that teachers in other departments are struggling to break out of.**

We can approach our classes as conversations or performances, and in my mind there is a world of difference between the two. A great performer may respond to his audience, but the play always evolves and turns out exactly as the playwright intended. Sometimes these performances are exhilarating, sometimes they are simply the meat and potatoes of language acquisition.

However, the notion of 'story-asking', the sometimes difficult art of nurturing a true conversation with students whose outcome is unknown, that is gradually being supplanted by something more mechanical. **We are losing the organic communicative classroom in favor of a factory model that fails to personalize the experience to the people who are actually in the room.**

I am reminded of a 2006 TedTalk by Sir Ken Robinson. You may have seen it; one of his key points is that **schools "ruthlessly squander" the innate creativity of children**. I re-watched that video recently and was struck by a vision of how that looks in our world of language instruction: it is the tightly-scripted curriculum, even a perfectly comprehensible one, that eliminates the chaos of the student voice. Batches of students move along a conveyor belt curriculum, being filled with just the right information at the right time, step by step along a linear sequence. That is an approach designed for an emerging industrial economy of the 18th century, not the creative economy of the 21st century.

> "Creativity now is as important in education as literacy...
> (but) we are educating people out of their creative capacities"
> - Sir Ken Robinson

This essay truly is not a critique of the content lessons available on Teachers Pay Teachers. I envision the 'second conversation' in the Two Conversation Classroom as a more presentational content lesson. I am certain that there is a strong place for story-telling within any language class. I even recommend that new teachers who are learning to manage their classes (or experienced teachers who are confronted with a particularly hard class to manage) lean heavily on these kinds of activities that simply supply a lot of good, comprehensible input: movie talks, cultural presentations, oral storytelling and using my advice to adapt target language TV and movies to the classroom.

However, the "student voices" activities encourage the teacher to approach these activities differently. Student voice activities are essentially interpersonal communication. **Like any real conversation, these activities must contain an element of unknown chaos or it is not true interpersonal communication.** This is where raw creativity enters our classroom.

When I speak of creativity, let's not imagining the beauty of a finished product. Creativity plays a part much earlier in the process, before the arduous refining and polishing that makes a finished product shine. Creativity can be ugly; it may evoke dark emotions of revulsion and rejection. In my writing group one teacher lamented privately to us that her students propose nothing but dumb ideas. Violence and stereotypes. We are writing class novels with our level one students; this is a group of teachers dedicated to honor student creativity and make it the centerpiece of their language classes. How do we nurture creativity?

Steps towards nurturing creativity
Creativity is a thinking tool used by all of humanity, not just artists but scientists, coffee baristas, landscapers... everyone. Fear chokes creativity, and that too can be useful. The logical part of our brain monitors our behavior and prevents us from blurting nonsense in front of colleagues. *Thank you logical brain!* It also criticizes our creative impulses, rejecting new ideas and preventing us from thinking deeply about a problem.

Experts who study creativity say that the creative process is often dogged by fear, and they are referring to the internal thought process of an artist. Our teaching reality is that the creative process takes place aloud, not hidden in the depths of our mind, and among dozens of other people, many judging us just as we judge ourselves. No wonder teachers want to stick to the script!

First, **re-imagine what creative expression looks like.** It does not look like sparkly unicorn dust. It is rarely a burst of inspiration, a thrill of laughter or excitement.

For example, in a student interview, don't prioritize coming up with 'interesting' or funny questions. **Instead, learn how to dig deep beyond the initial question to find something true about the student's life.** Composing a Write & Discuss text that quietly reveals a hidden truth about a student's life, making that student more human to her classmates, is a creative activity. It is also more meaningful than responding to silly questions designed to gain a laugh. This is a deeply creative activity that allows students to re-interpret their world by delving into what they discover about the life of one of their peers.

Work at it everyday. There have been studies on the work habits of scientists who make deep, creative insights in their fields. Over the course of a career, these studies have found that the scientists who manage to set aside a little time every day to focus on writing ultimately create much more than the scientists who mass their writing time into longer but less frequent sessions.

In the same way, rather than doing a One Word Image once and spending the next month privately evaluating whether it was worth it, plan to do the two day image plus story creation cycle every week with all of your classes. Perhaps you might only allocate twenty minutes for each of the two days, but do it often to give students plenty of exposure to the creative activity. **Focus on guiding them so that they become more comfortable, less inhibited, and less fearful of unexpected responses.** *A little bit frequently* is better than a lot infrequently.

Don't stigmatize mistakes. I am not simply speaking about grammar. The creative process requires revision. A predictable, lackluster plot in a class story can be revisited and reworked. This is part of the creative process that students unfortunately rarely participate in. **Don't throw away the first draft**; return the next day and point out elements that you would like to rethink. In my own writing the creative twists emerge in rewrites; rarely are they present in the first draft.

Trust the process. You may feel more comfortable delivering a lesson whose beginning, middle and end are already well-known to you, the teacher. **Accept that there are also great rewards following the uneasy path of interpersonal communication**. Minimize the fear of losing control of your class by planning to spend only twenty minutes on the "student interview that may flop", followed by a movie talk. Better yet, be sure to have a bailout move ready in case your planned student voice activity really bombs. But do it again next class. Continue to plan a different student voice activity every day. With time you will get better at guiding the process, and your students will get better too.

"If you are not prepared to be wrong, you'll never come up with something original."
- *Sir Ken Robinson*

The Art of the Bailout Move

Linguist Bill VanPatten likes to mischievously remind teachers that the language we plan to deliver in class is probably not the language that our students will acquire from us.

He is referring to studies that reveal that our students acquire language in a fixed natural order. We really have little insight into that order of acquisition, but we know that the brain will not acquire something until it is ready. Students can learn of course; we can teach students to apply grammatical rules on an explicit grammar test, but that will have no impact on their implicit language use and will quickly be forgotten. It will not be acquired. The best we can do is provide a steady stream of comprehensible language and the brain, which is a natural language acquiring machine, will sort out what it needs at the moment to continue down the path of acquisition.

I was chatting online recently with a teacher about the various activities in the Two Conversation Classroom. She told me that she would love to try more of the activities, but she just could not fit them into her curriculum. That was a person who desperately needs to hear Bill's message. There is no essential activity or sequence that must be followed precisely.

Language teaching is less like baking, which requires exact measurements for the final product to turn out well, and more like putting together a morning hash for breakfast. The activities in the CI Master Class help inspire the comprehensible conversations that will lead to efficient acquisition, but there is no requirement such as "speak in the present tense until students have mastered the stem-changing verbs, then proceed to preterit but not imperfect tenses". Instead, speak naturally, slowly, and make yourself comprehensible. The Natural Order Hypothesis is tremendously liberating; even if we did know the natural order, it is impossible to truly know where each student is along the way. **Just let the grammatical and thematic teaching sequences go!!**

The Bailout Move allows us to seamlessly transition between activities. Or better yet, let's refer to activities as 'language class conversations'. No one has the expectations for a 'conversation' that teachers have for 'activities'. We may have been trained to think in logical teaching sequences. For example, "in this activity students will learn to conjugate the subjunctive, followed by the next activity which will teach them three phrases that call for the subjunctive, followed by a third activity in which students start to form sentences with the subjunctive". Let's just throw away the hopes and dreams that we harbor for our 'activities' and instead call them language class conversations. **When a conversation dies out, nobody examines the rubble to realize in disappointment that students did not learn to manipulate X grammar.** A conversation is simply a conversation. We expect conversations to die down eventually, and when they do, we all have developed social responses to bailout of a dead conversation. It is the same with 'language class conversations'!

My favorite bailout move is simply to have students read independently for three to five minutes. We start class with 5-10 minutes of quiet pleasure reading. What a nice routine to put behind whatever chaos that happened in the hallways before class and calmly focus on our language class. Instead of returning books after the independent reading session is over, I have them place their books under their chairs so that we can resume reading if needed. Around 35 minutes into class everyone passes their books to the class librarian, who then returns the books to the correct place. I wish this could work at holiday parties! *"Okay, this conversation is ending, please take out your book while I find someone else to chat with."*

I often have a Textivate activity prepared and ready to go on my computer. It may be a Write & Discuss that we prepared two weeks ago. Once a class conversation loses steam I call a student up to the computer and we review the activity from several weeks ago. My school does not have 1:1 tech resources, instead we all look at the screen and the students verbally help the student sitting at the computer. Textivate is a great bailout move that keeps kids processing language while the teacher moves on to the next language class conversation. If you have never tried Textivate, read the essay on page --- for an introduction to this wonderful website. Textivate is a subscription website, but I think it is well worth it.

Bailout moves are an important part of my class management plan. Please see the essay on 'Bailout Moves and Extending the Input' on page 70. While I want large stretches of our class time to be focused on students, I want to minimize the opportunities to talk in English. When students are learning about each other it is natural to want to continue the conversation in the language that they are most fluent in, so these bailout moves provide a minimal amount of input in the target language that prevents students from 'filling in the holes in class' with chatting in English.

My recommendation is to plan one bailout move for the entire day. Use the same one all day, regardless of the section; either have it ready to go on your computer (Textivate will require a separate tab for each class since they should review something they have created previously together) or have a plan so that you can transition seamlessly and not leave any space for your students to occupy with English.

Extra long and extra short classes

Teacher from California: How would you modify or adapt your methods for working with a block schedule? We have traditional 50-minute classes on Mondays, then 90-minute blocks for odd/even periods the rest of the week. So I'm only seeing kids three times a week. Any advice?

Mike: One year I taught a similar schedule-- 109 minute blocks twice a week and one day with 40 minutes. In general I had two exit quizzes in the long blocks; one midway through and the other at the end. **The exit quizzes are not about pushing trivia into long-term memory but rather encouraging kids to simply engage and track the class**, so splitting the class into "two classes" with two separate quizzes worked well.

When I do a One Word Image in a block period, we do the image during the first half (20 minutes) and another activity (music, interview, movie talk, picture talk, etc.), followed by Write & Discuss and the first exit quiz. There is also 5-10 minutes of quiet pleasure reading at the beginning of class. During the 2nd half of class we make the story (again, only twenty minutes) along with another activity, followed by another Write & Discuss and the second exit quiz.

With only 90 minutes split into two sections (i.e. two 45 minute classes), you might have to make the second activity quite short so that you have time for the W&D and exit quiz. **Have a student take on the job as the timer to remind you when your time with each activity is over and stick to the schedule.** You might feel like a 10 minute picture talk based on a student photo has barely begun, but your students will love that each activity moves along fast. You will also grow to love having a breather planned in frequently.

Life gets even easier once you have a decent-sized class library so that you can take 5-10 minute reading breaks throughout class. Building a library takes time, but is worth it.

Finally, resist the urge of planning one mega-activity that will take up tons of time. The mega-activity approach exhausted me and led me to add less-than-efficient output activities such as frequent student pair/shares and quick writes. Being on stage for 109 minutes straight was tiring! A quick write once every three weeks is enough. Student pair/share whenever an admin wanders in and wants to see a 'student centered classroom' is enough. The efficient answer is to **plan enough 10-20 minute activities that, even with the block, class moves along fairly quickly.** Short activities with a couple of bailout moves not only makes it more engaging for the kids, but also gives you a bit of a break from being "on" all the time.

The Cool Generation

It happens without warning, catching me by surprise. We might be watching a video in which a Bolivian *chola* comes on screen, or perhaps a very dark-skinned person, an overweight woman wearing a hijab or a homosexual couple dancing in the background of a music video. I hear a snarky murmur, mean-spirited chuckling... nothing that I can precisely distinguish but I know what this is about.

You cannot let this fester. This has to be addressed immediately and unequivocally, but winning hearts and minds can be trickier than just shutting down the rude comments. **I have developed the perfect tactic to address this situation.** This is not an overall strategy (every teacher should carefully plan how to honor diversity in their classrooms), but rather a tactic to remind students of their better selves. I like this tactic because it rapidly turns the tables and invites them to join us in the 21st century.

When I sense such an undercurrent, I stop whatever we are doing and quickly say, "I thought yours is the cool generation, the generation that refuses to carry hate in their hearts, to hate people for what they wear, how they were born, for being different". I pause and frequently somebody in class will say, "we are". They really are the cool generation. "I admire that about your generation... all of that bullshit is over with your decision to end it here and now". Sometimes I make eye contact as I say, "right?", but often I am addressing the whole class when I say that. More students will respond affirmatively. "We're together on this one, right?", and the whole class responds affirmatively. Don't allow the few belligerent students to define your class culture; there really are good-hearted students who would prefer to define the class community *if you give them the space.*

Most often I can find a reason to fist bump the offending students within ten or so minutes, and they are fully back into our class community.

I do not know why this works so well, but every time I refer to them as *the cool generation* they immediately take it on as their identity. I am hoping that in the future when my students hear hate speech, when they see white supremacists in public spaces, when they observe powerful figures making harsh generalizations about minority groups, they will think to themselves, "that is not a cool generation, those are not my values".

'Calm & Clear' is better than 'Loud & Lively'

How do you nudge a group of timid Level 1 students to overcome their initial awkwardness with the target language and become adventurous, curious, talkative explorers... all in their second language?

Even the best of us have fumbled this, praising the few highly vocal students in September and then finding ourselves in March with a group of sullen, snarky adolescents who fill the classroom with grumbling or worse... in English, of course. You could log onto Facebook and gripe, "It is impossible to teach these brats!" but let me instead suggest something that could sting: *it might be your fault*. Let me explain.

Many teachers instinctively rely on a common sense approach to language acquisition called the *Skill-Building Hypothesis*. Those teachers present a rule and some vocabulary, lead students to memorize the words and practice the rule, and eventually, with lots of practice, the idea is that students learn to juggle it all in their minds fast enough to finally manage to speak the target language. It is very logical, seems so embedded in common sense, yet linguists who study second language acquisition tell us that the process that actually occurs in the brain is quite the reverse.

My first department chair in a suburban school near Boston explained it to me like this: you don't have to explain *why* X means Y, just tell them that X means Y without the explanation. "*Quería que **supieras***" means "*I wanted **you to know.***" Don't mention the names of tenses, don't explain that in another context you'll need to change the sentence structure, don't even say anything in English. Just write it on the board with the English written below, underline the part, and continue with the story, or the interview, or whatever communicative activity your students are engaged in. As long as they understand, with time their brains will naturally grasp how the language is put together with lots of exposure. **Everyone's brain works like this.** This is how children learn their first language. Just focus on communicating the "what," and their brains will unconsciously unravel the "how." This is the essence of Stephen Krashen's *Comprehension Hypothesis*.

Krashen's research tells us that our students need a lot more listening and reading (called input) before we ask them to write or speak (output). A LOT more. There should be so many comprehensible messages that the words eventually spill out of their mouths, without effort.

A few years later I had moved to a Title 1 public high school outside of Los Angeles where, at the time, completing homework was not really part of the culture and perhaps 20% of students went on to a four-year college. When we followed a textbook (which was a skill-building curriculum), the only students who managed to pass the AP® exam were students who spoke Spanish at home with their families. Then our high school transitioned to an IB approach, while our department also happened to be in the midst of a transition away from the textbook towards principles derived from Krashen's research. As department chair, I asked my colleagues to hold off on all speaking assessments for the entire first year of language instruction. Instead we focused simply on delivering comprehensible messages in oral and written form. Almost all assessments were comprehension quizzes, without any requirement that our students speak.

We knew we were on to something well before our first cohort took their exams. Still, it was gratifying to transform a department with lots of excuses as to why our students did not succeed into a department with a 100% pass rate on both AP and IB exams. Our program did not start in middle school; after four years of instruction in high school, 100% of our students passed their exams, **once we stopped stressing kids out with speaking assessments and instead simply focused on delivering comprehensible input.**

Sometimes adolescents are unpleasant for reasons other than our instructional choices, but forcing them to speak before they are ready leads to uncomfortable situations that rightly rouse their counter-will. It is the skill-building approach that indignantly cries out, "They need to practice speaking in order to learn to speak!" yet the resentment that many adolescents feel when forced to speak in front of their peers has no practical function in language acquisition. I can assure you that if you wait until the words effortlessly drop out of their mouths, their spoken language will flow naturally like a mountain stream. You might ask yourself, "Do I just talk all day and expect them to listen to me?" There are creative ways to deliver the massive amounts of comprehensible input that they need.

A language teacher who wants to maximize the amount of comprehensible input in their classes might spend portions of their class conducting student interviews, doing Movie Talks through a process originally developed by Dr. Ashley Hastings, story-asking, or even chit-chatting about the weekend. My favorite activity is to create a **One Word Image** with my students. However, it is essential for all of these oral sources of comprehensible input to be supported by a well-thought-out approach to reading.

Krashen's *Reading Hypothesis* is a special part of his well-known *Comprehension Hypothesis*. Just as students acquire language when they understand what the teacher is saying, the *Reading Hypothesis* emphasizes that students acquire language when they understand written texts. Seems pretty straightforward, right? So, why is this a big deal?

This is a very big deal because, in my practice, I have found comprehensible reading to be an incredibly efficient accelerant to language acquisition. Of course everyone needs to hear the target language, but the teacher needs to balance the amount of listening and reading in class so as to optimize the acquisition. I find that the quicker that students are reading regularly, the quicker they acquire rich language. In fact, I suspect that the most effective CI teachers are not necessarily the marvelous performers whose kids are constantly laughing in class; I believe that **the most effective language teachers** are highly aware of the balance between oral and written sources of CI and **are providing the maximum amount of appropriate reading to their students**.

I am not suggesting that we push students to read hard texts earlier. Instead, we need to provide more opportunities to read easy texts, texts that are so easy that students read them effortlessly. The best way to do this is by meticulously reserving the last 10 minutes of class each day for an activity called Write & Discuss (W&D). W&D creates a summary of the day's discussion through a class conversation that is recorded on the board. Linguist Paul Nation stresses that rereading is excellent for acquisition, and I think that is why W&D is so fantastic. Not only does it provide a context to immediately reread and redeliver excellent CI, it also really supports the literacy piece as we write out our summary in a way that is often more articulate than speech. We then save and reuse these comprehensible texts so that they serve as the very foundation of our reading program.

Provide a brief, independent reading time at the beginning of every class, and make class-created texts at the end of the period to ensure that there will always be something comprehensible for students to read. If you are a Spanish teacher, we are now in a golden age for the publication of comprehensible texts that even our Level 1 students can read independently. Learning to support a reading program with effective strategies for reluctant readers is a key professional development goal.

You do not have to be an entertainer, a clown, or even the perfect adult role model that effortlessly inspires respect. Perhaps that is a teacher goal, but **in the meantime try focusing on simply learning about your students, turning it into a text, and maximizing the reading experiences afterwards**. Quiet classes with lots of reading build language efficiently.

You might find, when you conduct an interview or lead a One Word Image, that students begin to take delight in their short time on stage. Thus surges forth the group of adventurous, curious, talkative explorers that we were hoping to develop all along.

The Problem with a Grammar Syllabus

On a Winter day in 2014 I visited a school on the East Coast that was in deep trouble. The Spanish AP test had just undergone a heralded transformation from grammar-based to communicative skills-based and the uncertainty among teachers, along with the intense community pressure for high AP scores, had driven the AP Spanish teacher to announce her early retirement... effective in January before the test! I sat with the department chair and the principal as the first snowflakes of a Winter storm fell outside. The school was emptying of students scurrying home due to early dismissal for Winter weather.

Everything felt ominous indeed.

And then the other shoe finally dropped. The Department Chair showed me the scope & sequence documents for their AP Spanish class. I had asked about the Spanish heritage language population in the district -- there was such a population, but the department chair did not know about them because those students were tracked into English only classes. That, I mentioned, is the low-hanging fruit to get some success in the AP Spanish program while restructuring the program to be communicative classes. The principal was a youngish Irish-American with a wide arm span, maybe he had played basketball, because he knew how to control a room. "Whoa", he said extending his arms, "I'm not looking for big changes, I'm just looking for an AP teacher". And that is when I realized that the job I thought I was interviewing for was not this one.

That weekend on the flight back to Los Angeles I wrote a version of the essay below, titled "The grammar syllabus is worth fighting against".

One of the things that I absolutely love about a comprehensible classroom is the way that **the method fosters an inclusive classroom**. As long as students are physically in class, they all acquire language because our class stories are compelling and entirely comprehensible.

Although this is a difficult skill for the teacher to master, students often comment that our 'classwork' is easy. The high-achievers who have been trained to differentiate themselves from their peers can display their brilliance through their independent reading choices and their timed writings, but class stories always move at the speed of the slowest processor. If I note any of my students experiencing difficulty I know that I am moving way too fast because at no point should students be actively thinking about trying to learn the language. They should be engaged with the story; if students cannot understand, then that was my fault!

Teaching advanced classes does not change what the literature tells me about second language acquisition. I focus on meaning and do not move on until my students are processing quickly. If I were to move on when the top 20% were getting antsy because, well, they've got it, then I would be reinforcing the message that languages are hard to learn to the remaining 80%. If I were to move on because I have a syllabus to follow, then I would be reinforcing the erroneous message that languages are hard to learn. If I were following a grammar syllabus packed with abstract concepts that leave 80% of my students confused while I push ahead, then it would not be a surprise that my program would become an anemic bastion of the so-called elite of learners.

As a public school teacher I am very aware that the elite learners are closely correlated with social class. It is devastating the way that educational institutions can function to reinforce inequality in society, and I personally believe that the packed grammar syllabus is our contribution, as language teachers, to reinforcing inequality.

It is not that I do not teach advanced grammar. I actually teach advanced grammar in Spanish 1, and my students acquire it as evidenced through their quick writes. What I do not do is separate the language into abstract units that simply confuse students. I do not devote a unit to the subjunctive, and then expect them to either reproduce it accurately (top 20%) or (for the other 80%) forget it after the test because we are moving on to the imperfect tense now.

Instead, within the context of a meaningful story, I use my skills so that my Spanish 1 students understand the phrase "yo quiero que seas feliz". My students were interested in this phrase because it was uttered by the father in the story, who had never bought a car but always rode an elephant to work. He finally overcame his moral objections to the oil economy and bought his daughter a car because he wanted her to be happy. He looked her in the eyes (student actor steps forward) and said, *yo quiero que seas feliz*. That is emotionally gripping.

I ask my students ¿ustedes quieren que yo sea feliz? (I want an elephant, by the way). I ask them ¿El Grinch quiere que seamos felices? We play with variations of this one phrase until it is natural, until they have acquired it. It takes a while.

A week later it showed up in a timed free write of a student who was writing about a boy who screamed at a girl; he wrote *el chico quiere que la chica sea triste*. That is language acquisition for 100% of my students: no conjugation charts, no forced deadlines for learning and yes, they will get it "wrong" before they get it right.

Recently I saw a scope and sequence for an upper level class that had quite a bit packed into the year. Every few weeks a new grammar concept, and then the last several weeks of the school year finally dedicated to "using all tenses at once". My issue is not actually with the grammar taught. It really is with the sequence. A sequence ordered by linguistic function is great for linguists… but for the majority of us humans, not so much.

All of our students will learn the complete grammar of the target language naturally if we do not shelter our grammar instruction into discreet units, but rather limit our vocabulary so that we remain 100% comprehensible. Many high school language departments still sequence their courses largely by grammar concept, making it very difficult for a good comprehensible input teacher to follow the dictates of research and conscience.

The grammar syllabus is worth fighting against.

Do Word Walls Help the Flow of Conversation?

I know what I want to believe... I want to believe that they do. I really would like that. Part of me is a teacher-artist who loves the notion of students picking words off the walls to express whatever is in their hearts. The other part of me, the scientist-teacher, is doubtful. As it turns out, it was something I tried out while learning a new language (Japanese, my fifth language) that helped me re-examine how I use word walls

Where Words Walls Go Wrong

Most of my study of Japanese has been focused on online iTalki tutoring sessions with bilingual Japanese tutors and, outside of class, frequently reading simple texts.

A struggle particular to learning an Asian language is learning to read the characters at the same speed that I can read letters of the Roman alphabet. とても should sound in my head like "*totemo*" the moment I look at it. In my case I am only concentrating on kana, which are far easier to master than kanji. I need to be able to sound out the words quickly enough that I can process a sentence for meaning rather than just sound. If you have ever worked with a young child learning to read, you know exactly what I am going through.

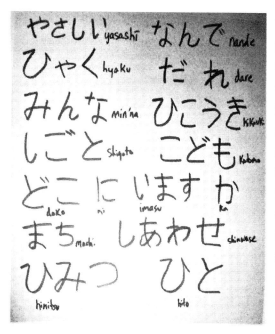

To provide a scaffold to use during my online tutoring lessons I decided to make myself a word wall full of some of the high frequency words that appear over and over again in our lessons. I affixed the poster to the wall facing me so that I would be staring straight at it during our session. These were not new words that I had targeted to learn but rather words that had appeared organically in previous sessions and were already quite familiar. Keep in mind that the words written in the Roman alphabet, know as *romaji*, are transparent in meaning for me, so for me at my stage this really does work as a high-frequency word wall.

My primary goal was to be able to develop a visual recall so rapid that the reading part of our lesson would move forward smoothly. It did occur to me, however, that creating such a word wall might also help me be creative during the speaking parts of the class.

That is how I think most teachers expect students to use word walls. Teachers create a list of target words hoping that students will gaze at the list while the teacher talks and then, when asked a question, the students will use the word wall to express something novel, compelling or at least adhering to the textbook unit.

> *Teacher*: "What do you need when you play football?"
> *Student*: "I need... (searches word wall)... a helmet."

I hope it is clear from the above example that word walls do not always help students create compelling conversation or even express "what is in their hearts". A conversation like the above in which *nobody really cares about the information being exchanged* is less conversation and more like a textbook drill. I think it is best to avoid that kind of approach!

What surprised me, however, is that my Japanese class still moved way too quickly for me to actually use the high-frequency word wall. I control the pace; I am the only student in the class. Yet I found it too confusing to switch between my tutor and my word walls. The only time the word wall was used was when I had significant time to gaze at the words and search for inspiration... which might happen in a classroom with 30 students but was nearly impossible in a one on one conversation.

You might react saying that, unlike our classroom word walls from first language to second language (L1 to L2), my word wall in *romaji* clearly prevented me from processing the meaning of the words quick enough to be able to incorporate them into conversation. Maybe. But I want to point out that kids-- even adolescents-- don't process L1 at the same speed as adults. You should expect a delay in language processing speed if you expect students to read word walls during class.

Word Walls that Work

Word walls that work are used frequently *by the teacher first*, not the student. If you are not actively using the wall, you can be fairly certain that students are not using the wall either. Worse yet, most word walls **reinforce the misunderstanding that we acquire language by studying discrete words rather than by understanding entire messages**. A thematic list of words on the wall does not aid acquisition in the way that frequently using those words does. A list becomes visual noise for the student.

A word wall is half a tool, like a mechanical pencil without lead. The teacher must commit to supplying the other half of the tool: frequently using each word in a comprehensible, compelling context.

I post the Sweet Sixteen verbs in the 3rd person present tense and refer to them constantly. Even in upper level classes, if I say "Si pudiera comer" and that phrase was out of bounds, then I pause, point at *puede*, repeat the phrase *si pudiera comer* and then write "*si pudiera comer* if he could eat" on the board. The Sweet 16 verbs are my constant crutch as we are creating language. I gaze at them trying to figure out how to express our ideas using these highest frequency verbs.

Elementary school teachers often have many ways to skillfully *extend the input*, which is a wonky way of saying "using the same words over and over again in new ways (rather than introducing new words) so that students deeply acquire what they are hearing/reading".

Nonetheless if you have to teach a thematic unit and cannot spread out the words over the course of the entire school year, then a word wall can help you (a) keep those words alive and present throughout the unit and (b) satisfy the demands of an intrusive department chair who insists that every teacher in the department pay closer attention to the textbook sequence than student interest.

I also use **this word wall of characters created by Craig Klein Dexemple** from SpanishCuentos.com. These are definitely low-frequency words, but I use the wall 2-3 times a week when we are generating new characters for our class stories. This wall, along with the Sweet 16 verb wall, is an essential crutch for my students

when they first start **writing their own fluency writes** *(see page 74)*.

If you cannot force yourself to routinely use the word wall, I recommend that you skip it altogether and create a story wall instead *(photo below)*. Walls with OWIs and their entire stories are the eye candy that students need when they are having a hard time focusing on class. Let them read the stories created by other classes and reminisce about their own classes greatest hits. Rereading is great for language acquisition.

My final conclusion is that, if you are going to take the time to construct word walls, **be sure that you are using them**. Students are busy processing language in class and, unless directed, most will not idly read the word walls. For those that do, it is better to have whole class stories posted rather than isolated lists of words.

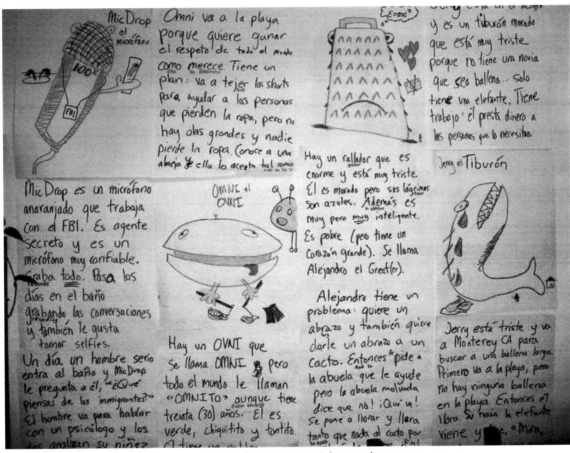

A story wall that I built after creating four OWIs with my classes.

Cognate Recognition Routine: Béisbol Baseball

Every year we start our Spanish 1 class with a **card talk activity** so that, from the very first hour of class, we are immersed in the target language. No singing the alphabet, no pronunciation drills, no awkward memorization of greetings. On the first day I am already using my Sweet 16 posters to focus on the highest frequency verbs.

I am careful to steer our conversation through a sea of cognates so that student comprehension comes easily, **but every year there is always someone who cannot hear the elephant in** *elefante*. And everyone, even my superstars, occasionally have their slow processing days when the word *hospital* in Spanish sounds nothing like *hospital* in English.

We have come up with the perfect class routine to tune all ears to the cognates. When I say a cognate I pause, then say the Spanish word *béisbol* to which the entire class responds "baseball!!". Now that they are alerted to the presence of a cognate I repeat the cognate and the students who understand (usually most of the class) shout out the word in English.

I love this little routine because students who did not instantly understand the cognate have a chance to process before I give them the answer. **The students who did understand it are proud that they can demonstrate their mental agility.** The quiet students who did not hear the elephant in *elefante* are able to comprehend without feeling humiliated and the entire routine is so quick that our class conversation is barely interrupted.

During live in-person classes I encourage students to discreetly use a hand signal to indicate that they are not understanding the conversation. Many students are so easily embarrassed that they would rather sit quietly through an incomprehensible class than stop the class for an explanation, so allowing them to discreetly call my attention is important. If you are teaching online, however, students have less options to discreetly attract your attention. In this context, you'll need to remain proactive and use a cognate recognition routine like **Béisbol Baseball!!** even when you think the cognate is easy to hear.

Comprehensible but rich language

CI teachers don't value incomprehensible noise.

Unlike other approaches that value immersing students in a sea of language noise, CI teachers range from **(group A)** those that want their students to understand 100% of what is said in class to **(group B)** those that want students to *feel like they understand* 100%.

I am in group B. I seek to create an environment of flow. I want class conversation to be so compelling that students are not even aware of processing the language; they are simply engaged with the messages.

Group A teachers often limit themselves to present tense in level 1 because they are trying to maintain very simple, comprehensible messages. Perhaps they built their program around a textbook scope & sequence. Perhaps they negotiated with non-CI colleagues to created a 'best-fit curriculum' in which they could at least teach as they see fit. But as a result, group A teachers tend to emphasize the target language, while group B teachers tend to follow the flow of conversation.

I suggest that you loosen the reins on your language (while remaining comprehensible) for one important reason: **your students are developing an unconscious instinct for the language based on what they hear**. This is the natural paradigm that Krashen speaks about when he says that **we all acquire grammar unconsciously**. Your students should be hearing and understanding the full grammar of the language as spoken naturally, but you should limit the vocabulary so as not to provide too much incomprehensible noise.

How do you do that?!

On the next page is a link to a 5 minute video excerpt of a class I taught recently in which I was trying to give a lot of comprehensible repetitions of the word "vas", or "you go", in Spanish. This is definitely a typical Spanish 1 situation. However, as you watch you'll see that I use the infinitive "ir" in a verb clause, I use the past tense "fuiste" (you went), and I even use a conditional clause ("if there were... would you go"). Watch my student's eyes: she understands without explicit explanations. I could have used the subjunctive and I am certain that she would have understood me if I used my hand gesture as I asked, "**When you go tomorrow**, will you eat more tacos" ("**Cuando vayas mañana**, ¿vas a comer más tacos?").

I use hand gestures to reinforce meaning. You'll also notice that when I used the verb "*irías*" (would you go) I also couched the unknown word within a context and language that made the meaning clear. **I did not explicitly define every word because that would have drawn too much attention to the language and interrupt the flow of the conversation, or the illusion of comprehensibility, although I did code switch judiciously using English as needed.** If I were teaching this in a classroom I probably would have written the word "vas" on then board, pointed and paused, and then ended the session with a Write & Discuss so that students could see the rich written language we produced.

https://vimeo.com/463313388/e0a81fed9d

Most CI teachers **don't shelter grammar** anymore; that means we speak slowly and choose high-frequency vocabulary so that students understand. Even if you are in a department that has agreed to only 'teach the present tense in level 1', you are doing your students a favor by still speaking in a more grammatically-rich manner. You don't have to assess the grammar and certainly don't ask them to produce it (you'll notice Tatiana says *come* when she should have said *comí*). You are building a foundation so that other tenses sound natural and will be acquired easily when ready.

For example, rather than waiting to teach "fue", it might come up on the very first day of school. During a student interview I ask what a student does after school (I am speaking Spanish but the words & translation is projected against the whiteboard). When the student says that they like to go to In-n-Out Burger after school, I then ask in Spanish:

    Teacher: ¿**Vas** a In n Out Burger? (Student responds: Sí)
    Teacher: Clase, ¿**va** a Burger King o In n Out Burger? (Class: In n Out Burger)
    Teacher: Clase, ¿Quién **va** a Burger King? (A few hands raise).
    Teacher: (Turning back to student) ¿**Vas** a In n out Burger hoy
        (write "hoy = today" on the board)? (Student: Sí)
    Teacher: ¿**Fuiste**...

(throw my hand behind my shoulder, then write on the board "fuiste = you went", say "Fuiste" again and throw my hand back),
Teacher: ¿**Fuiste** (throw hand back again) a In N Out Burger ayer? (Student: Sí).
Teacher: Clase, ¿**fue** Jon a Burger King ayer? (Class: No).

We focus on the Sweet 16 verbs, but use a natural diversity of verb tenses to discuss life. Students don't memorize the verb tenses, they get exposed to them in context and slowly acquire them without having to memorize them. Seeing the written language through a Write & Discuss at the end of the conversation will speed up the process of acquisition dramatically.

My collection of Spanish 1 short stories ("*Good Stories for Language Learners*", available in French, German & Spanish) is a year-long literacy module for level 1 that provides progressively more complex language in each story. Every two weeks I read aloud one of these stories. I don't expect my level 1 students to speak or write grammatically complex language, but I read and make comprehensible the language so that my students understand.

Within the first few weeks students are being exposed to small amounts of past tenses, and by the end of the year they have been exposed (through highly scaffolded, comprehensible situations) to many of the major elements of Spanish grammar.

Whether you use my stories in class or you create your own with your classes, don't be afraid to use natural verb tenses as long as you can remain comprehensible.

You are not on stage

The other day I pulled out a picture for picture talk and, remembering what had been successful in other classes, I started to describe the picture to my students with a particular 'story' in mind. I knew exactly where I wanted to go **and that was part of the problem.** My students had no real opportunity to contribute except in a mad-lib 'fill in the blank' kind of way. We have all taught lessons that went fabulously in one class and, upon trying to recreate the fabulous experience in the next class, it just falls flat.

Sometimes we might think that the problem is with the materials; "*if only I had a better picture, a better story, or a better video to describe*". This leads us down the rabbit hole of endless prep when there really is an easier, no-prep solution.

Have you ever gone to a social event and, remembering the great time you had at a barbeque the day before, tried to wrestle every conversation to replicate that great barbeque experience? Of course not, because real conversation is unplanned and has active participants, not an audience.

The search for better materials leads us to believe that if we were better performers, more interesting on stage, then our students would pay more attention and acquire more. *False! It teaches students to be even more passive, critiquing our teaching performances as interesting or not.*

It is worth the effort to learn to become a good conversational partner rather than a performer in class.

All we need to bring to class is something that creates the smallest of sparks. A funny picture dies on stage because there is nothing to say beyond the few chuckles. Instead we need a mild photo from which we can kindle a few questions while sitting in a circle, not on a stage. If there is humor or sadness, laughter or anger, it comes from the students, not the picture. **Resist the urge to make your classroom a theater.**

We should be able to use the same picture in all of our classes, all levels, because the questions we ask (and the responses we receive) will naturally mirror the level of our students. There is no 'level 1 Movie Talk', but rather only developmentally appropriate questions and responses. As this sinks in you'll find that multi-level classes don't have to be difficult to manage.

Here are some concrete tips to become a better conversational partner for your students:

(1) Ask more questions. Tape the **Basic Skills Cheat Sheet** (page 55) in your line of sight while you teach as a reminder.

(2) Use the Sweet 16 verbs to add a greater diversity of questions. Physically touch the posters on the wall while you speak.

(3) Every question is worthy of exploration. Connect any question word with any of the Sweet 16 verbs to make an unexpected question. Model the curiosity that you want your students to develop. "Where does the guy playing guitar put... (glance at the photo to figure out how to finish this question), ah, the money that people give him!"

(4) Build the back story. You are teaching students to actively consider the questions you pose. Build an image in their minds that extends far beyond the picture talk. When we imagine the family circumstances of people in pictures, their motivations, their problems, when we imagine their unique lives then we help our students build empathy for humanity.

If your students just stare at you and never participate, I get it. Schooling has trained them to turn off. Tell them to answer with just a few words in English. Then put their ideas in the target language, slowly and deliberately. Are they still silent? Turn and write it on the board. Point at it, read aloud and pause. Then ask another question. Don't give up. Don't respond to the need to fill the space. **You are not on stage.**

Become comfortable with awkward silence. You are not there to entertain them; you are building social skills that many young people have not developed. When students become engaged, curious and actively consider your questions, they enter that state of flow where language is acquired effortlessly through good, comprehensible conversation.

5 Scaffolds to improve class outcomes

Many experienced CI teachers are not as effective as they could be simply because they have bought into one of the oversimplifications about comprehensible input. It is the shining promise that attracts many educators to CI in the first place.

Before CI, my classes were guided by large vocabulary lists, 'drill and kill' and complex grammar explanations. Recognizing that students (at best) memorize the content for a quiz and promptly forget it, many educators are drawn into the CI community by the promise that **'if you plant the seeds, with time the language will grow'**. Speak freely, play games, and the language will emerge with time.

In practice, this is an oversimplification and is the root of why so many CI teachers quietly retain so many legacy methods (i.e. flash cards, vocab lists, vocab drill games, conjugation assignments, assessments that students must cram for). Teachers are frustrated that 'just talking' doesn't lead quickly enough to the learning outcomes they expect. We need proof for stakeholders that our students are learning. 'Just talking' is like scattering seeds on hard ground hoping that some plant will sprout. Plants do sprout that way, but we can help move the process along.

Today I will describe five scaffolds that you can **apply to every class session so that you do not simply scatter the seeds of language on hard ground**. Instead, cultivate a lush language garden for your students to harvest.

(1) A Place for Written Language

I am often surprised at how many teachers simply speak, letting the oral language disappear into the air. In my Japanese classes, my short term retention of a new word orally spoken is *very* short indeed. I have filmed the classes and timed myself; within 10 seconds an unwritten new word is gone from my memory. Sometimes that is okay if my teacher is trying to get me comfortable with a structure that is repeated in various guises. I don't have to *remember everything* that I understood, especially in early stages of language acquisition, but if we want the language to stick quicker it is well worth the time to turn and write it down.

In face to face classes teachers use the white board to write notes (sometimes individual words, even better if the word is embedded in a short phrase) so that we can point and pause at the word. We also have our verb posters that we use to point and pause. Online classes should also include a place to write notes while we teach.

There are many ways to do this. I am a fan of simplicity; whichever way is easier for you is the best approach. It could be that you actually have a small whiteboard that you physically lift up like Diane Neubauer does in her Chinese classes. I have seen teachers simply share their screen opened to a word doc so that students see the word doc and their teacher in a small box. Simple. Or you might feel comfortable writing with a stylus on a projected screen like Terry Waltz does in her Chinese classes.

I have a drawing tablet & stylus that I already use for illustration; while teaching I use a background with my question words and Sweet 16 verbs already posted around the borders and simply write with the stylus. In face to face classes I often simply write on the board, but for the final Write & Discuss summary I also am a fan of writing straight into Textivate (see page 72). However you do it, make sure that you have an arrangement that is easy for you to manage. Nobody wants to fiddle with tech tools in the middle of class!

(2) Monitor engagement

In face to face classes we have a host of techniques to monitor engagement and comprehension, including teaching to the eyes, artful questioning, choral translations, developing gestures, physically moving through the classroom and standing purposefully next to the student who needs us there to hold their attention. Engagement is essential, even if it is a low-level engagement that simply ensures that students can pass a simple exit quiz at the end of class.

Two teachers who are truly rocking the "monitoring engagement" skill for online teaching are Brett Chonko, the CI teacher behind the ComprehensibleRVA blog, and Josh Rooke. They both use a system called Desmos to monitor student engagement live during in class. If you are in an online setting, check out Brett's tutorial series on using Desmos on his website ComprehensibleRVA. If there were only one tech tool that I could learn for teaching online, it would be this one. Other teachers have wholeheartedly recommended Peardeck.

(3) Write & Discuss review

We create oral language in class *for the purpose of writing it up*. I really believe that if you skip the Write & Discuss routine at the end of the class period, you are giving up the most valuable part of the class. Even if you have carefully written your class notes on the board or online word doc for all to see, a W&D text serves two extremely important functions. First, the random words scribbled on the board are now embedded in a complete, grammatically coherent, comprehensible message. This is how languages are acquired on a most fundamental level. It feels satisfying when we finish class with a board filled with notes and drawings made to scaffold comprehension of the class conversation. However, remember that for learners those disconnected words and phrases have a very tenuous link in their minds until the words are cemented in place by forming complete messages. The bonus is that, by writing out a complete message, we will include all of the necessary grammar that is essential for learners to develop an unconscious paradigm of how the language functions. In my Japanese class the other day one of my tutors was shocked that I tentatively used a compound verb *yomihajimemashita (I started reading)* because I had never been taught the phrase before. In fact, I already knew the vocabulary *yomimasu (to read)* and *hajimemasu (to start)*, but I must have observed the grammatical pattern elsewhere. The compound verb just kind of popped out when I needed it. That is how grammar is acquired.

Second, the W&D text provides a good context to re-experience familiar language. This is so important that I am tempted to add to Krashen's famous conclusion that "we acquire when we understand comprehensible messages" to make a more useful bumper sticker for language teachers: "we acquire **much more** when we are **re-exposed** to messages that we have **already understood**". Not as catchy.

(4) Always Give an Exit Quiz
I used to think that this is a necessary trick to improve my students' engagement, whether face to face or online, but I am realizing in my Japanese classes that this is another very compelling excuse to review the input provided in class. If you follow Brett's lead (above, with Desmos) you will probably use the results of the questions posed in class as your recorded exit quiz. That is okay; you can still give a quick oral quiz 'for fun'. For fun?! Yeah, **it is actually very empowering to end class with an oral quiz that everyone does extremely well on**.

(5) Start Class with a Review of the Last Class session's W&D
Let me explain this with a really catchy slogan: we acquire **much more** when we are **re-exposed** to messages that we have **already understood**. Are you beginning to warm to it?

These are the foundations of effective & efficient language acquisition. You may already have great conversation topics prepared for class: fascinating lessons, brain break activities, and media that students are excited to consume. However, without these five scaffolds, the seeds you plant will have a harder time taking root. Make the most of good language learning material by making sure that all of these scaffolds are present in your classes.

The Balance of the Two Conversations

Once a week I take an intermediate French class with Alice Ayel, a marvelous language teacher whose approach centers around providing language that is natural as well as easy to understand for her students. Perhaps you have seen her wonderful videos (search "Alice Ayel" on YouTube). Her live classes are fabulous. Today she read us a poem and, as I was enjoying her reading, I realized that it has been quite a long time since I have sat down to read a poem on my own for pleasure. In fact, that is how I often respond to her class; surprise and delight upon hearing a folk tale, a myth, or a fable.

This is exactly how I imagine the impact of the second conversation in the daily "Two Conversation Approach". **The first conversation is student-centered**; a student interview, a card talk or a creative activity like a One Word Image that inwardly explores the world inhabited by our students. **The second conversation opens the door to a wider world.** In neither conversation are students struggling to remember vocabulary or grammar; instead they focus on the delight of learning about each other (first conversation) and some small piece of human culture (second conversation). To make sure students focus on content rather than form, we end class with an easy four question exit quiz generated in the moment.

Enjoying the French poem reminded me of a poem that I read with my Spanish classes. This poem, by Chilean poet Nicanor Parra, seems to me perfect for an audience of adolescents keen to criticize the imperfect world they are inheriting. I preface the reading explaining, in Spanish, that in our world there are love poems and poems about beauty, but this poem is neither. Sometimes it is important to say an uncomfortable truth. *"Eating with your mouth open is repulsive."* It hurts to hear that when your mouth is open & full of food. But of course there are far worse things in this world that need to be denounced: racism, gender stereotypes, class oppression, violence. In this poem Parra announces to the reader that he is not going to apologize for writing poetry that may offend you. Read at your own risk:

La montaña rusa
Durante medio siglo la poesía fue
el paraíso del tonto solemne.
Hasta que vine yo
y me instalé con mi montaña rusa.
Suban, si les parece.
Claro que yo no respondo si bajan
echando sangre por boca y narices.

You might ask why I explain the poem to my students before reading it. First of all, I agree that 'explaining' a poem cuts short possible student interpretations. Yet what I want to avoid is confusion. This conversation will last from 15 to 20 minutes and I want students to be amused by the imagery. I want them to understand the context in which Parra situates himself. I want to get straight to the delight of the poem. I don't want my students' first impression of Chilean poetry to be confusion. Rather, I'd like to present a window into another world, or possibly a mirror through which they recognize their own thoughts and feelings reflected in Parra's poetry.

The second conversation is not always so grandiose, but when I am teaching really well I have tapped into my students' sense of self in the first conversation and then, in the second conversation, provided a bridge, a window or a mirror so that they can stretch out and identify themselves in a broader human culture.

Crosswords: Boring or Fabulous?

April is the perfect time to deeply immerse students in reading. After having spent the year focused on the 'two conversations each day', students have acquired enough language to be able read on their own with the teacher providing a loose scaffold to make sure that all students are successful.

In today's newsletter I want to describe how I modify several traditional reading comprehension activities so that they don't negatively impact your students' reading pleasure and provide them with just the information they need to keep everyone reading successfully.

The ideal crossword puzzle for a CI class is a reading activity, not a decoding activity. We are not providing clues in English. In addition, they are very quick to do. I post these

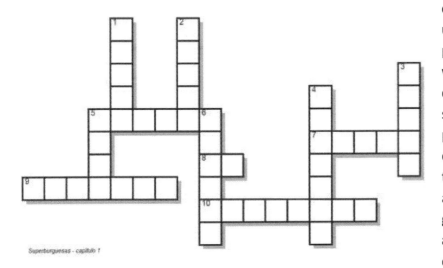

crosswords as a warm-up activity by projecting them on the white screen and I don't even need to spend time photocopying. When done as a warm-up the purpose of the activity is not to get a grade but rather **to allow students to confirm that they really did understand the reading** even before our class conversation.

The clues are full sentences that refer back to the plot of the novel. Members of the online Master Class and their students have free access to the eBook version of my novel *Superburguesas* (look in the **Reading Module** in the essay titled "Free Access..."). I have also placed lots of free resources on my **Superburguesas homepage,** including a detailed description of how I teach the novel, crosswords, word walls and comprehension questions for every chapter.

https://mygenerationofpolyglots.com/my-tprs-novels/

ACROSS

5. El señor Superburguesas tiene que ____ el restaurante porque nadie quiere comer las hamburguesas.
7. Rodney es un empleado que nunca se lava las ____.
8. Bobby le ____ la comida a Fifi porque no quiere comer.
9. Rodney grita el número trescientos ____ y ocho.
10. En el baño Bobby ve a Rodney, el ____ malo.

Superburguesas - capítulo 1

DOWN

1. Bobby cree que el restaurante es perfecto porque no hay ____ allí.
2. A Rodney le gusta que nadie va al restaurante porque le gusta hacer la ____.
3. Una superburguesa tiene ____ secreta.
4. Después de ir al baño Bobby vuelve a la mesa con las manos ____.
5. Fifi ____ las dos superburguesas y Bobby no dice nada.
6. A ____ no le importa que haya perdido el trabajo en el restaurante.

The crossword puzzles can be an even better experience when wrapped inside an exciting group activity. This is a variation of Jason Fritz's activity "running dictations". Students work in groups of three. Each group has one copy of the puzzle (without clues). The clues are taped outside against the wall, in the hallway. Each group member is assigned one job. One student, **the runner**, goes outside to read the clues. **The writer** stays inside guarding their clue sheet (one per team) and writes the answers. The last student is **the reader**, who can consult the novel to find answers that the runner does not know.

When I say Go! the runner runs out into the hallway where the clues are posted and then returns to the writer to fill out the crossword or discuss with the team's reader if s/he does not know the answer. I allow group members to tag out so that they can all run, but only one can run at a time. These "running dictation" crossword games are meant to be short... just a quick burst of movement to keep the blood flowing.

You can find free crossword creators online if you are reading another novel.

pistolas, casa, civilizada, hombres, devolver, dónde, quiero, pregunta, pintura, matar, ver, padre, dame, limonada, Fifi, enojada, problema, ciudad

Superburguesas - capítulo 9

We also have word walls for every chapter in 'Superburguesas' as well as the stories in 'Good Stories for Language Learners' (also available in the Reading Module). These word walls can be used for pre or post reading activities. As a post-reading output activity you could ask students to either talk in pairs or write individually producing a summary of the chapter, with only the word wall as a guide. Author Margarita Pérez García told me she uses these word walls to build her student's confidence as a pre-reading activity.

Margarita writes:

"Hi Mike, thanks for these resources. I will be reading Superburguesas during the second term (January-March) with my classes, so I'm super grateful every time you publish resources for the novel. I tried a word cloud activity yesterday as a pre-reading for a short story. First, I did the cognate challenge. The students loved it, in particular those with ASD. I asked them to count how many they could find, and even if they were beginners they could say "tengo 8". I copied the names of the students and the number of cognates on the board with many repetitions of "tiene/tienen" + rejoinders of amazement. All very quick. Then I asked the group with less cognates to give one, and I moved up to the groups that found more cognates. In few minutes, we had a comprehensive list of cognates that weren't unfamiliar any more. After that, I asked them to read again the words of the cloud, and I asked "¿Quién?", then "¿Dónde?", then "¿Qué va a ocurrir?, using "es posible" and "a lo mejor". Then they got to the reading, they were much more confident. Such a great idea, these word clouds. Thank you!"

Finally, whenever there are sets of comprehension questions I almost always review them orally in class and ask spontaneous follow-up questions for each written question to keep the conversation organic and lively. Use your question word posters and your Sweet 16 verb posters to keep the questions unexpected.

I would not simply assign the questions and accept written answers as proof of comprehension... that would be way too tempting for students to fall into 'playing the game' and copying homework in the hallway without understanding what they are copying. Instead you want to make sure that students are truly understanding the language in the moment. When they waver, you've learned what you needed. Rescue them immediately and transform the question into an either/or question: I ask in Spanish, "What does Mr. Superburguesas want?" and if the student wavers I fairly quickly ask, "Does he want the dog or the painting?" as if that were my original question all along.

After so many experiences with the language of the novel I think it is perfectly valid to ask for output-- for example a five minute fluency write in which students describe what happened and what they think might happen in the next chapter. A more open-ended assessment tends to be perceived by students as a more empowering exercise. Let them demonstrate what they are capable of!

However, if you really want them to focus on the details and finely demonstrate their reading comprehension I have a few summative assessments for Superburguesas including a chronology quiz and a fill-in-the-blank paragraph. They are available on the Superburguesas homepage described in the beginning of this essay.

A Small Bucket of Language

We know that most students need to listen and read *a lot* of the target language before being able to speak. However, **how do we best lead them to speaking?** Do we provide lots and lots of listening with comprehension checks and simply don't expect them to speak for a very long time (like Krashen & Mason)? Do we circle around one sentence and continue hammering variations of that one sentence until all students are speaking (like Blaine Ray)?

Both of these approaches work, but they are the extremes. I propose that a reasonable approach focuses on the Sweet Sixteen verbs to structure your class conversations. Let the highest frequency verbs of the target language guide the conversation, **allowing for a truly student-centered experience while still limiting the language students hear**. Find the balance so that students can experience some early success speaking in the target language.

This is the reason I start the school year with student interviews and card talks. These activities are inherently interesting to students as they are student-centered, **but the nature of the conversations make it easy to continuously loop back to the Sweet Sixteen verbs**. When I eventually move on to creating One Word Images and picture talks we are still pursuing a student-centered curriculum because it is the students' ideas and pictures that generate these conversations. I am still referring back to the Sweet 16 verbs as well. I am very gradually expanding their language through these activities, but I am even more dedicated to repeating the Sweet 16 in a variety of contexts so that my students firmly acquire these highest of high-frequency words.

Krashen has argued persuasively that the case for natural language use in the classroom is clear: **students who hear and comprehend natural language acquire even the trickiest grammar concepts unconsciously while attending to the meaning**. When I say to a student in class, "*quiero que seas feliz*" (I want you to be happy), students are not thinking about conjugations, rules of use of the subjunctive or change of subjects. Instead they are determined to solve the problem that a student has articulated because, after all, *we all want this student to be happy!* When this happens frequently in class (every Tuesday our OWI faces a problem that we solve), students hear the grammar enough to acquire it and be able to use it unconsciously, without hesitation.

Here is a mental image created by a clever educator to explain why we need to repeat so much. You might imagine all of the not-fully acquired target language sloshing about in a learner's mind as if it were in a bucket. Every time the learner understands a phrase, you've added another drop to the bucket. Once the bucket overflows, then the learner can confidently speak. Here is the trick; **the more vocabulary that you expose learners to, the bigger the bucket and therefore the longer it takes before the bucket overflows**.

Students speak & write quicker in the target language if you provide a smaller bucket of language for them to process.

Don't get me wrong; **students need huge amounts of input (listening & reading) before they are ready to output (speaking and writing)**. But if we tightly control the language used in class so that there is very little new language every day (i.e. a small bucket of input rather than a big lake) students will move from listening to speaking quicker.

The trick to teaching beginners is to remain interesting while introducing as little new language as possible... which is exactly why I begin my year with student interviews. If you are teaching beginners I suggest that you really limit your language in the first weeks of school so that everyone experiences some early success with output. This early success is what impresses both students and parents and motivates students to become lifelong language learners.

I limit my language by posting the Sweet 16 verbs and using those verbs to guide every step of our class conversations, every day. When a level 1 student reveals during an interview that she moved over the summer, I glance at my Sweet 16 verbs and use IR (to go) instead of MUDARSE (to move). **Simplifying is often not about shorter sentences, but rather re-using the high-frequency verbs that we already know**.

I also use whole language from the first day of school-- full sentences so that students are not just following a conversation but are hearing all of the verbs conjugated in the appropriate forms.

> *¿Tú tienes un perro? Yo* (hand placed on my chest) *no tengo perro. Tengo* (hand placed on my chest) *un gato. "Miau", dice* (walk over and touch the dice poster) *mi gato. Clase, ¿quién* (walk over and touch ¿quién? on the interrogatives poster) *tiene* (walk over and touch the tiene poster)... *¿quién tiene un perro?*

The Write & Discuss that we create after our class conversations help keep our language bucket very small as we move slowly, ever so slowly, towards fluency.

Is 'non-targeted' language an efficient use of class time?

We have very little time with our students. Over the course of a four-year program, we typically have anywhere from 450 to 600 class hours. Research suggests that it takes thousands of hours to acquire a second language. Students may expect to leave our programs "fluent", but most language teachers understand that we are truly aiming to develop enough language so that students can continue the process on their own.

Over the course of my career, I transitioned from being a very targeted teacher to eventually following a mostly non-targeted approach. **'Targeting' is when you know exactly which phrases you'll be teaching on any given day, and you make plans to repeat those phrases as much as possible.** For example, I used to start class every day with three phrases written on the board that we would use over and over during the period. The idea is to provide enough focused repetitions of key phrases that students fully acquire the language one step at a time. It is logically satisfying for teachers who want a very orderly process. Everyone learns the same thing at the same time, and we all build our language skills in synch. That makes assessment easier too. Sounds beautiful!

Except, language acquisition is a very messy business. Linguist Bill Van Patten often delighted in pointing out to teachers that learners acquire at different paces. There is no guarantee that learners will acquire what the teacher targets. Neither can we be certain of the exact order of acquisition. While we do know that the brain can memorize all sorts of language trivia that we can train learners to use to pass tests, when it comes to true spontaneous language use the brain only acquires what it is ready to acquire. And even if we did have access to that black box, every student is on their own trajectory.
All of this uncertainty is often ignored in grammar-focused language classrooms.

My non-targeted approach, on the other hand, exposes students to lots of less planned language through student-centered conversational activities. The grammar is unsheltered, but the vocabulary is limited. This used to be highly controversial in the CI community but now, I believe, it is a common practice. We can speak in past tenses on day 1 as long as we make ourselves comprehensible. The subjunctive is not avoided, and we use meaningful complex expressions when needed... as long as we take the time to make sure it is highly comprehensible.

Of course, nobody is arguing that students *fully acquire anything* on first exposure. **Both targeted and non-targeted approaches have to recycle language so that learners eventually encounter the language when they are ready to acquire it.**

The real question in my mind isn't whether language is recycled. All good CI teachers are skilled at recycling high-frequency structures. **The real question has to do with the richness of the language that students encounter, starting from day one.** When I was a teacher who closely followed daily targets, my classroom language was simple and comprehensible. But what if you could expose students to language that is rich and at times even complex, while still being highly comprehensible?

That is what I find in my non-targeted student interviews. **Rather than a pretext to use the three target-phrases repetitively, the language is a bridge to make unexpected discoveries about my students.** We follow up an interview with a Write & Discuss, and inevitably there are complex phrases included that I would have never included if it were not part of that student's unique interview.

Since I center much of my intentional speech in class around the Sweet 16 verbs, I know that there is a lot of repetition and recycling of language in my classroom. However, having a set of daily activities that are focused on developing unplanned, student-centered stories & narratives leads to much richer (and more interesting) language.

When I transitioned to a non-targeted approach my main concern was whether I could provide enough repetitions of core, high-frequency language. I wanted students to thoroughly acquire the high-frequency language rather than just remain in a perpetually confused cloud of "I-kind-of-sort-of-understand". I knew that, given enough exposure to interesting & comprehensible language, they would acquire it eventually. My question: **is there enough time in a school**

day so that *eventually* comes quick enough? Or is a tightly targeted curriculum better suited for the reality of preparing students to fly on their own someday.

I have written before about how CI is a humane, inclusive method which allows students to blossom at their own natural pace. The non-targeted lessons based on One Word Images also move as slowly as my best targeted lessons did. Nobody is getting left behind; everything is as comprehensible as before. **I think the interest level is higher because the personalization of the story is deeply embedded into the DNA of the activity**, whereas my targeted stories are about as personalized as a Mad Lib activity. Kind-of personalized, but the kids see right through it.

My biggest surprise with the non-targeted approach is the realization that I have more opportunities to differentiate for fast processors while not losing the slower processors. In the past I would spend time trying to find student jobs and other ways of occupying the busy minds of my fast-processing students. Part of their classroom experience was learning to remain focused and to not blurt out answers before the rest of the students had the opportunity to process the language. Now I am reaching the high-fliers like never before.

The 10 commandments of easy CI

Write on the board

Ask artful questions
Who? What? When? Where? How? yes/no this/that

Require choral response

Point & pause at language frames (online) & posters (on walls)

Increase processing speed; don't memorize

Ask students, "what did I just say?"

Default to Sweet 16 when talking in class

Choral translation

Write & Discuss

Exit quiz

In **our Tuesday night Zoom workshops** we made that set of "commandments" for easy CI, however you decide to practice it in your own classroom. I think if you follow 7 or 8 of the commandments, you'll be a superstar. But who needs that pressure? Print it out and try to do 5 of them every day. You choose which five and I am sure it will up your game.

On the last page are images of the quick writes produced by a few outstanding Spanish 1 non-heritage learners. These are just beautiful and **demonstrate a richness of language that I would not expect, and certainly would not have targeted**, for students in their fifth month of language classes. Some of the words I expect will drop out of their active vocabulary (maceta, semilla). But some of the expressions are not actually coming from this specific story. It is pretty darn cool.

Harness the power of choice to develop a smooth-running class

You don't have to run yourself ragged while students passively watch

This essay is only partly about student jobs. I have always found most student jobs to be a further burden on my mental energy as I keep track of what everyone is supposed to be doing. I'm looking to make my teaching life easier. **The greater insight in this essay is about how we can harness the power of choices to lead our students to choose a smooth-running classroom.**

Classroom management gurus often tell teachers to offer a choice rather than an ultimatum: "you can either give your sunglasses to me or put them in your bag; I'll be back in a moment to see which you choose". This technique uses the same psychology but applied to the whole group.

Let's start with a common issue that drives teachers crazy: lack of student engagement. You are trying to conduct a student interview, make a One Word Image or do some guided creative writing but your students are just so passive that you can't get anywhere with them. In fact, the harder you try and the crazier you dance in the target language, the more passive they seem!

There may be several things going on here, but I want to encourage you NOT to continue pouring out your energy in class hoping to ignite a spark. It is perverse, but **the more you perspire, the further students recede into passivity.**

Instead, I have a three-part strategy to develop student allies who advocate within their peer group for a smooth-running class.

First of all, tell them what you want, when you want it.

It seems simple, but students may sense your frustration while not really understanding what you want. Think about the contradictions that can emerge in a CI classroom from the perspective of a student: "teacher tells us we don't have to speak until we are ready (*lots of input before a little output*) but then she asks us to all speak", "teacher tells us to listen listen listen, but then she tells us to speak at the same time (*choral response*)", "teacher is constantly shushing me (*one person speaks everyone else listens*) but then gets mad when I don't talk".

From an adolescent perspective, having a side chat with a friend might be the same in their mind as answering a student interview question: it's talking.

I tell them what I want *in the target language* if my students understand, and I verify their comprehension. At the beginning of the school year, I might do this in English.

> **Teacher**: "(in the target language) Voy a hablar (make talking hand gesture) con Katelyn (gesture towards Katelyn). Katelyn va a hablar (talking hand gesture again) conmigo (touch my chest with my palms). Ustedes (waving my hand towards the entire class) van a escuchar (bring hand to ear). Ahora, (in English) *what am I going to do?*"
> **Class**: "Talk"
> **Teacher**: "What is Katelyn going to do?"
> **Class**: "Talk"
> **Teacher**: "What are you all (wave hand towards whole class) going to do?"
> **Class**: "Listen"

I'll do a version of that routine in all levels from 1 through AP **every time we do a student interview.**

The moment that students in the audience start a side chat, ask the entire class, "**what** are you all doing (wave your hand out to the whole class just like in the initial instructions so that the memory is activated, and they respond: "Listening"). If the side chat has not stopped, try asking again but punching the "**you all**" part of the question: "what are **you all** doing?"

Most times you will not need to speak directly to the students chatting. The power of the entire group responding reinforces, "**We** are listening". If you have to, you can even hold two palms facing up as offering a choice and ask the whole group in the target language: "Who is speaking? Katelyn and I... or all of you?"

Having the whole group enforce the norms of the activity is powerful and also establishes a **calm tone to the class in which the teacher is *not* losing her cool**.

This is also how you'll train your student allies to remind the class how you want the class to function. Remember, students have 5 or 6 other teachers with 5 or 6 other class expectations. Students will forget your expectations if you are not reinforcing them every single day, all year long.

Second part of the strategy: when the interview doesn't go well because the student does not engage

I don't want Katelyn to feel bad about her moment on the class stage, so I simply say, "This isn't going as planned. Sorry Katelyn, I think I got you up here before we were ready. Thank you thank you thank you for being a good sport and playing my game with me".

Then I turn to the class and say, "okay, let's use these next ten minutes instead on a Write & Discuss comprehension quiz. Take out your notebooks and read the W&D from last Wednesday, October 15th (or whatever date, but choose one from about a week ago). You have five minutes to read the W&D and then it's all notebooks away for the quiz. No sharing notebooks-- this is a notebook quiz."

Of course, this only works if you have students keep a W&D notebook, which I think you should.

Many teachers have a place in the classroom where students store their notebooks so that losing the notebook or forgetting it at home does not become a problem. In that case, be sure to have getting the notebook at the beginning of class and returning it at the end of class a part of a class routine.

Linguist Paul Nation's research indicates that revisiting texts a few days later or even a week or two later has a greater impact on acquisition than the first read through!!! So, I often have students copy the W&D into their notebooks and about once a week I ask them to translate the text at home to an adult (if they take their notebooks home).
We also use these notebooks as a transition activity: when the interview isn't going well then I might say, "okay, this isn't going as planned. Let's try something else. Open up your notebooks and read the W&D from November 15th. You have 5 minutes and then we will close all notebooks and take a short comprehension quiz".

If you do that when you first start using notebooks, students learn to take good notes and KEEP them! They also learn to participate in the interview and to "do their 50% of the work" in the conversation, or we have a back-up plan that is less enjoyable. You'll hear other kids coaxing them along because everyone understands that if the current activity falls apart, they may be reading for a quiz.

The third part of the strategy, in future days, is to simply give the class a choice.

In the early days of the school year, I'll ask them whether they want to continue with the student interview (followed eventually by an exit quiz) or reread a W&D text for a reading quiz. Whichever they choose, it's good input!

However, often you'll have student allies coaxing their peers to continue with the student interview. Later in the year I might offer a choice between the interview and student choice reading of a novel from the classroom library. I don't even mention a quiz; it's simply a choice between two activities. But students have been trained to feel investment in whichever choice wins out. Either activity leads to acquisition. In fact, whichever activity has more student buy-in will probably lead to greater language acquisition.

Keep in mind that this is truly a long-term strategy, not a "spur of the moment tactic". It builds a class culture in which students feel more in control of their learning and students are given space to advocate for their favorite use of class time.

This strategy goes hand-in-hand with the way I assign class jobs. Essential jobs in my classroom are (1) the librarians to whom students pass their independent reading books about 2/3 of the way through the period so that the librarians neatly return the books to the shelves, (2) the computer kid who sits at my teacher desk and controls the computer which is projected against the white screen at the front of the room, and (3) the class artists who illustrate our One Word Images and define the visual branding of each class.

In each case, the jobs are often assigned to a willing student in the beginning of the year and are rarely changed. The computer kid sits in the comfiest chair in the room and often raids my candy drawer... but is so integral to a smooth-running class that I keep that candy drawer well-stocked! The librarians protect the books from damage; I don't mind if they miss a few minutes of class conversation while they do their job. The artists provide endless discussion in the days and weeks after creating a OWI as we glance at the back of the room where the OWIs are hung.

These are all student allies that help our class work smoothly.

And the student allies who actively advocate for one choice or the other move the class energy forward rather than stagnating in a miasma of "we don't want to do anything that you suggest".

What are grades good for?

In this essay I want to describe the many practical things I do to get grades into my grade book. We should recognize that grades and assessment are separate issues; I might examine the texts that my students produce through fluency writing in order to assess what kind of language my students need from me, but I record a line of mostly A's in my grade book that indicates simply that the students are progressing as expected.

In my somewhat renegade opinion, there should be no effort to correlate grades with student performance at certain proficiency levels (for example, *"Level 1 students who perform at intermediate low by years end will receive an A"*). **Language acquisition is an unconscious process; putting it on a timeline is like grading kids based on their growth spurts.** It is not only ridiculous, it is deeply elitist and against the best interests of our students.

In my classroom, **grades encourage students to simply engage in the daily conversations**. It is the daily engagement that leads to language acquisition, so the bulk of the grade is based on their performance on daily exit quizzes. I make those exit quizzes easy enough to simply measure whether the student was engaged during the conversation; they should never test memorization of trivial details brought up in class.

If we accept the research that language acquisition is largely an unconscious process, it does not make sense to assign a grade based upon a students perceived proficiency or linguistic performance in class. This is not a class where students study hard to pass an exam; **their performance is based upon the *quality* and *quantity* of comprehensible input that students have received**.

Use grades to help students improve behavior that they can control. Students are in control of whether they are present in class and whether, while in class, they track the conversation. My grades reflect those two variables.

However, **much of their acquisition is *out of their control***. Should I base grades on the biological speed at which their brains form a paradigm of the target language? Whether their parents built up their reading stamina by reading aloud to them as young children? Should I punish them with poor grades if they do not have books in their home (and a text-poor home) or if I have an off week and fail to provide highly-compelling input? I often receive emails from teachers who want to know *'where their students should be'* at X point in the semester. That is simply not a useful question for student or teacher. A more useful question might be, *"how do I know if my students are acquiring at their maximum efficiency?"*

I am deeply disturbed by the shift in resources towards proficiency testing. Tests that attempt to level students by their performance on a proficiency exam are big business. **These tests do nothing to promote language acquisition; students cannot be motivated by tests to acquire quicker** in the way a test may motivate a student to memorize the periodic table in Chemistry or examine the impact a historical event in a History class.

Worse yet, the time and financial resources used on testing could be allocated to better purposes. Experienced teachers understand that committing to doing one thing means denying ten competing projects. I say, let's focus on developing more and more compelling ways to have conversations in class.

Compelling language experiences motivate students to acquire faster. Great conversations draw them into the class culture, seeking more compelling input. Take the $20 per student needed to administer one of these exams (and that is on the cheap end) and instead buy a few CI novels for each student to read at home– that would actually move students further down the path to proficiency in the target language.

Shifting the focus from grammatical accuracy towards proficiency is a positive development in our profession. It cues teachers to pay attention to how languages are actually acquired. **Endlessly tracking students performance and attempting to correlate performance with proficiency levels is not useful**.

If grades in my classes do not attempt to describe my students abilities with the language, what do my grades say about my students? Let's return to the question I posed above: *"how do I know if my students are acquiring at their maximum efficiency?"*

The following all correlate to whether students are (a) present in class and (b) attending to meaning (either understanding or stopping me when they do not understand). Krashen tells us that as long as students are comprehending the messages that they are receiving, their brains are acquiring language. It will happen faster if those messages are truly compelling, but making it compelling is the work of the teacher. For students, we just need to hold them accountable for understanding the messages we communicate (and stopping us when they do not understand). Here are the categories that appear in my grade book:

1. **Exit quizzes** are the largest weighted category in my grade book, making up 65% of students' grades. I record a grade for an exit quiz almost every day.

    The rest of the categories are lumped into one grading category in my gradebook, making up 35% of the students' grades. I do this so that, if I only grade one or two assignments from any given category, it will not have an outsized impact on the final grade.

2. **Fluency Writes**
3. **Homework**: i**llustrating Write & Discuss**
4. **Quick translations**: paragraphs that reflect input delivered in class such as **the second approach to movie talk**, a prepared reading based on **an oral storytelling session**, or simply a Write & Discuss text.
5. **A content comprehension quiz** based on a **cultural presentation** or content lesson about the target language culture, delivered in the target language of course. Unlike the exit quizzes, these are usually Friday quizzes given after several days of instruction. Students take notes and study from those notes.
6. **Classroom activities**: This is a catch-all category. Not everything we do is graded, but occasionally I put in a grade for a **gallery walk**, for example, or student led book talks (in upper levels). The grades are based on completion or active participation, not performance, but in the case of a gallery walk I don't rush to make that clear to students.

I offer extra credit for activities that deliver more comprehensible input. I offer this mainly for students who have missed class and need to replace a zero on an exit quiz or other grade.

1. **Reading** while eating lunch in my classroom. Usually I require two lunch periods (total 30 minutes) to substitute for one exit quiz (one class period is equal to 55 minutes).
2. **Attend a lunch time OWI session.** I have advanced heritage language learners trained to lead OWIs twice a week during lunch. Students of any level are welcome to attend and must pass a quick exit quiz at the end of the session to substitute for any grade recorded in the grade book. Students can save these up in a 'bank' over the course of the semester and if they have 10 saved up by the end of the semester I bump their overall grade up an entire letter grade.
3. **Some student jobs.** If a student holds a job consistently and responsibly throughout the semester I justify a small amount of extra credit if that job makes the class run smoothly so that I can deliver even more CI in class. Often student jobs pull students attention into the class, so there is no reason to grant extra credit. The job itself is making the class more compelling for the student. On the other hand, I once had an outstanding student librarian whose organization made our class run so smoothly that we routinely had an extra 5-10 minutes of class conversation every day. She was also extremely dedicated to student government and missed too many classes, but I felt justified in excusing some of her missing exit quiz grades.

Acknowledgements

This approach to language acquisition emerged through conversations and a history of collaboration among a large community of educators: the TPRS community, and later the CI community, who developed techniques and laid the groundwork for all of us to follow. Susie Gross and Berty Segal Cook are two educators that I met briefly, but impacted me profoundly, and there are many more whose contributions I am grateful for although I don't know them by name. The educators whose works have been my teachers and guides include Grant Boulanger, Jason Fritz, Bryce Hedstrom, Anne Matava, Blaine Ray, Karen Rowan and, especially, Ben Slavic. Over the last decade conversations with Elicia Cárdenas, Brent Chonko, Anny Ewing, Alina Filipescu, Ben Fisher, Cynthia Hitz, Cécile Lainé, and Margarita Pérez García have helped focus my attention on a conversational, student-centered approach full of pleasure reading opportunities. I increasingly came to see the need to provide a counterbalance to interpretations of CI teaching that are more presentational in nature. As 'story-asking' has faded from the lexicon of new teachers, our teaching community has lost something crucial which this book attempts to restore.

I want to thank the many school districts that have brought me in as a consultant; without your support I would never have been able to complete this book. Likewise, I am grateful to the Colorado Congress of Foreign Language Teachers, the Hawai'i chapter of AATSP, the Philadelphia chapter of AATF and the Indiana Foreign Language Teachers Association for their support and feedback. Special thanks to members of my writing collective, for improving my writing and leading me to appreciate the need for many voices in a classroom library.

Thanks to my Japanese tutors Kaho and Yuki who kept me grounded over the past few years, constantly reminding me what it is like to learn a new language.

Made in the USA
Las Vegas, NV
03 October 2023

78510065R00153